Clint Eastwood

Clint Eastwood

Christopher Frayling

for Thelonious, Crispin and Justin — the wild bunch

First published in Great Britain in 1992 by
Virgin Publishing Ltd
338 Ladbroke Grove
London W10 5AH

Copyright © 1992 Christopher Frayling

The moral right of the author has been asserted

A catalogue record for this book is available from the British Library
ISBN 0 86369 307 5

*Typeset by Typeout, SW16
Printed and bound in Great Britain by*
Cox & Wyman Ltd,
Reading, Berkshire.

Contents

Acknowledgements

Thanks: to Budd Boetticher who discussed his work with me at his Equestrian Centre in Ramona, Southern California; to Philip Kaufman, who talked with me about his script of *The Outlaw Josey Wales* in his office at Berkeley, Northern California; to the late Sergio Leone, with whom I had several genial conversations in Rome and London – after a long-suffering translator had read all 288 pages of my book *Spaghetti Westerns* to him; to Burt Kennedy, who discussed his films inside a facsimile log-cabin interior in his garden near Los Angeles; and to Clint Eastwood, who reminisced about his career over a bowl of fruit and nuts, in a suite of rooms at Claridges Hotel, London, and in the process enabled this book to happen.

Others who helped were: librarians at the New York Public Library, the American Film Institute and the British Film Institute; criminologist Robert Reiner, with whom I once taught an evening class entitled 'Blue movies – the image of the police in film from Keystone to Kojak'; Adrian Turner (sometime organiser of the *Guardian* lectures at the National Film Theatre) who opened a lot of doors for me; Alice, in the office of the *Carmel Pine Cone*, who gave me access to the file on Eastwood's mayoral election campaign; the Publicity Department at Warner Brothers (London); and Paul Barker, who first encouraged me to publish parts of my Eastwood interview, in a different form, in the *Independent Magazine*.

Christopher Frayling
London, January 1992

Illustrations

1   So help me Randolph Scott

Veteran film maker Budd Boetticher's original screenplay for *Two Mules for Sister Sara* (written in the mid-1960s) begins by introducing the reader to the central character – a professional gunslinger, who is riding alone through the bleached white rocks of the Sierra Madres.

'As we scan the terrain we discover an almost imperceptible movement mostly hidden in the long evening shadows tight against the rocks. Zooming closer we recognise the figure as a lone rider astride his horse, followed by a pack-pony, loose, who trots to keep up with the long-legged animal before him . . . The man is tall and lean, dressed in the colours of the desert and the rocks. The tans, and the browns and the grays of his tight-fitting outfit are only broken up by the black and yellow beaded Indian moccasins which he wears instead of boots . . . And now we get out first real look at the man himself. It is impossible to determine his age. He could be thirty, or maybe even forty, but we'll never be sure because the wrinkles around his eyes and at the corner of his tight lips could have come into being from the desert sun.

'He wears his sweat-stained hat low down over his eyes to shade them from the fading light, but there is a sparkle of all-consuming awareness in those eyes that makes you feel certain that not even a lizard mor'n half a mile away could skitter across the sand without his knowing which way it was headed . . . One word passes through your mind: *gunslinger*. This man is a *pro* – and you know it.'

He is also a man who, Boetticher later tells us, has chosen to become a 'pro' as the direct result of a personal tragedy: 'The sounds of the wind, for the gunslinger, are unpleasant sounds – the bickering of a nagging mother; the shrill laughter of his schoolmates (as he never was much at book-learnin'); the startled gasps of the men he has gunned down in his own particular line of duty; and the last soft moans of the woman he once loved and still, fitfully, dreams about – the girl who had carried his son until the very last days of pregnancy. And then he had lost them both in a filthy Indian hovel in Arizona . . .'

In the Sierra Madres he approaches the rise of a hill, and hears the sound of drunken laughter. He dismounts, loads a shell into his long gun – a Winchester – and lights a thin brown cigar. Then he registers exactly what is going on. Three men are staggering and dancing around a terrified girl, whose naked white back is all he can see: 'Their wardrobe and their sidearms reveal them for what they are . . . cattle thieves, robbers, killers and now, most certainly, rapists. They could be German; Irish sons of Irish brothers from the Civil War; or North Americans who have found a bloody sanctuary across the Rio Grande. There isn't a chance that any one of the three could be mistaken for a Mexican.'

While the lone gunslinger stands above the rocks and shouts 'Hold it!', two of the rapists open fire on him and he shoots them dead with his Winchester. A third, who is a kid, gets hold of the girl and threatens to blow her head off: 'I mean it fella! So help me God!'

'Still the youth sees only the death-like immobility of the rocks, and hears only the eerie silence of the desert. But suddenly there is a sputtering sound wafting toward him through the air, and then a foot-long stick of dynamite, its fuse sparkling with fire, plops onto the sand a scant fifteen feet from where he holds the girl. The boy takes one hurried glance at the explosion growing next to him; untangles his fingers from the blond curls and makes a beeline for the nearest cover. He fires once, almost crazily, at the figure of the gunslinger as he bursts from behind the rocks and dashes towards the stick of dynamite. But the tall man fans his Colt three times at the man and the kid spreadeagles to bury his bloody face deep into the sand.

'The gunslinger re-holsters his revolver as he slides into the dynamite and draws his Bowie-knife in one long sweeping movement as he lands on his left hip a foot from the sputtering fire. The long knife flashes once in the last rays of sunlight, and the fuse is severed an inch from the stick. He rises to one knee and pops that last inch into his mouth to chew out any remaining spark of danger. And then, for the first time, he takes a long, CLOSE-UP, look at the girl . . . finally he says, "Well, don't jes sit there, lady. Go put your clothes on. It's gonna git cold."

Boetticher had originally intended Robert Mitchum or John Wayne ('my John Wayne, not John Ford's'), or perhaps Steve McQueen, to play the gunslinger and Silvia Pinal (from Luis Bunuel's *Viridiana*) to play the girl: and his screenplay had been written, in the Hotel Diplomatico, Mexico City, with these personae very much in mind. In the event, when *Two Mules for Sister Sara* was turned into a film, several years later in 1970, by director Don Siegel, Clint Eastwood was the gunslinger and (after Elizabeth Taylor had dropped out) Shirley Maclaine the girl: the screenplay – adapted by Albert Maltz 'based on a story by Budd Boetticher' – had been radically rewritten, to suit the character of the Man With No Name from the Italian 'Dollars' films which had been belatedly released in America (with fantastic results at the box office).

Siegel's film even had a musical score by Italian composer Ennio Morricone, which boasted a main title theme consisting of two mules braying followed by children singing the Latin words for 'lead us not into temptation', while steel-stringed acoustic guitars provided the rhythm section.

Budd Boetticher went to the premiere in Hollywood, accompanied by his friend Ron Ely (a one-time cinema and television Tarzan) and was sitting immediately in front of Clint Eastwood and Don Siegel. Morricone's score began – almost like an overture – and the curtains opened, to reveal the wide screen and the colour photography of veteran cameraman Gabriel Figueroa.

A professional gunslinger was riding alone through the snow-capped mountains at sunrise: he had a trotting pack-pony in tow. You could tell he was in the wilderness, a very long way away from civilisation, because the camera kept panning from all manner of wild beasts to the single-minded gunslinger, who was apparently paying no attention to them: first an owl, then a big fish in a stream, then a jackrabbit, than a snarling wild-cat, then a rattlesnake, and finally a tarantula – which struggled through the mossy grass, only to be trodden on by the front hoof of the gunslinger's horse. This hero wasn't just a pro, a man of experience: he had adopted a personal style which was unbelievably cool. He still wore a sweat-stained flat-top hat low down over his eyes, but he seemed to be doing so because it was *stylish*, like his shaggy waistcoat, which looked from a distance like a cutaway Yak coat from the Kathmandu Trail. The dark brown hat was made of leather, not felt, and it was tilted forward, whether or not the gunslinger was facing the sun. It was only in the old-time 'B' movies – the ones where the cowboy still kissed his horse – and in some television Westerns, that hats (to be precise, white felt hats with three or four dents in their high crowns) were worn during leisure hours on the *back* of the head. And in Eastwood films – where the competition was no longer between goodies and baddies, but between perhaps goodies and very-very-baddies – white hats were most definitely *out*.

The sequence, starting with the silhouette of a leafless tree against a Mexican sunrise, had so far neatly provided a series of dark spaces against which to project the credits. It had also, and this was the point, reintroduced us to a big-budget variation on the Man With No Name. Boetticher's sunset had been turned quite literally into Eastwood's sunrise; by the late 1960s you didn't *begin* a Western with a sunset, unless it chronicled the adventures of a senior citizen.

As he approaches the rise of a hill, our hero hears the sound of drunken laughter. He looks quizzical for a moment – or rather, squints. He dismounts and strides over to a rock overlooking a desert canyon: the sound of his spurs is amplified on the soundtrack, and we get a subjective shot of his approach to the rock. He immediately takes in exactly what is happening. Three men are dancing around a terrified, half-naked woman: they are evidently drunk. The gunslinger fires his Colt to attract their attention, and snarls, 'The party's over. You men can git movin'.'

The three men – all of whom have the pock-marked, plug-ugly physiognomies of Spaghetti Western villains, and two of whom look very like Mexicans – pause, as they consider their position. He has the high ground and the sun behind him, but there are three of them.

'I don't know who y'are – but, er, why be a *hog* man – she can have four of us.'

'We also got some mighty fine whisky here.'

'Waiting for yer.'

The gunslinger, eyes of flint narrowing, coolly shoots two of the rapists as they run. The third grabs hold of the woman, while our hero ducks behind the rock.

'Now what're you goin' to do, you *bastard*? You might get me, but you sure as hell ain't gonna get any part of her – unless . . .'

The gunslinger lights his brown cigar, striking the match on the sole of his boot. He then takes a stick of dynamite, lights the short fuse and tosses it over the rock. It lands just by the villain's feet. In a panic, the boy shoots almost crazily in the rough direction of the gunslinger then runs for it. Eastwood stands up and shoots him in the back three times, an action accompanied by the trademark scowl and gritted teeth.

The gunslinger strides purposefully – but still coolly – towards the sputtering stick of dynamite. His spurs jangle as he holsters his Colt. He reaches the stick, treads on the fuse, then extinguishes its tip in his mouth and tucks the stick into his shirt pocket. And then, for the first time, he takes a long look at the woman. Morricone's music starts again, on the soundtrack.

Eastwood: You keep standing around like that, the sun's gonna burn the hell outta you.

Maclaine: They told me . . . they were going to kill me . . . they told me . . .

Eastwood: Well they ain't tellin' you much now – so get dressed, huh?

As he says this, in his breathy Californian voice, the gunslinger walks straight past the Sister (for that is who she is) without even looking at her, towards the three bodies he intends to loot.

At this moment during the premiere, Ron Ely – who had lived through the script with Boetticher, and knew exactly what he wanted – said to his friend Budd, 'Let's turn around and hit those two sons of bitches.' To which Boetticher laughingly replied, 'I tell you what, you hit Clint and I'll hit Don.'

'Actually,' Boetticher recalls, 'Siegel called me the next day and said, "Thank you for not walking out; I knew this wasn't what you wanted." ' Clint Eastwood's response to the man who was sitting directly in front of him has not been recorded.

So, why such an extreme reaction from Boetticher?

In the first place, the hero of the story – called Lucy in the original version, Hogan in the film – had changed beyond all recognition. As Boetticher says, 'He had really become the man without a name. It's the difference between [Italian director] Sergio Leone and what I do. We have a different style of talking about men. My men have become tough for a *reason:* maybe the character in *Two Mules* would have been a cowpoke if his wife had lived, and they'd had their son, but it didn't work out that way and fate intervened, and all of a sudden here's a guy that's angry, who says what we all would say in the circumstances: "Why me?". You know, "I was going to settle down and okay, screw it, now I'm going to become a gunslinger", and he got a *job* and his whole idea is when he doesn't trust anybody "never get involved, don't give a damn about anybody", and then he goes and falls in love with a nun! Well, how screwed up can you get?'

In the second place, the hero also seemed to be much more concerned about personal style – about cultivating his ironic, detached stance in order to enhance his status as a walking piece of mythology – than about behaving in a remotely credible way: he was forever 'getting his act together' (in the cult phrase of the day) and this act had to be stylised, laid back and elegant.

'When the gunslinger put out the dynamite, I was disgusted,' Boetticher continues. 'It disgusted me because the minute he walked casually down to stop the dynamite from exploding, I said, "We're gone – how are you going to get anybody to believe the rest of this picture?" And that's the minute Ron turned to me and he said, "Jesus Christ, that's not the way you do it." And I thought, "My God, we're going to have another Eastwood thing" and Clint can be so good or so bad. To see what I had written for Robert Mitchum destroyed by this situation, which was mostly the producer's fault – I just couldn't believe it. I mean, if I was to throw dynamite to get rid of those guys, I wouldn't *walk* down to that dynamite. In my script, the gunslinger went *flying* down there, slid into it like third base, grabbed it in his mouth, and now you come to the nun who was naked. Three dead guys are all around, and he chews it until it stops sparkling and he says, "Put your clothes on. It's going to get cold". He didn't walk down there like Douglas Fairbanks senior, who'd never have done it that way anyway. It was awful.'

In the third place, the plot, with its various 'mysteries' which were revealed as the action progressed, seemed to have become less important than the $4 million spectacle – Eastwood's prowess with gun/dynamite; a bridge plus locomotive blowing up; a night-time battle between Juaristas and a French garrison – all added to Boetticher's script in an attempt to give the piece a 'roadshow' feel. And a great deal less important than the detailed variations on a successful theme:

'I wrote a very serious picture that was funny,' says Boetticher, 'and they made a very funny picture that isn't funny. I didn't tell anybody that the girl was a nun, and that the nun was a prostitute, until the end of the picture, until the last two minutes. The whole idea of the story was these two dreadful people – one, who you believe is a nun, becomes a beautiful person because she falls in love with a bum, who becomes a beautiful person because he is in love with an unobtainable woman. He is in love with the only thing he has fought all his life – the Church. And he can't have her because she is *for real* . . . She didn't smoke a cigar in the second reel and wink at the audience. I loved the review in the *Hollywood Reporter*. It said, "the only one who was surprised when she became a hooker was Clint Eastwood". I mean the most stupid guy in the theatre *had* to be the leading man, because she's been smoking cigars and taking shots of liquor. It wasn't about a war. It was about two people – people you are *involved* with – who become good from being very, very bad. I was told that the producer Martin Rackin – the man who stated *in print* that he would remake *Stagecoach* to see if this time it could be done *right* – also admitted that he didn't even know who the second mule was!'

The conclusion from Boetticher's point of view was, "Damn it, I sure felt sorry for Sister Sara. She was a hell of a nice nun while she lasted".'

The reason I have described this story, which took place between the mid-1960s and 1970, in such detail is because the story of the transformation of Budd Boetticher's screenplay *Two Mules for Sister Sara* into a Clint Eastwood star vehicle in a Western setting represents a key moment in the recent history of American popular culture, which is to say global culture. It also reveals a great deal about Eastwood's important and distinctive contribution to that story.

Two Mules isn't a particularly interesting film in itself; on the contrary, in the list of Eastwood's achievements as an actor, it comes fairly low down (partly because it is one of the most vocal of his major roles, partly because of the miscasting of Shirley Maclaine). But the contrast between Boetticher's work (which arose out of the 1950s Western and, long before that, the origins of the genre itself) and Eastwood's (which brought a new 'image' to the American hero – an image which Eastwood would spend the next two decades exploring and developing and even satirising) is a pivotal one. It had already been demonstrated, eighteen months before, in Eastwood's first film with Don Siegel *Coogan's Bluff*, the story of a deputy sheriff from Arizona who treats the streets of modern New York City as though they all lead to the OK Corral, that the image worked just as well in a contemporary setting as it did in the wild Southwest. Just as well for Coogan as Hogan.

Budd Boetticher, who had worked with John Ford in the early 1950s, had attracted much critical attention – especially from the avant-garde film magazine *Cahiers du Cinéma* in Paris – for the cycle of low-budget Westerns he had made between 1956 and 1960, scripted by Burt Kennedy and starring Randolph Scott, *Seven Men from Now, The Tall T, Ride Lonesome* and *Comanche Station*. In these films, sometime romantic lead and Western hero Scott played characters with names like Stride, Brennan, Brigade and Cody, who represented integrity, resolve and inner strength in a barren wasteland peopled with drifters who were sadly lacking in all of these attributes. Scott was already in his mid-fifties (the same age as William S. Hart, whom he resembled, in *Tumbleweeds,* 1925, and as silver-haired William Boyd when he started reappearing as Hopalong Cassidy on television). As Boetticher put it, he was 'moral, warm and he could be funny . . . a Western hero whom everyone related to'. Sometimes, the Scott character would go too far, as when his own tragic history led him to put personal revenge before more social forms of morality (almost a trademark in Boetticher Westerns). Sometimes, his values, like his physical appearance, seemed archaic. But such ambiguities and imperfections meant that the films were dramas rather than parables – and that they could be taken seriously by adults. His actions always made some kind of sense, within Boetticher's (and Kennedy's) symbolic landscape where, as one critic put it, 'life goes on with no meaning other than the sense of worth and purpose that strong individuals bring to it'.

Scott rode through these stories, which usually took the form of journeys, with a clear sense of what was noble, a complete lack of self-consciousness, and an unshakeable belief in the credo 'a man's gotta do what a man's gotta do'. In short, he epitomised 'the Westerner' in the sense that critic Robert Warshaw gave to the term when Randolph Scott was at the height of his popularity. 'He fights not for advantage and not for the right, but to state what he is, and he must live in a world which permits that statement. The Westerner is the last gentleman and the movies which over and over again tell his story are probably the last art form in which the concept of honor retains its strength.'

George Macdonald Fraser, in his book *The Hollywood History of the World,* sees this 'Westerner' as coming in two distinct – well, fairly distinct – varieties: Randolph Scott and John Wayne:

'Scott is the old-fashioned ideal, quiet, slightly grim, self-possessed, eyes on the horizon, unfailingly courteous, touching his hat-brim to ladies and calling them "ma'am" (he could even remove a note from Marlene Dietrich's garter with perfect good breeding), meeting trouble with a poker face and a lightning draw. Was he ever heard to swear? I doubt it. Wayne was a harder article altogether, a rugged expansionist with a short fuse, given to strong language and physical violence; even when complimenting a schoolmarm on her cooking he did it with a deep-breathing deliberation which suggested that he was preparing to go out and wreck a saloon, preferably with Scott inside it . . . Asked to define their screen religions, I should have put down Scott as an Episcopalian and Wayne as a lapsed Presbyterian.'

The two characters did, in fact, meet in the wartime version of the Klondike yarn, *The Spoilers* (Ray Enright, 1942), and the medium-term result was that a bedroom, a stairway and a saloon were broken to smithereens in a fist fight which lasted the best part of a reel. At one surprisingly 'in-joke' moment in the film, Scott bumped into the table of a moustached man who was observing the action from a distance, sipping whisky and writing: the man turned out to be none other than the poet Robert Service (or rather, an actor impersonating him) in the process of writing one of his famous prairie poems (or 'pomes', as they were known) – such as 'The Shooting of Dan McGrew' or 'The Cremation of Sam McGee'. Shortly after seeing the film, the elderly Robert Service himself was inspired to write his only (so far as I know) poem about the movies, called 'John Wayne and Randolph Scott'. The two great 'Westerners'. Forty years later, in a very different era of movie mythology – the era of the mature Clint Eastwood and the immature Arnold Schwarzenegger – President Ronald Reagan would recite 'The Shooting of Dan McGrew' *in toto* as his favourite party-piece in the White House, to remind himself of the good ol' days, when men were men and women seemed still to like it that way. In *The Spoilers,* incidentally, John Wayne won the fist fight (despite having a spitoon and half the contents of a furniture warehouse chucked at him), for Randolph Scott was playing a crooked gold commissioner over a decade before he was ennobled in all those Ranown Westerns for Budd Boetticher in the 1950s, and so became a Westerner.

The central character in Boetticher's screenplay of *Two Mules for Sister Sara* may have done those things he oughtn't to have done and left undone those things he ought to have done, but by the end he too has proved himself, all in all, to be a 'Westerner', rather like the Randolph Scott character in Sam Peckinpah's *Guns in the Afternoon* (also known as *Ride the High Country*) – itself an elaborate homage to the Boetticher Westerns.

In *Guns*, Joel McCrea, playing a highly principled ex-marshal, has been shot: Scott, playing (apparently against type) the less-than-principled gunman who was once McCrea's friend, rushes to his rescue. As McCrea lies dying, Scott solemnly promises that he will, after all, return the gold he has stolen to its rightful owner. McCrea's last words are, 'Hell, I know that. Always did. *You* just forgot it for a while, that's all.' To which Scott adds, 'I'll see you later' as he prepares to ride back to the low country with its sidewalks, its traffic congestion and its suburbs.

The Clint Eastwood character in the film version of *Two Mules* would never have returned that gold. Indeed, at the end of Sergio Leone's *For a Few Dollars More* he grabs hold of a saddlebag of gold, which he knows to be stolen, before riding off in the opposite direction to the sunset. He lives on his wits; he much prefers survival to honour, revenge to community spirit; he will protect his own privacy and independence before almost all other things. He is a loner who will not admit to having had a history (which might make him vulnerable); one of his main ambitions seems to be to exploit the injustices he sees all around him (rather than attempting to put them right); he doesn't do things because 'a man's gotta do what a man's gotta do' but because he's being paid for doing them. And perhaps above all, he is highly self-conscious about the way he presents himself to others – about his personal style, which has more to do with Latin machismo than American toughness.

As critic Scott Simmon has written, 'Audiences loved this guy, not because he stood for honour and home but because he was the coolest, the best, the *survivor*'. Also because he was relatively *youthful* – Eastwood was in his mid-thirties at the time of the 'Dollars' films – when most of the old-style Hollywood heroes were heading for the last round-up. To put it more simply (as Clint Eastwood himself did, when *A Fistful of Dollars* first opened in America), 'I do all the stuff John Wayne would never do.' He could well have added with even more emphasis that Randolph Scott would never do. The only consistency between the two – apart, of course, from the Western genre itself, with its repertoire of settings, stories and ideologies – was that the Eastwood character, like Wayne and Scott, was certain of himself as rugged individualist but uncertain in nearly all his relationships with others. Unlike Wayne and Scott, however, he never expressed this uncertainty (about relationships with the opposite sex, anyway) by muttering 'Aw, shucks' and talking with rising gorge to the schoolmarm about a little ranch in the prairies: instead, he kept himself to himself and just walked away. Wayne and Scott yearned for commitment, for the pursuit of an ideal. Eastwood preferred to believe that he who travels alone travels furthest, and his terms were strictly cash. The hero with no answers.

One reason why the Eastwood image, whether in Westerns or in contemporary adventures, 'clicked' with American audiences from the late 1960s onwards was that it seemed to embody the values (or lack of them) of the only credible hero in the era of Vietnam. American audiences saw *A Fistful of Dollars* (three years after their European counterparts) at the same time as the launching of the Tet offensive. *For a Few Dollars More* and *The Good, The Bad and The Ugly* were released when the My Lai massacre was making headlines on television and in the press.

Michael Herr reported in his *Dispatches* from the front to *Esquire* magazine that John Wayne's 'Vietnam' adventure, *The Green Berets,* was proving popular with the troops *as a comedy* rather than as a war movie: 'It wasn't really about Vietnam, it was about Santa Monica.' The film may have named its Green Beret outpost Dodge City, and featured Wayne as Colonel Kirby (a direct reference to John Ford's *Fort Apache*), and even delivered the traditional fade-out with John Wayne ambling into the setting sun (as a perceptive critic added, 'into the South China Seas to the east of Vietnam'), but it didn't work as a Western movie either. The traditional Western story about a hero fighting against the odds for his code of honour, and eventually winning, simply would not 'fit' the experience of the Vietnam war. As Herr relayed, in his zappy rock'n'roll style: 'Mythopathic moment: *Fort Apache,* where Henry Fonda as the new colonel says to John Wayne, the old hand, "We saw some Apache as we neared the fort," and John Wayne says, "If you saw them, sir, they weren't Apache." But this colonel is obsessed, brave like a maniac, not very bright, a West Point aristo wounded in his career and his pride, posted out to some Arizona shithole with only marginal consolation: he's a professional and this is war, the only war we've got. So he gives the John Wayne information a pass and he and half his command get wiped out. More a war movie than a Western.

'Nam paradigm: Vietnam, *not a movie,* no jive cartoon either where the characters get smacked around and electrocuted and dropped from heights, flattened out and frizzed black and broken like a dish, then up again and whole and back in the game; "Nobody dies", as someone said in another war movie . . .'

True, adds Herr, his conversations with conscripts led him to believe that 'Somewhere all the mythic tracks intersected, from the lowest John Wayne wet dream to most aggravated soldier-poet fantasy', but the fact remained that *Catch 22* became a Nam standard 'because it said that in a war everybody thinks that everybody else is crazy', while the *The Green Berets* was popular only because it was so bad. Lieutenant William Calley (of My Lai notoriety) evidently did not get the joke: he recalled of his time in Vietnam, in all seriousness, in 1968: 'I felt alive, as I never had in America. I felt *helpful,* even if I couldn't build a spaceship or something spectacular. I built wells, I showed the Vietnamese movies. I even showed them *The Green Berets.*'

Fort Apache, directed by John Ford in 1947, had ended with a powerful epilogue where John Wayne's Captain Kirby Yorke describes his late commanding officer Lt. Colonel Owen Thursday (Henry Fonda) as if he was a great American hero, even though Yorke *knows* that Thursday was obsessed and not very bright. John Ford later said of this sequence, and of its obvious parallels with the historical Custer, 'We've had a lot of people who were supposed to be great heroes, and you know damn well they weren't. But it's good for the country to have heroes to look up to . . . ' So print the legend.

Fade to the late 1960s when Ford was invited by the United States Information Agency to oversee the production of *Vietnam! Vietnam!*, a documentary film which was intended to be 'good for the country', from the official point of view. Ford's role was to ensure as far as possible that American troops came over as 'heroes to look up to'. In the event, as Joseph McBride described the film: 'Glib as it may sound, Ford's view of the war is reminiscent of a Western. The Vietcong are the bad guys, the peasants are the terrorized farmers, the Americans are the Earp brothers come to clean up the territory so that decent folks can go to church and set up schools. Such an innocent vision of society is charming in the archaic context of the Western genre, but debilitating and ridiculous in a documentary of modern war'. The result was that the film was shelved, in cans marked 'Not to be shown publicly in this country'. It was obsolete even before it was finished.

Another reason why the Eastwood image 'clicked' so effectively from 1967 onwards had to do with longer-term tendencies within the Western film itself, which pre-dated America's involvement in Vietnam. Writer Larry McMurtry — the author, then, of *Horseman, Pass By* (filmed as *Hud*) and *The Last Picture Show* — wrote an essay about these tendencies in 1967 with the mock heroic title 'Cowboys, Movies, Myths and Cadillacs: an excursus on ritual forms in the Western.' As a figure of high romance and myth, wrote McMurtry, the lone cowboy in the Wild West still packed a considerable punch: 'He has outlasted the noble red man, Johnny Reb and Billy Yank, GI Joe, and any number of sports kings and entertainers; he has successfully absorbed the figure of the pioneer, and with luck may even outlast acid-rock.' But there were definite signs that the cowboy's function as a mythic figure in relation to genre and to society was a'changing:

'Indeed, a certain change has already taken place, and was taking place when Robert Warshaw wrote his essay in 1954. If one can apply to the Western the terminology [literary critic] Northrop Frye develops in his essay on fictional modes, we might say that in the fifties the Western began working its way down from the levels of myth and romance *toward the ironic level which it has only recently reached*. Westerns like *Shane* [George Stevens, 1953] and *The Searchers* [John Ford, 1955] are in the high mimetic mode, with the hero still superior to other men and to his environment. In *The Gunfighter* [Henry King, 1950], this is not the case — we have moved to the low mimetic . . . *Hud* [Martin Ritt, 1963] is a recent example of the low mimetic Western, though it tends at several points toward the ironic.

'There are comparable developments in fiction: Thomas Berger's *Little Big Man* is a brilliant ironic performance. Its nearest cinematic equivalent is *Cat Ballou* [Elliot Silverstein, 1965] in which Lee Marvin won an Oscar for a role that parodies the Gunfighter. No doubt high mimetic Westerns will continue to be made as long as John Wayne is acting — he wouldn't fit in any other mode — but in number they are declining, and the figure of "the Westerner" is gradually being challenged by more modern figures.'

According to this analysis — which derives, distantly, from Friedrich Nietzsche's view that art forms have a tendency to travel from high art (where the artists mean it) to the ironic (where the artists both mean it and don't mean it, at the same time), with all the various stages in between, first time as history, last time as farce − Western films up to the 1950s provided myths and romances, and characters who were exemplars within them, that helped to sort out the story of 'America' and retell it as an epic journey. The heroes were played by the likes of John Wayne, Gary Cooper, Randolph Scott and James Stewart. Then came Westerns which, while staying within the rules of the genre, saw their purpose as 'de-mythologising' the West: films such as *The Gunfighter* (where the central character just wants to retire peacefully, but his mythic status won't let him) and *High Noon* (where the townspeople, the silent majority, behave as if *they* are the baddies).

The end of the cycle − until a reworked myth appears which will 'fit' the changed expectations of the audience − comes when irony and parody begin to ride the range, sending up the old rules without bothering to think about what the new ones might look like. A sort of shootout at deconstruction pass.

As Nietzsche wrote in the section of his *Untimely Meditations* which asks the question, 'Are there no longer any living mythologies?': 'The oversaturation of an age . . . implants the belief, harmful at any time, in the old age of mankind, the belief that one is a latecomer and epigone; it leads an age into a dangerous mood of irony in regard to itself and subsequently into the even more dangerous mood of cynicism: in this mood, however, it develops more and more a prudent practical egoism through which the forces of life are paralyzed and at last destroyed . . .' The net result of these dangerous moods of irony and cynicism and the rise of 'a prudent practical egoism', continues Nietzsche, is that you reach a point where 'nothing can affect the age any longer. Good and right things may be done, as deeds, poetry, music, art: the hollowed-out cultivated man of this age at once looks beyond the work and asks about the history of its author.'

To me, this sounds very like much contemporary film criticism (where the critic is much more interested in the budget of the film or its fraught production history than in what is seen up there on the screen; or art criticism, where it is the catalogue, rather than the artworks, which are the focus of the critic's attention). Nietzsche was writing about the historical mythologies of *his* day − and exactly what their relationship was to other tendencies of his age. No wonder he was taken up with such gusto by theorists of post-modernism in the 1970s: the twentieth *siècle* would appear to have begun its *fin* rather earlier than the previous one.

Where the cycle of American Westerns was concerned, the decisive shift from films which pack iron to those which pack irony was perhaps reached, long after McMurtry wrote his prophetic article, when Mel Brooks made *Blazing Saddles* [1974]. In this part-parody, part-farce, the black sheriff of Rockridge asks the townspeople to allow him twenty-four hours to save the town with the words 'You'd do it for Randolph Scott', at which point a heavenly choir repeats the words 'Randolph Scott' as the townspeople reverently remove their hats. *Blazing Saddles* must have been doing something right: it turned out to be one of the most successful Westerns ever at the box office, outgrossing all of John Ford's classic Westerns put together. More subtly, some critics – including the film-maker Paul Schrader – have argued that *all* important Westerns since the mid-1960s have at some level been parodies. This would include *True Grit* [Henry Hathaway, 1970], with its self-consciously 'naive' patchwork-quilty style (yes, John Wayne could engage in self-parody); *The Wild Bunch* [Sam Peckinpah, 1969], with its over-the-top inflation of the gunfighter Western to Wagnerian proportions; and *Butch Cassidy and the Sundance Kid* [George Roy Hill, 1969], with its smart-ass, Beverly Hills dialogue and ever-so-hip references to other Westerns. As another critic has put it, 'Eventually Westerns started to *look* like they were no longer preaching to the converted, and could hear the rude noises from the side aisle.' Or, as the respected citizen Howard Johnson observes in the town meeting sequence of *Blazing Saddles,* 'You know, Nietzsche says "out of chaos comes order" ' – to which the townspeople reply, 'Oh, blow it out your ass, Howard...'

Larry McMurtry had concluded his essay with the optimistic thought that 'in time Hollywood will grow tired of parodying the Gunfighter and the ironic will yield to the mythic again; the Italian-made Clint Eastwood films mark, already, the re-appearance of the archetype'. Yet here was another paradox: a larger-than-life mythic super-figure had emerged (perhaps owing more to Nietzsche than merely his sense of timing), but he had emerged from within a series of stories which were themselves 'brilliant ironic performances'. He was for real, but he also and simultaneously had tongue in *chic*. An American icon who was also an iconoclast. An all-American anti-hero, as he has been called, who had learned his lessons from the Marlon Brando/James Dean generation *as well as from* the Westerners of his youth. A careful craftsman who liked to appear as casual as hell.

Clint Eastwood was to base his entire career as an actor and as a film-maker on the fact that he learned his trade in a Hollywood which still called itself the dream factory, but he became a star – an old-style star – in a Hollywood which no longer had that confidence.

As Deyan Sudjic has recently written in *Cult Heroes* – a book which, in its search for post-Warhol celebrities who manage somehow to be famous for more than fifteen minutes, unaccountably omits any mention of Clint Eastwood: '. . . the qualities of the new cult heroes have very little in common with the virtues attributed to heroes in the past. Chivalry and modesty are conspicuous by their absence. But then the new breed are rarely presented as role models in the way that heroes once were. Today's cult hero is seen by the audience as a focus for the projection of their dreams, more than as a model for emulation.'

This transformation – from chivalry to efficiency, from warmth to cool or even coldness, from affection to affectlessness, from life-experience to lifestyle, however you want to put it – this transformation seems to have happened (or more accurately accelerated) in the movies, in advertising and marketing, and in popular music, some time during the 1960s, in the era of James Bond, Pop Art and The Man With No Name. By the 1980s, it had become the cornerstone of a significant growth industry. The hero as style warrior or as corporate image. Sudjic continues, 'These changes amount to something rather more fundamental than the shifting back and forth of large amounts of cash. Perhaps the nature of the change can be explained partly by the isolation and anonymity of life in the big cities. There is an apparent yearning for hero figures [of the new breed], . . . to service that demand, a handful of individuals have moved beyond celebrity to become cult heroes. They have a presence, whether it is created artificially or not, which has a powerful economic role . . . The heroes who last are the ones who have the stamina to adapt to adjusting circumstances. Partly it is a question of substance. The cult hero needs to have more than one good idea. But it is also a stylistic issue.'

In the late 1960s, when the films of John Ford and Budd Boetticher were rediscovered by classrooms full of style-conscious European cinéastes, this search for the new cult hero led to some strange reinterpretations of what the films had meant first time round. Of the Randolph Scott/Burt Kennedy/Boetticher Westerns, it was the last – *Comanche Station* made in 1960, the year before *Dr No* – which stimulated the most speculation. Knowing that Boetticher himself had trained as a bullfighter in Mexico, and had spent as much time as he could afford in and around the corridas of Tijuana (as well as making two bullfighting pictures earlier in the 1950s), cinéastes began to reinterpret the Randolph Scott hero as some kind of a matador – a strutting, machismo figure whose behaviour has as much to do with style as substance.

The opening sequence of *Comanche Station* (which in fact resembles the equivalent sequence in the script of *Two Mules for Sister Sara*) seemed an excellent case in point. Randolph Scott, as Cody, is riding out of a rocky canyon – with a pack-mule in tow – when he is suddenly surrounded by a band of Comanche warriors, on their pinto ponies: as is usual in 1950s Westerns, the Indians hold the high ground, the hero is trapped in the bowl of the canyon; what is unusual, is that the Indians form a circle, rather than the usual line along a ridge, around the hapless hero. Boetticher recalls a film seminar in Paris, during which this sequence was discussed: 'The students in France were *so disillusioned* when they found out they'd been completely wrong about me, and everything I did in those pictures, but for the last question one of the fellows said – and he'd scratched out all the stuff he'd written for his thesis – he said, "let me ask you one thing, I just *know* I'm right about this", and all the kids got their pencils ready, they were so delightful it was terrible to disillusion 'em. He said, "During the opening of *Comanche Station,* Randolph Scott is the matador in the middle of the ring of Indians who represent the *plaza de toros,* right?" And I said, "Wrong!" He said, "What do you mean?" I said, "He's not a matador – he's a cowboy in a hell of a lot of trouble." And they said, "Well, what about the arena – the circumference – isn't that a bullring?" I said, "No, that was a convenient way to circle someone, they could have done it in a square; with the Indians, it would have been the same situation. He still wouldn't have been going any place."

'You see, my hero isn't a matador performing before the crowds in a bullring, he is a very simple man, who's educated from the Church, he's religious, he believes in his morals, he believes in the things that I believe in. And he has a job to do. As simple as that. And he does it. But, to make him more attractive – to help the audience relate to him – Burt and I put opposite him really attractive, deadly, colourful guys to play off him.'

In the years when Clint Eastwood was fast becoming the world's number one box-office star, the ageing John Ford had moved 150 miles away from the film community to a ranch-style house in Palm Desert on the Old Prospector Trail. There he surrounded himself with mementoes of history and legend which he had collected during his seventy-eight years. They included a war bonnet from the Battle of Little Big Horn, a pair of gloves worn by Buffalo Bill in the Wild West Show, Wyatt Earp's rifle, a statue of the Virgin Mary, a portrait of Abraham Lincoln, photos of assorted American admirals (including himself), six Oscars, and a rosary. He had lived from the gung-ho days of Roughriding Teddy Roosevelt right through to the American withdrawal from Vietnam under smooth-talking Dicky Nixon, and he was much given to saying that 'Our ancestors would be bloody ashamed if they could see us today'. Hollywood had lost interest in him as a working film-maker, but film buffs the world over (to him, the lowest form of human life) were determined to turn him into a national monument. He talked of new projects – even, on one bizarre occasion, a Western to be financed by the Italians – but they all came to nothing. He spent much of his time watching television in the bedroom, with a bottle of Guinness to hand. One evening, shortly before he died in 1973, he happened to see Don Siegel's *Two Mules for Sister Sara*. His old friend Budd Boetticher recalls exactly what happened:

'John Ford called me and this was the whole conservation. The phone rang, and I picked it up and he said,

'"Budd, Jack Ford."

'I said, "Yes sir, how are you?"

'He growled, "Did you make that piece of shit I saw on the tube last night?"

'I said, "Er ..."

'He said, "What the hell were all the mountain lions and the hawks and the tarantulas? All that crap, What *is* that?"

'I said "Jack, I didn't make it – the only credit I have is the story and it's my title. It's certainly not what *I* would have done."

'He said, "I didn't think so."

'Bang, he slammed down the phone. That's the way he was with me. But I loved him. And it *was* a piece of crap.'

You can almost hear The Man With No Name whispering, in a voice as gentle as ever, 'When you say that about me, *smile* ...'

2 He doesn't know how good he is . . .

Ever since he became a name above the title, in the mid-1960s, Clint Eastwood has tried as far as possible to prune the scripts in which he has chosen to act: any dialogue that is 'too expository' tends to get cut away before a foot of film is shot. This usually means that the co-star talks a bit too much – like Richard Burton in *Where Eagles Dare* or Shirley Maclaine in *Two Mules for Sister Sara,* or the *Dirty Harry* films where the over-talkative ones tend to be the out-and-out punks, while Eastwood comes over as monosyllabic man: his actions speak far louder than his words.

But the moment you meet Eastwood you are struck by the differences between his screen persona and his own personality. Rather like that other actor-turned-director Woody Allen, the closer you get to him the more you realise what a conscientious and craftsmanlike actor he must be. When I met Eastwood – in the wide-open spaces of a suite of rooms at Claridges Hotel in London, where he sat carefully munching fruit and nuts – he seemed both articulate and relaxed, give or take a few long silences and a tendency to leave his answers trailing in the air. More like Josey Wales or Bronco Billy or the country-and-western singer Red Stovall in *Honkytonk Man,* than The Man With No Name or Harry Callahan.

There are more obvious differences, too, between the magnum star and the real man. In the 'Dollars' films of the mid-1960s, the bounty hunter always had a small cigar in his mouth: but Eastwood does not approve of smoking (although he admits, for that role, the cigars 'kept me in the right kind of humour – kind of a fog'). Harry Callahan fires his .44 Magnum at the advancing baddies while

21

chewing on a takeaway hamburger: Eastwood is, in fact, unimpressed by violent solutions to everyday problems, and, a careful eater who believes in a substantial daily intake of vitamins and minerals, he tries, where possible, to avoid red meat. These days, there are almost as many words written about him in books with titles like *Life Extension: a practical scientific approach* or in monthly fitness magazines, as there are in the movie journals. Then again, the avenging High Plains Drifter is cruel to everyone in town – and especially to the women (whether local floozie or sensible lodging-house keeper): but Eastwood was delighted at the overstatement when a critic, referring to the meaty parts he had offered over the years to talented actresses, dubbed him 'Hollywood's most feminist film director'. 'Remember,' Eastwood says, 'I grew up watching films with all the strong women like Joan Crawford.' Such characters certainly help to offset his own larger-than-life persona and, certainly since the mid-1970s, most of his films have attempted to take apart the macho image which made him famous. He has often observed of his own attitudes, 'People who are confident in their masculinity don't have to kick in doors, mistreat women or make fun of gays.'

Most of the cowboys and cops he has played have been accused, at one time or another, of a 'fascist' mentality. Yet, far from being a Bay Area Mussolini, Eastwood seems to believe in a strange mixture of anarchism, Republicanism, populism and individualism. I say 'seems' because, although he has been mayor of his home town of Carmel, he is uncomfortable talking politics and he feels strongly that actors and entertainers should not thump tubs about their personal views on public affairs. People who have tunnel vision about their political affiliations, he once said on the stage of London's National Film Theatre, tend to be boring and inflexible people, difficult to have a conversation with: but, he added, good luck to them 'so long as they don't hurt anyone else'.

The characters he plays on screen, by contrast, tend to have rather more closed minds. As Robert Mazzocco has written: 'With Clint Eastwood, the topical referent has been nostalgic, the average man's growing uneasiness over the eclipse of the old paths, old truths, from the Silent Majority to Moral Majority, what some now call "the politics of resentment" ... In Eastwood's movies, frustration and aggression are dominant . . . Understandably, such a persona, more Yankee than Puritan and more "Lonesome Traveler" than either, is pre-eminently a man with a project: a battle to win, frontier to cross, criminal to collar; evocative of patriarchy, yet aloof from it, with little belief in Providence but lots in provender. He is a "closed" rather than an "open" personality, without unction and without "feminine" traits; a graduate of the school of hard knocks.'

Confronted by such analyses, Eastwood the actor, unconsciously echoing Budd Boetticher, tends to say things like 'I've conducted cinema classes around the world, and people will sometimes put the wildest interpretations on something you've done.' Unlike Boetticher he continues, 'Whatever they say, I say "That's right". It's their *participation* that I want. What counts is what gives *them* the best enjoyment.' But he is prepared to concede that the characters he plays have a cinematic precedent in the form of director Frank Capra's heroes of the 1930s, Mr Deeds and Mr Smith, who were heroes because 'they were different', because they stood out as individuals against faceless bureaucrats, *and* because they were able to express themselves: 'Some people still cling to the idea that the *Dirty Harry* films are some kind of right-wing statement . . . but you can interpret them as other things too, if you want to take the time to think about it . . . as an individual going against the system.' Whatever the intentions behind the *Dirty Harry* project (Mr Deeds never actually blew people's heads off, as I recall) one thing is for certain: Eastwood in person is a great deal more 'open', less dogmatic, than the characters he plays, even though he is in fact a graduate of the school of hard knocks. He is a herbivore who has become the most famous film actor in the world by pretending to be a carnivore.

The only points of contact between persona and personality are his soft Californian voice, whence seldom is heard a discouraging word, his eyes (one of his most charismatic features, on film) which tend to turn glacial when he's confronted by a pretentious question, and a lean craggy profile, which gets leaner and craggier with the passing of the years.

He doesn't like talking about success. Nevertheless, he seems gratified that after thirty-six major features as actor or director or both over the last twenty-seven years, he is at last getting good notices and serious critical attention in America as well as in Europe. 'Maybe,' he says, 'it isn't all some cowboy or cop who happened to click.'

And maybe those films which didn't happen to click first time round are the ones which will last the longest: '*The Beguiled* has always been well thought of in Paris, so it works well for me in the long run. It's even been suggested to me by a friend of mine that those kinds of films – with *Bronco Billy* and *Honkytonk Man* – may rise higher as time goes on, because they were films which were turning points in my career.' *The Beguiled* perhaps paving the way towards his own films as a director; *Bronco Billy* towards an examination of losers rather than winners; and *Honkytonk Man* towards the confidence to be more autobiographical.

It wasn't always thus. Until the early 1980s, the Spaghetti Westerns starring Eastwood tended to be dismissed (especially by the New York weeklies) as 'too heavy on the bolognese'; his *Dirty Harry* cop films were macho, 'fascistic' and evidence of Hollywood losing whatever social conscience it once possessed in the good old days; and his own personal explorations of the American dream (like *Play Misty for Me*) were 'vicious and emetic'. In other words, this was entertainment for meatheads and rednecks (or equivalents) the world over. But opinions have changed.

'It's interesting,' muses Eastwood. 'The more intellectual community' (he says this looking directly at me) 'seem to ask more about, are more anxious about, the Western movie than the man in the street.' In 1980 the Museum of Modern Art in New York ran a retrospective of his entire *oeuvre*, centring on the recently released *Bronco Billy*. Both in 1985 and 1988 he appeared on the platform at the Cannes Film Festival (where screenings of *Pale Rider* and *Bird* were shown in competition). He has been presented with a fistful of compliments by Norman Mailer, who wrote: 'Eastwood is an artist . . . I'll go further. I'll say that you can see the man in his work just as clearly as you can see Hemingway in *A Farewell to Arms* or John Cheever in his short stories. Hell, yes, he's an artist. I even think he's important . . . Not just a fabulous success at the box office, but important . . . (but) I'm angry with him. He doesn't know how good he is. I don't think he tries hard enough for what's truly difficult.'

This macho prose style – which reads like a good ole buddy-movie in essay format – may have been an attempt to outgun the *New York Review of Books,* which had featured Eastwood's name on its cover in April 1982 (the cover actually promised 'Clint Eastwood/ Wittgenstein/G.B. Shaw') to draw attention to an impeccably liberal article entitled 'The Supply-Side Star' by Robert Mazzocco, which concluded: 'The Eastwood phenomenon, I think, lends itself to an examination of how the "convictions" of free spirit and rugged individualist, which found root in our soil long before the industrial-isation of America, continue to fascinate, despite their archaic air . . . Yet what's most distinctive about Eastwood, a latecomer to the ranks of rugged individualists, is how effectively he struggles against absorption into mere genre, mere style, even while appearing, with his long-boned casualness and hypnotic presence, to be *nothing but style*.'

Card-carrying cinéastes had a chance to put some of this to the man himself when Clint Eastwood held a press conference in Cannes to discuss *Pale Rider*, his first Western for nine years. Given European attitudes towards gung-ho American popular culture at the time, the event could well have turned into a shootout, but instead, a genial exchange along these lines took place.

FRENCH CINÉASTE *(evidently recovering from total immersion in the* écrits *of psychoanalyst Jacques Lacan):* 'Monsieur Eastwood, your own Western films as *auteur*, zay have a certain tendency to represent an Oedipal destruction, 'ow you say, of your cinematic father Sergio Leone – *n'est-ce-pas?*'

CLINT EASTWOOD *(after a long, long pause):* 'Sergio Leone my father? Serge, uh, Sergio and I are both the same age, so if he is my father, Sergio must have conceived me at a very early age.'

Shortly after this, a visiting American critic in Cannes quite rightly pointed out that 'the Eastwood phenomenon' (as members of the more intellectual community tend to call it, like isolating a not entirely malign virus) wasn't about psychology at all but about mythology: so it was bizarre in the extreme to apply neo-Freudian analysis to a body of work from which 'the inner man' was almost entirely absent.

Eastwood's film *Bird* opens with a much more apt quotation, from F. Scott Fitzgerald: 'There are no second acts in American lives'. This does not, of course, fit Eastwood's *own* second career as a film-maker but it certainly fits his film mythology, built on the powerful, ironic image which he projected through his work as an actor in the mid to late 1960s. The image, as we have seen, is that of the eternal outsider, who walks gracefully and stylishly along the main street (Eastwood has the most distinctive walk in movies since John Wayne strode around the Big Mitten, Monument Valley), his eyes squinting into the sunlight, streetwise about everything that's going on around him. During *City Heat* (1984), the otherwise dull homage to Warner Brothers crime movies he appeared in opposite Burt Reynolds, there's a knowing comment on this image. Reynolds has been hiding himself from a gang of vicious hit men, while Eastwood has been coolly trying to save him. 'I've been doing it all wrong,' moans Reynolds. 'I've been hiding — you just walk down the middle of the street, huh?' Like Hogan walking down the slope towards the dynamite in *Two Mules for Sister Sara*. It is an image Clint Eastwood carefully nurtured, and about which he has few illusions: paying customers tend to go into the cinema feeling frustrated and they come out feeling great. As he admitted to Norman Mailer: 'People in the audience just sit there and say, "I admire the independence. I'd like to have the nerve to tell the boss off or have that control over my life." In the society we live in, everything is kind of controlled for us. We just grow up and everything's kind of done. A lot of people are drawn to an original like Dirty Harry. The general public interpreted it on that level, a man concerned about a victim he'd never met . . . And I think a lot of people believe there isn't anybody who's willing to expend that kind of effort if they were in that situation.'

At which point Mailer asked, 'Do you think this is one reason why blacks like your movies so much?'

'Well,' was the cautious reply, 'maybe blacks feel that he's an outsider like they felt they've been.'

Actually, ethnic audiences, especially in America, have been loyal supporters of the Eastwood persona since the days of the Italian Westerns — when Jamaican Ska musicians released numbers with titles like 'For a Few Dollars More' or 'There's a Stranger in Town'; when Jimmy Cliff went to see a Spaghetti at the Rialto, Kingston (Jamaica), in Perry Henzell's *The Harder they Come*, before embarking on his life of crime; and when Eastwood's appearance – complete with poncho and cigarillo – made him look as though he was equally at home in both first and third worlds. In Britain, a popular reggae singer even adopted the name 'Clint Eastwood'.

Paradoxically, where the *Dirty Harry* films were concerned, young black males – together with drug addicts, 'militants' of all descriptions and other inhabitants of the run-down inner city areas of edge-city-by-the-bay, San Francisco – tended, inevitably, to be the baddies as well. Which brings us back to the 'politics of resentment' and the controversial question of closed minds. A question to which Eastwood tends to reply, 'Dirty Harry has a broad appeal [to black audiences] because he's fighting the bureaucracy. He's trying to get things done. And it's hard to get things done. You're not only fighting the criminal element, you're also fighting the bureaucracy of society.' Which brings us *right* back to 'the politics of resentment'.

Having created the Eastwood persona – a hero who is distanced from being a hero, a hero about heroes – especially in the Italian 'Dollars' films of 1964 – 7, and in his early films as a director from 1971, he has, as he modestly puts it, proceeded to 'pick up things that work for me – and just kept adding on'; kept adapting to adjusting circumstances. In other, perhaps more pretentious words, the second act of Clint Eastwood had involved deconstructing the first while still keeping the 'act' going.

'If I just wanted to go out and make some dough,' he says, 'I could gun 'em down as good as I ever did. But I'd rather not do movies where there are 800 guys in the theater and one chick who was coerced into going by her brother.' But his process of 'adding on' is not, according to Eastwood, a rational process. Rather, it is instinctive – from the 'gut, or soul, or heart, or wherever you want to place it . . . I can't start thinking about how I function within my image instead of how I function as an actor. It leads to a circular thing, worrying about my conception of the audience's conception of who I am. The audience reacts by instinct. So I have to produce in the same way they react.' If you start making a movie with a particular audience – or even reviewer – in mind, 'you'll get fooled every time.'

Perhaps this is why, although Hollywood executives have frequently cautioned him about tampering with his hard-won image, he has in nine cases out of ten taken a loyal mass audience with him. Others, such as Burt Reynolds, Charles Bronson, Sylvester Stallone and Chuck Norris, have not tried quite so hard: they've preferred to perform endless encores. As Norman Mailer put it in his inimitable way: 'What separated Eastwood from other box-office stars was that his films (especially since he had begun to direct them) had come to speak more and more of his own vision of life in America. One was encountering a homegrown philosophy . . . Burt Reynolds also gives us a private vision of the taste of life in America, but it is not so much a philosophy as a premise. East high on the hog, Reynolds suggests. The best way to get through life is drunk. Since it's possible that half the male population of America under forty believes this, Reynolds is endlessly reliable . . . The car gets totalled, but Burt is too loaded to be hurt. He leaps to his feet, pulls the fender off his neck with a sorry look, and we laugh . . . Eastwood is saying more.'

Although Eastwood and Reynolds appeared together on the cover of *Time* Magazine in 1978 ('Good ole Burt, Cool-Eyed Clint'), although Reynolds himself has said, 'We both have a particular audience that is loyal to us no matter what the critics say'; and although their careers (television Westerns/Spaghetti Westerns/Hollywood) are very similar, in the last fifteen years Eastwood has allowed himself to develop while Good ole Burt has not, at least not to the same extent. Burt has continued to wink at the camera, and watch himself being ever-so-macho. It is a question of how one uses fame, and the economic power it brings. As Eastwood has said, 'If you're not willing to stretch out and do different things, what's the use of being in a fairly good position to do them? This is a great era for actors. Any actor who's doing well can have a certain amount of control. In the old days, it was "Here's your next picture, Mr Bogart." Today, you're a free agent.' To put it another way, when, in the 1960s, film people used the word 'agent', it tended to refer to James Bond. Today, it refers to the people who run Hollywood.

Perhaps his unusual ability to 'add on', to keep in touch, is partly sustained by Eastwood's mistrust of the usual corporate methods of market research – questionnaires, computer analyses, screenings in executive suites: 'The studios love to throw the thing in hoppers and computers – but I just go on, er, instinct.' He prefers to visit the local cinemas in Carmel-by-the-sea, or Monterey, sometimes in disguise, to see and hear for himself the audience reaction to his work. Not your typical middle American audience, admittedly, but more typical than a group of impressionable Hollywood wives. In recent years the result of his participant observation has been that Eastwood has alternated a shoot-'em-up (usually a cop movie) with a more personal project. Like Woody Allen, whom he much admires ('He's still reaching out. There's a seriousness about him, even in his humour') he buys the possibility of being ambitious by sometimes producing work which is less ambitious. But unlike Woody Allen, whose image remains closely associated with the angst-ridden life of smart people on the upper east side of New York, Clint Eastwood's territory is still expanding all the time.

However, the late 1960s image is still powerful enough to cause a long-standing public confusion, characteristic of big-budget moviemaking, with its attendant publicity, between Eastwood and 'Eastwood'. ('Everybody keeps asking about Harry Callahan.') Shortly after the local newsletter, the *Carmel Pine Cone and Carmel Valley Outlook* (total circulation 10,000), announced to the unsuspecting world on 30 January 1986 that Clint Eastwood would be running for the $200-a-month job of Mayor of Carmel, endless Clint-runs-for-Mayor jokes began to play on this confusion. In Garry Trudeau's *Doonesbury* strip cartoon, the mayoral candidate, represented only by his cowboy boots, was asked, 'What's the greatest problem facing municipal government today?' His reply was 'Punks!' And countless 'Clint for Mayor' or 'Clintville-by-the-Sea', or even 'Clint for President' T-shirts made visual reference to the same sequence in *Dirty Harry* and *Magnum Force*, by showing a finger itching to squeeze the trigger of a Colt .44 Magnum. In particular, this image recalled the famous monologue written by the young John Milius (which has become the late 1980s equivalent of 'Play it again, Sam' or 'Come up and see me sometime'): 'I know what you're thinking – "Did he fire six shots or only five?" Well, to tell you the truth, in all the excitement, I kind of lost track myself. But being this is a .44 Magnum, the most powerful handgun in the world, and would blow your head *clean off,* you've got to ask yourself one question: "Do I feel lucky?" *Well do you, punk?'*

The mayoral opposition preferred to produce a collaged poster which had Eastwood as Josey Wales, clutching ice-cream cornets rather than handguns: 'law, order and ice-cream'. To compound the confusion, when Eastwood won the local election (by 1330 votes, or 72 per cent of the poll), President Reagan immediately phoned to congratulate him. As Eastwood later recalled the conversation, 'I said that he had used my "Go ahead, make my day" line from *Sudden Impact*, so I had borrowed his "Get government off our backs" line. He said he was envious of the vote margin.' The headlines in the *Carmel Pine Cone*, throughout the campaign, had been along the same lines: 'Eastwood fires away at Carmel City officials'; 'Eastwood shoots from the hip'; 'Clint jumps into the fray'; 'Can he quell the "make my day" jokes and begin to tackle the issues?'; and on 10 April 1986 – 'CLINT WINS'. The *Pine Cone*'s introduction to the campaign summed it up:

'An old fable: Man One comes across Man Two beating his donkey to make it move. Stopping him, Man One says, "That's no way to act. You have to talk to it." Man Two steps back to allow Man One a try. Man One then goes to the side of the road, picks up a two-by-four and smacks the donkey squarely between the eyes. "Wait a minute," exclaims Man Two, "I thought you said you have to talk to it?" "Yes," says Man One, "but first you have to get its attention."

'If anyone can swing the two-by-four of fame it would be Carmel resident and businessman, Clint Eastwood.'

It was all *very* post-modernist.

There was even talk, serious talk, of political office in Washingon, which in the Reagan era didn't seem too far-fetched. But Eastwood scotched all rumours and brought the subject right down to earth by saying that he only became 'mayor of a small community' because he wanted to do something about the tight planning regulations (and to do something about restrictive local ordinances on such heinous crimes as eating ice-cream, throwing frisbees and wearing high-heeled shoes), and he only chose the mayoral office because it was for a two-year period, while 'a seat on the council would have been for a four-year term'. Let Ronald Reagan get on with his job, he concluded, 'And I'll do mine.'

By the time he was quoted as saying this, Clint Eastwood was fifty-six years old – and was the only living film star to have been in the top ten list of box-office champions for over fifteen years: this put him in the same league as John Wayne and Gary Cooper, and marginally ahead of Clark Gable, and unlike them he was playing Western heroes, anti-heroic cops and tough gunnery sergeants at the same time as directing the movies they appeared in. But at the time when they had been at the very top of the bill, Eastwood had had no idea at all exactly what kind of job his might be. And when Ronald Reagan had first made his name in Californian politics (having become adept at the Hollywood variety), the summit of Clint Eastwood's ambition had been to be a well-established television star in a steady job on a long-term contract. It took a very long time for him to decide 'what he wanted to do with himself', and when he had decided, it took him almost as long again to learn how to do it well.

3 'My teeth needed capping, I squinted too much'

When I wrote an article about Clint Eastwood for the *Independent Magazine* in November 1988, I received a letter – signed by several of the residents in a nurses' hostel – asking whether or not there was any truth in the rumour that he was really the son of Stan Laurel (of Laurel and Hardy fame): his eyes, said the letter, were so like Laurel's, and wouldn't it be terrific if he turned out to be the son of a music-hall comedian from Ulverston, Lancashire. In fact, it would *make their collective day*. I had to write back saying that there was no known evidence for this piece of genealogy, and that whoever the journalist was who started this particular story, he had made a 'fine mess' of his job.

In fact, Clint Eastwood was born Clinton Eastwood Jr on 31 May 1930, in San Francisco, the son of Clinton (Sr) and Ruth Eastwood who were, apparently, 'very young parents'. His father was of Scottish-English descent, his mother of Irish ancestry – several generations back. He grew up in towns and schools all over Northern California during the Depression years, as both of his parents searched for work: another child, his sister Jean, was born while the family was still 'drifting'. Eastwood has recalled that the family was sometimes reduced to living 'in real old places out in the sticks' and that 'I never saw my father in a specific profession' (the jobs, or rather the economy of makeshifts, ranged from accountancy and minor management roles at one end of the spectrum to pumping gas at the other).

Such recollections have led to another Eastwood myth – the myth, as expressed by Norman Mailer, of a young boy growing up 'in a mix of Okies also wandering up and down California searching for work': images which have a satisfyingly rags-to-riches feel to them – they conjure up in the movie mind thoughts of Henry Fonda in dungarees talking to Ma Joad in an overloaded jalopy, with bucketfuls of studio dust courtesy of John Ford – but which do not quite fit the facts. As Eastwood has recalled, the 'Okie' bit can be considerably overdone where his family is concerned. The migration of 400,000 agricultural workers from the dustbowl (as well as from Texas and Missouri) to California in the 1930s, where the often inhospitable Californians labelled them 'Okies' and their communities 'little Oklahomas' because of their distinctively 'hillbilly' Southern accents, labouring clothes and extreme poverty, was very different from the circumstances of his own upbringing. Yes, he did grow up in about ten different locations and ten different schools, but no, he never drifted around with the Okies or even remotely belonged to their communities and he never went hungry, but was often told to eat up everything that was left on his plate. In short, his was more like a middle-class family down on its luck, and his father always remained hopeful with maxims such as 'You've got to outlast yourself' and 'You don't get anything for nothing'. Eastwood reckons that his father (as drifter and outcast from his own people) and his grandmother (as the solitary, resourceful owner of a chicken farm near Livermore, with a few horses as well) were the two most influential people in his early life. His mother, by contrast, is conspicuous by her absence from his public utterances on the subject.

Eventually, Clinton Eastwood Jr registered at Oakland Technical High School in Oakland, California, where Clinton Sr had become an industrial efficiency expert with the Container Corporation of America, and where his mother Ruth had landed a job with IBM. He graduated from High School in 1948, having excelled at athletics (although not in team sports – he was apparently too introverted and too much of a loner for that), coasted in academic subjects, learned how to play piano and trumpet, and having acted the lead in a school play (type-cast as 'an introverted kid'), an experience which proved so terrifying for him that he vowed never again to get involved with anything to do with acting. His school yearbook entry for 1948, next to a tiny photo-portrait of a callow youth sporting a striped tie with a straight parting in his hair and slicked-down quiff, was cryptic in the extreme: 'Eastwood, Clinton – Senior Day Committee. Senior Banquet Committee'.

One of his close friends and classmates at Oakland – and still a close friend and executive in his company, as well as being the producer of *Any Which Way you Can, Tightrope, City Heat* and *Heartbreak Ridge* (among other films) – was Fritz Manes. Iain Johnstone quotes Manes as recalling (in the late 1970s): 'Clint hasn't really changed that much. He was always a tall lanky kid (six foot by the age of thirteen, six foot three inches by fifteen) and didn't necessarily dress the way the rest of the kids did. It was our first day in grammar school and it was just one of those things, we instantly identified with each other. We weren't that excited about going to school; both being sort of non-joiners, non-members of the pack. Clint had tremendous athletic ability all through school but not being a keen-spirited type guy, never really followed it through.'

Clint's year after leaving school followed the by now familiar pattern of drifting: he worked as a haybaler, a lumberjack, a truck-driver, a furnaceman at a steel mill, and a filler-in of invoices in the parts department at a Boeing plant, all in Northwestern America. He 'longed for independence' (he later remembered) but hadn't the first clue as to where or how to find it. A chance visit to a concert by Bob Wills and his Texas Playboys, combined with his parents' move to Seattle, encouraged him to apply for a course in music at Seattle University.

But before he could begin the course, he was called up to serve at Ford Ord military base near Monterey, California: after completing the regulation sixteen weeks of basic training (which he found a lot easier than many of the other Californian conscripts) and while most of his contemporaries were sent on active duty to Korea ('my name just didn't come up'), he became an assistant army swimming instructor, part-time bartender at the NCO's club and relief cinema projectionist.

The only active service he saw, apart from fishing raw recruits out of a long swimming pool, was when a small navy plane on which he had hitched a lift from Seattle to San Francisco, after a weekend's leave with his family, crash-landed in the sea off Point Reyes and he found himself swimming for his life with no one around to pick him up. But his stint in the army did serve two important purposes: it introduced him to Carmel-by-the-Sea ('I used to go there when I had a day off'), and it introduced him to various actors and musicians – including David Janssen (later to become television's *The Fugitive*), Norman Bartold (later to appear in *Breezy*) and Lennie Niehaus (with whom Eastwood played in a weekend jazz band at Ford Ord and who was later to become orchestrator and composer for the Malpaso Company). These men were to influence the next stage of his life, a time when 'I still didn't know what I wanted to do'.

After completing his national service, Clinton enrolled at Los Angeles City College (away from his parental home), with a grant on the GI Bill majoring in Business Administration: it was, he later said, the sort of subject you choose when 'you don't know what to do', rather like History used to be at university in Britain. To supplement his grant, he pumped gas in the afternoons, was janitor at the apartment house where he lived and at weekends a part-time lifeguard. On 19 December 1953 he married Maggie Johnson, a blonde 5ft 7in graduate from Berkeley, who, following their honeymoon in Carmel, at first supported her twenty-three-year-old husband by working in an export company and modelling swimsuit designs for Catalina and Caltex. They were eventually to have two children, Kyle in 1969 and Alison in 1973.

According to which written account one reads, it was either a friend of Eastwood's from Fort Ord named Irving Lasper, by now a stills photographer at University Studios, or a Hollywood film director named Arthur Lubin (who'd met Clinton Jr in Los Angeles when he was still pumping gas) who first encouraged him to take a screen test in the form of an 'interview-on-film'. It may even have been both of them. Whoever it was, the test (not a fully-fledged screen test of a performance) was directed by Lubin and photographed by cameraman Irving Glassberg during a lull in the production of the Universal-International film of *Francis the Talking Mule*. It took the form of a series of shots of Clint Eastwood (as from now on he liked to be known) 'just standing there' in his swim-shorts trying his best not to look too self-conscious as he looked to the left, then to the right and then straight at the camera, all the while answering questions about his name and address. As he has recently recalled 'They were talking to me off camera, trying to get different expressions, but the only expression I could manage was one of sheer terror.' Nevertheless, it landed him a six-month contract at Universal at $75 a week, as well as a place on the studio's training/talent programme in 1954 – 5. Simultaneously, he registered on a drama course at night school, preferring this to his Business Administration course, which he never completed. The in-house programme taught him such essentials as how to ride a horse in a photogenic manner (the Western was still the staple produce of Hollywood – just); how to rush up and down stairs while wielding a sword (this was also the era of *The Black Shield of Falworth* and *The Flame and the Arrow*), how to dance ('Fred Astaire never had to worry'), how to hold a knife and fork in the correct way while at the same time conducting a coherent conversation (just in case he should ever appear in a drawing-room comedy) and how to pose in plaid swim-shorts, surrounded by hopeful young starlets, in order to illustrate aspects of something called 'body conditioning'. The evening course, which he continued, on and off, 'with my eyes open and my big mouth shut', for the next *fifteen years*, was eventually to teach him that he should only attempt the parts 'that interested me and that I knew I could handle'. On one memorable occasion, according to Arthur Lubin, who was to direct Clint Eastwood in four of his first eight film appearances, during a 'reading session' of the studio's talent programme Eastwood was given extracts from the Leslie Howard part of Alan Squier in *The Petrified Forest*, and his attempt to play in the style of a ruminative, mild-mannered Englishman, almost resulted in him being given the sack on the spot. Clearly, he had yet to learn the lesson he was later to understand very thoroughly indeed: 'I'll try anything', he was to say in the early 1970s, 'that fits within my physical make-up . . . I hardly think of myself as playing Hamlet or Oedipus or something from Noël Coward . . . I have no interest in miscasting myself.' By then he could add, though, that actors who were good in *Hamlet* or *Private Lives* weren't necessarily (or even likely to be) good at the more 'physical' roles. British casting directors tended to look for new talent in drama schools: Hollywood casting directors had the sense to go first to the gymnasium or, come to that, the swimming pool.

Clint Eastwood's early film roles at Universal tended to take the form of, as he put it, 'the young lieutenant or the lab technician who came in and said "He went that way" or "This happened" or "Doctor, here are the X-rays" and he'd say "Get lost, kid".' They were all very small roles, and all in one uniform or another. In his first film, *Revenge of the Creature*, a 3-D sequel to *The Creature from the Black Lagoon,* he was directed by Jack Arnold, who cast him as Jennings, a white-coated lab technician who helps to do research on the scaly Gill-Man, and, incidentally, to pad out the script:

JENNINGS: Doc, there were four rats there in that cage when I changed my lights. Now there's only three. It's my considered opinion that rat number four is sitting inside that cat.
(Close-up of a black and white cat, with three white rats, in a wire cage.)
DOC: Are you sure you fed them *all* this morning?
JENNINGS: Here! I always feed them *(puts his hands in his pockets of his lab coat, and produces a white rat from one of them).* Uh-oh. What're *you* doing here?

Then he played, again for Jack Arnold, a bomber pilot who drops napalm on to a gigantic *Tarantula* in the great American desert: unfortunately, for this role, his face was almost entirely covered by a helmet and rubber flight-mask, and, as for the words, the role was even less verbal than Jennings:

PILOT: . . . *(crackle, crackle)* . . . dropping napalm − follow in order . . . *(crackle, crackle)*
(We see another bomber peel off; through the pilot's cockpit window.)
PILOT: Here goes . . .
(The pilot's plane swoops down on the magnified spider.)

It was something like a Cold War movie equivalent of the young Shakespearian spear-carrier saying 'I will my lord, with all convenient speed.' Much later − thirty-five years later, to be exact, in *The Rookie* − Clint Eastwood was to show an extract from this sequence of *Tarantula* on the wall of video monitors which flickered behind him as the sadistic spider-woman Liesl (Sonia Braga) tied him to a chair, sat in his lap and 'raped' him. By then, his early career had become an excuse for a blink-and-you'll-miss-it visual reference.

After playing a distinctly *un*-Shakespearean 'First Saxon soldier' with fustian jerkin, a quiverful of arrows and a mid-fifties quiff, in Arthur Lubin's *Lady Godiva of Coventry* (starring a chaste Maureen O'Hara as the Saxon damsel – who is well covered throughout by her long and curly red tresses) and a naval pal of Donald O'Connor called Jonesy in the same director's *Francis in the Navy* (fairly difficult stuff – they both had to stare in bewilderment at a talking mule whose talk would only be dubbed in later by Chill Wills at post-production stage), Eastwood again put on a technician's white coat for *Never Say Goodbye,* based believe it or not on a Pirandello play, where he appeared in an X-ray lab sequence with Rock Hudson (one of the 'big three' at the studio in the mid-1950s, the other two – Eastwood recalls – being Tony Curtis and Jeff Chandler):

> (*Enter the Lab Technician from behind a screen, as Doctor Parker inspects an X-ray plate through his black-rimmed spectacles.*)
> DOCTOR PARKER: What is it, Will?
> LAB TECHNICIAN: Telephone, Doctor Parker . . . good luck with your speech, Sir.
> DOCTOR PARKER: Thank you, Will. I'll need it. As a public speaker I should stick to orthopedic research.

After which, Universal began its policy of pulling out of the studio training/talent programme, and started the process by failing to renew Clint Eastwood's contract as well as that of his army buddy David Janssen (who had also appeared in *Francis* and *Never Say Goodbye*. His first roles as a freelance actor were with RKO, the studio which director Arthur Lubin had joined (he, too, having been given his marching orders from Universal).

In Lubin's *The First Traveling Saleslady,* the story of steel corset retailer Rose Gillroy (Ginger Rogers) and her chanteuse friend Molly Wade (Carol Channing) who together try to sell barbed wire in the Wild West at the turn of the century, Eastwood was given a 'featuring' credit (after 'starring' and 'also starring' and shared with four others), for his part as callow Lootenant Jack Rice of Teddy Roosevelt's Rough Riders. It was the most verbal part he had yet played and the *Hollywood Reporter* actually noticed it: 'Clint Eastwood', said the *Reporter,* 'is very attractive as Miss Channing's beau.'

His first appearance comes when Carol Channing, having belted out the song 'A corset can do a lot for a lady, whenever a lady wants what she ain't got', walks past a recruiting poster for the 'US Volunteer Cavalry, the Rough Riders' in the foyer of a Kansas City hotel. There, at a desk, sits the young Lootenant in a cavalry jerkin, a cowboy hat covering his slicked-back hair and sideburns.

MOLLY: Pardon me, but what *is* a Rough Rider?
   (*He stands up gawkily, removes his hat, and offers her a recruiting paper.*)
MOLLY: Oh, don't be silly, I don't want to join, I can't even ride . . . What's your name?
JACK (*shifting from foot to foot, in an uncomfortable way):* It's Jack Rice.
MOLLY: You're handsome, and brave too I'll bet — do you like girls?
JACK: Yes, ma'am, I do (*smiles*).
MOLLY. Well I'm a girl.
JACK: Yeah, you sure are!

A little later, Molly introduces him to Rose Gillroy.

ROSE: Pleased to meet you, *all* of you.
JACK: Likewise, ma'am.

His second appearance comes when he enters the hotel dining-room, in full uniform, to say farewell to his new friend Molly:

JACK: I didn't want to leave without saying goodbye.
MOLLY: Leave?
JACK: Yeah. For the Rough Rider camp at Poker Flats Texas, in about an hour.
MOLLY: That's not very long is it?

JACK: No, sure isn't.
MOLLY: Sorta crowded in here, for saying goodbye.
JACK: Yeah! Sure is.
MOLLY: Do you think we could take a little walk maybe . . . ?
JACK: (*smiling in a shy way*) Sure could.

His last big moment comes when he rides at full speed to Joel Kingdom's (James Arness's) ranch to rescue Carol Channing from the baddies and puts on a (not very effective) Texas accent:

MOLLY: Why, it's Jack Rice, my wonderful Rough Rider.
   (*He dismounts.*)
JACK: I've come here to git Miss Molly Wade. Don't try to stop me, Mr Kingdom – if you do, you're gonna meet up with a pack of trouble.
KINGDOM: She's all yours, boy. I got trouble enough of my own.
MOLLY: Oh, Jack. I guess you're just about the bravest man in the whole world, defying Joel Kingdom in this way . . .
JACK (*smiling*): Oh, come on . . .

And that, give or take a few more trying-hard-to-be-magic moments with the manhunting Miss Channing ('There's a strange man in the room/Oh, keep dreaming . . .'), is about it. In one scene, she looks again at the Rough Rider poster, and the face of grizzled Teddy Roosevelt turns into that of a smiling fresh-faced Clint Eastwood. Amid all the jokes about corsets, women drivers, Eastern ladies and Western louts, and the feminist movement, Eastwood's function throughout was evidently to be 'a nice young man – you know, the *right* kind', good looking, not particularly bright, slightly self-conscious but able to deliver when the occasion demanded, much better at actions than words. ('For a shy man,' says Molly, 'when that Jack Rice says goodbye it's almost like saying hello.') The film, in short, is a sample of Clint Eastwood's persona – and the opportunities he was offered to show it – during his apprenticeship in the mid-1950s. And it got him his first review, albeit of two column inches.

But the excitement must have been short-lived. For, in Arthur

Lubin's next film *Escapade in Japan,* Eastwood was demoted to being one of those single-sequence airplane pilots again, this time a rescue pilot. An American diplomat's little son, named Tony, is flying unaccompanied from Manila to Tokyo. The Mid-Pacific Airliner on which he is travelling suddenly develops engine trouble over the sea. The local USAF rescue squadron is alerted, and the civilian pilot is told that 'One Dumbo is on the way to intercept'. We see the One Dumbo flying boat on its way, and then:

RESCUE PILOT: Pilot to radar operator. Let me know as soon as you get him on the scope, will you? (*He is wearing a blue hat, earphones, a lifebelt and he is speaking into a microphone. Cut to the cockpit of the Mid-Pacific passenger plane.*)
CIVILIAN PILOT: This is Nan Charly 351, calling Dumbo Victor – can't keep her airborne much longer. Have you got radar lock yet?
RESCUE PILOT: No, you're too far out.

And that was it.

After two long years in the movie business and at drama school, Clint Eastwood was appearing in a film for a grand total of ten seconds, without his name even appearing on the credits. 'I will, my lord, with all convenient speed'. The only consolation, maybe, was that a credit with RKO wouldn't have been of much use anyway: the studio was shut down by its proprietor, Howard Hughes, shortly afterwards. It was during this period in his life, 1957 – 8, that Eastwood had to supplement his irregular income by digging swimming pools for a property company: indeed, some sources claim that he made more money from labouring than from acting. It seems likely. He also earned the nickname 'Slick' at this time. A few of his close friends today (his 'inner circle' tends to be made up of buddies from school, army, apprenticeship and television years, rather than from Hollywood) still call him 'Slick', *and* they have lived to tell the tale. Maybe it was originally a reference to his hair rather than his style.

The film roles he did land remained very small. There was *Lafayette Escadrille* (known in Britain as *Hell Bent for Glory*) directed by William Wellman (of *Wings* and *The Ox-Bow Incident* fame), in which Eastwood – dressed in a zip-up leather bomber jacket, but still with his fifties quiff – played a First World War flying ace named George Moseley. It was his first film for a major director, his first role (and last, until *White Hunter, Black Heart* in 1990) as a real-life character, and his first for Warner Brothers, a studio to which he would not return until the early 1970s, for the *Dirty Harry* series, and which has released nearly all his films since 1980. But, despite all these firsts, it was yet another walk-on pilot, with no dialogue at all this time. He had a name, but it didn't feature on the opening credits. Possibly after reading the reviews, the great William Wellman decided to retire from movie-making.

And there was *Star in the Dust* (this time a one-off for Universal, made in twelve days), his first Western proper in which he played an anonymous and uncredited ranch hand for producer Albert Zugsmith who was much more at home with unusual 'B' movie *films noirs* such as *Touch of Evil* and the delirious *Confessions of an Opium Eater*. Also *Ambush at Cimarron Pass* for 20th Century Fox (a low-budget Western made in nine days that was, according to Eastwood, 'even worse than the title') in which he played an impetuous ex-Confederate cowboy named Keith Williams with memories of the Civil War (again described as 'a good boy, just young') who has to learn – in the course of a journey escorting the latest rifles and numerous engagements with the Apaches – to settle his differences with Union sergeant Scott Brady. Eventually, there is the inevitable fist fight – which Eastwood loses, after a single well-aimed punch – followed by a final-reel reconciliation: Eastwood survives the Apache attack, a sure sign that director Jodie Copelan reckoned that by then the drive-in audience would be identifying with him.

It was watching this film with his wife Maggie which nearly convinced the twenty-eight-year-old actor to quit. 'I finally got to a state where I was really depressed,' he has recently recalled. 'You know, I was married, no kids . . . Well, the movie finally came out and I went with my wife down to a little neighbourhood theatre, and it was *so* bad . . . I said to Maggie, "I'm going to quit, I'm really going to quit. I've *got* to start doing something with my life."'

Okay, the film was shot in colour in stunning RegalScope for the Regal Company, but its visual quality – or rather, the lack of it –

still embarrassed the hell out of its no-longer juvenile lead. Even then, he has more recently remembered, he took a craftsman-like interest in the technical side of film-making, and especially 'the cheap quality of the production and the lack of technical know-how . . . The photography was the most uneven I'd ever seen. One minute it was so light you needed sunglasses to look at the screen; the next second the print was so dark you couldn't make out anything.' The review in *Variety*, on 12 February 1958, was even more succinct than his last one: 'Fine portrayals also came from Margia Dean, Frank Gerstle, Clint Eastwood and Dirk London'. No wonder he was depressed. This man had *peaked* in *The First Traveling Saleslady*.

In between times he had landed a few television parts. They allowed him to ride a motorcycle for one episode in *Highway Patrol* (the series which had made its debut in 1955, where Broderick Crawford always said into his car-mike, 'Twenty-one-fifty to headquarters . . . Ten-Four', a catch phrase of the day even though no one understood what on earth it was supposed to mean); to march around the quad and play American football for twelve episodes as a military cadet (in *West Point*, about which he recalls 'We'd open an episode with some strong dramatic line like "You stole my laundry!" Where do you go from there?'); and to do his own stuntwork for individual episodes of *Navy Log* and *Men of Annapolis*, a series produced and directed by low-budget-horror-king William Castle.

But, in general, he was told by casting directors all over Hollywood that 'my voice was too soft, my teeth needed capping, I squinted too much, and I was too tall: it was the same old story'. He may have been born with the monosyllabic first name and duosyllabic surname of Rock Hudson, Tab Hunter, Jeff Chandler, and most of the other Hollywood role-models of the mid-1950s, but despite the best efforts of a succession of directors he didn't look like them, act like them or even photograph like them.

He has talked a great deal about those five years when he hung around the margins of Hollywood. He is, evidently, still bitter about the experience: 'I absolutely hated it. I tell people if you really want to do it, then you must be willing to study it and stick with it through all opposition and having to deal with some of the most no-talent people in the world passing judgement on you. They're going to pick the worst aspects of you or of anybody else that they cast. If you can take all that and keep grinding until some part comes along that fits you and your feelings, then sometimes the odds will come up for you . . . People think I play "anger" well; all you have to do is have a good memory'.

When, in the late 1960s, Eastwood began to call the shots, the first thing he did was to form his own production company (Malpaso – Spanish for 'bad step', and also the name of a hillside drive and a stream above the road between Carmel and the Big Sur) to ensure that only he, plus a few trusted friends who went back a long way, would in future be passing judgement on 'Eastwood': also, to try out some less extravagant production methods than he had seen, first hand, in Hollywood. It would appear that he had (and has) a much thinner skin than the characters he plays.

4   Livin' high and wide . . .

The part that did come along, in 1958, was that of ramrod Rowdy Yates in the *Rawhide* series – number eleven in the avalanche of 'adult' television Westerns (adult, that is, compared with Roy Rogers, the Cisco Kid and the Range Rider) which was started with Warner Brothers' *Cheyenne* in 1955: already, *Gunsmoke, Wells Fargo, Have Gun Will Travel, Sugarfoot, Wagon Train, Lawman, Wanted – Dead or Alive, The Rifleman, Bat Masterson* and *Maverick* were slugging it out in the ratings charts. Indeed, the market was so saturated that *Rawhide* initially had trouble finding a sponsor. After shooting ten episodes on spec (at an average cost of $40,000 per hour) rather than the more usual method of making one pilot episode, CBS were forced to postpone the screening of episode one from autumn 1958 to January 1959, when it struggled on to the air as a mid-season replacement sandwiched between *Hit Parade* and the *Phil Silvers Show*.

Eastwood had been so sure the series would be shelved that, in the meantime, he had accepted a part (not even a guest spot) in an episode of *Maverick*, with James Garner. He was, he thought, about to become the star that nobody had ever seen; a pity, since he had rather enjoyed his outing to Nogales, Arizona, where the credit titles, location inserts and some of the more spectacular episodes were filmed, before the crew returned to Universal Studios – their base for the rest of the series.

But, on the night of 9 January 1959, Clint Eastwood could have read in *TV Guide*: 'Eric Fleming and Clint Eastwood are the stars of a new hour-long Western series to be seen each week at this time [eight p.m. Standard Time]. The stories will revolve around the

Western legend of the cattle drive from Texas (San Antonio) to Kansas (Sedalia). Frankie Laine sings the *Rawhide* theme music which was written by Dimitri Tiomkin and Ned Washington. The series was produced by Charles Marquis Warren who was producer-director of *Gunsmoke* in its early days on TV.'

A little later, the reviewer of *Rawhide*'s opening episode – 'Incident of the Tumbleweed Wagon' – in the *Hollywood Reporter* was less excited by the prospect: 'Selection of this one as the debut episode (actually, the ninth to be shot) was unfortunate, especially since its top-liners Eric Fleming and Clint Eastwood were subordinated to the point where the average viewer, without the benefit of a credit sheet, might well say "Who stars in this series?" '

Even at the beginning of the second season, the *Reporter*'s Hank Grant still remained not entirely convinced: 'Ostensibly, producer Charles Marquis Warren tried for a change of face on this, the first ['Incident of the Day of the Dead'] of a new *Rawhide* batch after a summer of re-runs. The change of pace couldn't have been more of a radical one, with all regulars save co-star Clint Eastwood completely eliminated in the opener. Whether or not this particular change of pace sat well with viewers is a matter of conjecture but it did serve to give Clint Eastwood his strongest showcase on the series to date and he did acquit himself ably, appearing as he did in practically every scene in the hour.'

But these were in a way criticisms of the series' strengths – it *was* unconventional at times, and it *did* try to depict the cattle drive as a team effort – and, in any case, Clint Eastwood had at last found a part that seemed to 'fit'. Even if it didn't fit at first, there was plenty of time for it to wear in. The first episode of CBS television's *Rawhide* was aired on 9 January 1959, the last – 217 hour-long episodes and eight seasons later – on 7 December 1965, which makes it the fourth longest-running television Western ever after *Gunsmoke*'s twenty years, *Bonanza*'s fourteen years and *The Virginian*'s eight years.

At the beginning, one of *Rawhide*'s great selling points was that it was a more 'realistic' series than some, and reference was made to the real-life diary of trail boss George C. Duffield dating from the 1870s on which Charles Marquis Warren (whose own early career had been helped along by F. Scott Fitzgerald) had based the series.

But 'realism' is, of course, a highly flexible concept in such circumstances. Yes, there was a lot of dust, and yes, the actors could ride, and yes, there was that emphasis on teamwork, but for the first few seasons every single episode opened – to the strains of Frankie Laine singing 'moving', movin', movin', keep those dogies movin' ' (not 'dawgies' as some critics have written; that was *Rin Tin Tin*) – with a head of cattle trotting at breakneck speed past the camera. As Larry McMurtry has pointed out: 'The moviegoer usually sees cattle being driven across the screen at a pace so rapid that even the wiriest Longhorn could not have sustained it the length of Hollywood Boulevard without collapsing. The trail herds of the eighteen-seventies and eighties were grazed along at a sedate eight to ten miles a day – anything faster would have been economically disastrous.'

Perhaps *that* explains why they put off reaching the town of Sedalia and why the drovers never did get to start 'livin high and wide'.

The novelisation of *Rawhide* (by Frank C. Robertson, 1961) describes Rowdy Yates as 'Standing a little over six feet, a good-looking kid mature beyond his years, with a shock of tawny hair that seemed habitually in need of cutting, and honest, sometimes challenging blue eyes. He was dressed much like his boss.' He wore a checkered calico shirt and leather chaps over his buttermint pants, he smiled a lot, he acted as spokesman for the other drovers, he sometimes behaved like a tearaway college boy who dated a girl in every town, and in one episode Eastwood sang a song called 'Unknown Girl', released in the States by Gothic Records.

Rowdy's behaviour in the series provided an essential counterpoint to that of Gil Favor (played by Eric Fleming), the authoritarian Confederate (or should that be Korean?) veteran who was also trail boss: in the first two series, Rowdy provided most of the romantic interest, was kidnapped, was shanghaid to do jury service, was falsely accused of murder (twice), was forced to hold a lynch mob at bay, broke in a killer stallion for a beautiful Spanish contessa, and contracted a rare disease normally restricted to cattle. Together with the drovers' never-ending battle against the elements – searching for strays/waterholes/common grazing land; avoiding prairie fires/ electrical storms/tornadoes/Chubasco winds, fighting off wolves/ pumas/crazy civil war veterans/escaped convicts or native Americans, who tended to be either impossibly noble or impossibly savage – Rowdy Yates's 'hell-raising' (and the running gag of his complaints about the cooking of Wishbone and his slow-witted assistant Mushy) helped to keep the series movin' on almost as much as the weekly guest stars; but, in the end, if any 'incident' threatened to upset the tightly controlled camaraderie of this locker-room on the hoof, Rowdy was certain to side with his boss. 'I'm just his ramrod, I'm not supposed to judge whether he's right or wrong.' Eventually, when the pre-credits sequence was changed from Favor shouting 'Head 'em up, move 'em out' – not 'Get 'em on', as one critic has recalled (that was what over-excited late 1950s male teenagers shouted back, or was it perhaps 'Get 'em off'?) to neo-Remington sculptures of all the drovers doing their jobs, Rowdy's horsemanship would have looked good on the mantlepiece of any suburban home.

In the film which provided the immediate stimulus to Charles Warren's *Rawhide* formula, Warren's own *Cattle Empire*, (1958) – a film which first introduced Paul Brinegar as the short-tempered cook and Steve Raines/Rocky Shahan as cattle drovers, later to play Jim Quince and Joe Scarlett in the TV series – trail boss Joel McCrea was not in a position to make friends with *any* second-in-command. But the conventions of the late 1950s TV Westerns (like the conventions of the 'B' Westerns they supplanted) demanded a sidekick – James Arness and Dennis Weaver in *Gunsmoke*, Ward Bond and Robert Horton on *Wagon Train*, James Garner and Jack Kelly in *Maverick* – and the scripts required someone to speak up for the cattle drovers, so Rowdy Yates became a pulp version of Montgomery Clift's Matthew Garth (to Gil Favor's Tom Dunson) from Howard Hawks's *Red River*. When Rowdy took over from Favor as trail boss it was inevitable that the tone of *Rawhide* would change dramatically. Favor had been a stern, demanding, almost obsessed trail boss (like John Wayne in *Red River*, and Joel McCrea in *Cattle Empire*), the kind who always earned the respect of the men in time for the fade-out, and who took the major decisions – to bail the drovers out, to negotiate over grazing rights, to sell part of the herd, to hire and fire, to 'head 'em up, move 'em out' in the first pace – on his own, without consultation, with the minimum of words. In 'Incident at Dragoon Crossing' (episode 57), when Favor is unwell, it never occurs to him to delegate responsibility to his ramrod, and it never occurs to the ramrod to ask. Instead, veteran trail boss John Cord (Dan O'Herlihy) is invited to take over, with dire consequences. Five years later, when he was promoted, Yates proved to be an easy-going leader, more willing to listen to his men (without a go-between) and more open-minded (he employed a black drover named Simon on the team, played by Raymond St Jacques – a nice touch of 'realism' since a lot of working cowboys were, in fact, black, and the only time a featured black actor appeared regularly in a TV Western at that time).

But by then, the cowboys of *Rawhide* had outstayed their welcome. By 1965 the emphasis had shifted away from 'community on the move' Westerns such as *Wagon Train* and *Rawhide* to 'property' Westerns such as General Motors' *Bonanza*, so of the planned thirty-nine episodes with Rowdy as trailboss, only twenty-two were in fact made (not networked in Britain), after which the series was junked. The next serious attempts to revamp the *Red River D* story came in the early 1970s – on the big screen – with William Fraker's *Monte Walsh* (the story of unemployed cowboys who know they are the tools of anonymous Eastern accountants calling themselves 'Consolidated'); and Dick Richards's *The Culpepper Cattle Company* (with its message that 'cowboyin' is somethin' you do when you can't do nothin' else', and its classic exchange between a little boy and a cattle drover – 'What's the name of your horse?'/'Sonny, you don't give a name to something you may have to *eat*!'). Any cowboy caught kissing his horse was likely to be certified as insane. Ten years after *Rawhide*, the Western had changed beyond all recognition, in significant part through the efforts of the subject of this book who wisely stayed away from herds of trotting cattle after his experience on the series.

Eastwood, however, kept in close contact with some of the people he had first met in the *Rawhide* years. Ted Post, who had directed seven episodes in the first two seasons of the show (1959 – 60) went on to direct *Hang 'em High* and *Magnum Force*; Dean Reisner, who had helped write some episodes in the early 1960s, went on to contribute to the screenplays of *Coogan's Bluff* and *Dirty Harry*; Paul Brinegar, who had played the long-suffering cook Wishbone in

Rawhide, went on to play the equally long-suffering barman in *High Plains Drifter*; Sonia Chernus, who had worked in the script department at CBS, had first tipped Eastwood off about the series, and had written the story of episode 104 of *Rawhide*, called 'Grandma's Money', was later invited to join the Malpaso production company as a script reader, and adapted Phil Kaufman's screenplay for *The Outlaw Josey Wales* – a film about a family of marginal Americans on the move, with The Man With No Name as trail boss. Eastwood also hung on to Rowdy Yates's gunbelt and Colt gun (with snakes on the grips) and used them in most of the movie Westerns he made after that time.

Curiously enough, one of Clint Eastwood's very first experiences of the film world had involved meeting the director of *Red River*: 'I regret not working with Howard Hawks and John Ford, all of those people. I remember when I was a kid living in Oakland, California, I went to Los Angeles from high school in the vacation, for a few days with some other kids. We drove down there – you know, teenage kids on a weekend thing – we were out at a friend's house in Westwood and some horses were running right down the main street, so we stopped these horses and led them back up the street, and this man came down and he thanked us very much, and the man's name was Howard Hawks. Though I'd never had any idea about the movies, I was kinda inspired by meeting a big, famous movie director like that. And later on, when I was in films, I thought it would be nice to work with somebody like that – John Ford in his heyday, Hathaway, Hitchcock – but all these people had either retired or some of them had died, and none of the rest would see me in my early days, because I didn't fit into their scheme, so I sorta missed out the whole era.' The film in question might even have been *Red River*: the dates certainly fit.

The experience of working on *Rawhide* for seven years, day in day out, six days a week, was like going to the finest of film schools (if such institutions had existed in the later 1950s). As Eastwood recalls: 'I was playing the second guy, and always the very youthful part. It never was much. But I enjoyed playing the character. I learned an awful lot from doing it. We did over 200 hours of that show. I think I learned more from that then almost anything I've ever done.'

He had worked with directors of such varying talents as Jack Arnold, Buzz Kulik, Andrew V. McLaglen, Ted Post, Charles Marquis Warren, George Sherman, Stuart Heisler, Joseph Kane, Bud Springsteen, Tay Garnett, Laslo Benedek and Christian Nyby, and he had seen just how inept some of them could be. On one occasion he watched a director shoot an elaborate cattle stampede with a single camera from some distance away, and wondered why the camera couldn't be mounted on horseback, in the middle of the action: he was told that things simply weren't done that way. On the other hand, he had also 'worked with many fine directors; unconsciously I must have absorbed some knowledge from them. I wanted to direct, way back when I was doing *Rawhide*. I'd been assigned to direct an episode, but the network CBS reneged, because someone on another series had gone way over schedule and way over budget – so they sent down a memo saying that no one who acted in the series could direct. So I directed some trailers, and various coming attraction things for the next season of the series, then I let it lie.'

He had also observed many different styles of film acting with the weekly guest stars, from Victor McLaglen (his last appearance, in over-the-top 'Irish' John Ford-style with Harry Carey Jr in the same episode) to Brian Donlevy (a classic 1940s Western heavy), to Mercedes McCambridge (*Johnny Guitar* hysterical) to John Cassavetes (a talkative version of 'the method') to Peter Lorre (a bizarre character performance) to the new generation of clean-cut heroes James Coburn, James Franciscus and Jack Lord. In general, he observed that the most effective performances on film were not necessarily the ones with the most 'acting' content in them. 'My old drama coach used to say, "Don't just do something, stand there". Gary Cooper wasn't afraid to do nothing.'

Yet, although there was much to learn and to observe, Eastwood began to get itchy feet after only three years (let alone seven) on the series, and the acting experience, plus the exposure, had already given him the confidence to speak up about it. He told the *Hollywood Reporter* on 13 July 1961: 'I haven't been allowed to accept a single feature or TV guesting offer since I started the series. Maybe they figure me as the sheepish nice guy I portray . . . Believe me, I'm not bluffing – I'm prepared to go on suspension, which means I can't work here, but I've had offers of features in London and Rome that'll bring me more money in a year than the series has given me in three.'

This was the golden era of TV guest appearances – in one particularly choice example, Gary Cooper stood uncomfortably in front of a curtain and a live audience, and sang 'Bird Dog' with the Everly Brothers – but the available evidence shows that, after that single episode of *Maverick*, the only TV guesting offer Eastwood was able to accept was playing himself opposite a studio-trained talking chimpanzee in the series *Mr Ed*. The episode was produced and directed by his patron from the early days, Arthur Lubin, who had presumably picked up the essential skills with *Francis the Talking Mule*. *Clint Eastwood Meets Mister Ed* (a title which does not appear in his official filmographies) first went out on 22 April 1962. The experience can't have been too traumatic, for fifteen years later he acted opposite a hyperactive monkey again, in *Every Which Way But Loose*. (*Francis in the Navy* had opened with a mule telephoning Donald O'Connor, to let him know that he – the mule – was about to be sold off as navy surplus. After that, *Mister Ed* must have seemed almost normal.)

The interviews Eastwood gave at this time weren't *all* about working conditions on his first steady job, however: he was already working hard on his own physical fitness, and had strong views about diet and exercise which he revealed to any interviewer who was prepared to listen. *TV Guide*, for example, after referring to him as 'one of TV's finer physical specimens', asked what the secret was: 'Stay away from carbohydrates,' he replied, 'especially rich desserts. Keep a scale in your bathroom. Proper rest, not noon to four a.m. Try to be optimistic. Eat fruits and raw vegetables. Take vitamins. Watch the amount of liquids you consume and skip beverages loaded with sugars. Avoid alcohol in excess.' Above all, take exercise: 'The worst exercise you can get is with a knife and fork.' And *don't smoke*. This advice (presumably released by CBS) may read like a Sunday supplement piece from the positive thinking/new age decade of the 1980s, but it was said and written in the early 1960s. In California, clearly, they are very quick on the uptake about such things.

The irony is, though, that Eastwood's next big breakthrough involved serious smoking and lashings of pasta . . .

5 An American in Rome

It was episode 91 of *Rawhide*, dubbed into Italian, which thirty-five-year-old film director Sergio Leone watched on a television set in Rome and which convinced him that the man who played Rowdy Yates could be just right for the lead part in *A Fistful of Dollars*. Originally, he had aimed for Henry Fonda or James Coburn or Charles Bronson (who judged the script of *Fistful* to be the worst he had ever read – 'What I did not know was what Leone would do with it'): but they were all too expensive, on a total budget of $200,000. Then he tried various American actors living in Germany and Italy, and one of these – Richard Harrison, who had already appeared in the early Italian Western *Gunfight at Red Sands* – suggested that Leone look at an episode of *Rawhide*. I once asked the late Sergio Leone whether he could remember his reaction: 'What fascinated me about Clint, above all, was his external appearance, and his own character. I first saw him in that forty-eight-minute episode of *Rawhide* called 'Incident of the Black Sheep'. I hired him because Jimmy Coburn cost too much for our limited budget – Jimmy cost $25,000 in those days, and Clint $15,000. And when I saw "The Black Sheep", what struck me was that Clint didn't speak much. He was the second lead supporting Victor, I mean Eric Fleming, but I noticed the lazy, laid-back way he just came on and stole every single scene from Fleming. His laziness is what came over so clearly. When we were working together, he was like a snake, forever taking a nap five hundred feet away, wrapped up in his coils, asleep in the back of a car. Then he'd open his coils out, unfold and stretch. This attitude he had – slow, laid back and lazy – was what he maintained throughout the film, and, when you mix *that* with the blast and velocity of the gunshots, you have the essential contrast that he gave us. So we built his character on this, as we went along – physically as well, giving him the beard and the small cigar that he never really smoked. When he was offered the second film, *For a Few Dollars More*, he said to me, "I'll read the script, come over and do the film, but please I beg of you one thing only – don't put that cigar back into my mouth!" And I said, "Clint, we can't leave the main protagonist, the lead actor, at home. We can't possibly leave the cigar behind. It's playing the lead!" '

Although Leone was joking when he said this, it is quite true that the 'props' surrounding the character of The Man With No Name (actually named Joe in the original script of *Fistful*, and occasionally in the film itself; Manco in *For a Few Dollars More* and Blondie in *The Good, the Bad and the Ugly*) played a key part in that character's success: the beard, the poncho, the sheepskin waistcoat, the cigars, the brown suede boots, the shrunk-to-fit jeans. Leone specifies: 'Clint Eastwood was a little sophisticated, a little "light", in the part of Rowdy Yates, and I wanted to make him look more virile, to harden him, to age him for the part as well – with that growth of beard, that poncho which made him look broader, those cigars.'

The cigars, incidentally, were usually *toscani*, a particularly obnoxious type of Italian weed. As G. Cabrera Infante has written in *Holy Smoke*: 'They are the hardest cigar in the Italian West. That's why skinflint Clint seems to be lighting them up forever to become somebody with a name. Sometimes he just doesn't seem to bother and keeps chewing it between his clenched teeth. This proves that Clint is full-time foreigner. Had Eastwood been Italian, like the rest of the roaring cast (dubbed), he would have cut his *toscano* in two with his penknife and then, only then, proceeded to light it.'

The match used by Clint is, it seems, also of interest: 'Back at the ranch, other smoking gentlemen preferred that reliable regular, the Strike Anywhere Match. These smokers were called Gary Cooper, John Wayne, Randolph Scott and, lastingly last, Clint Eastwood. All of them were capable of striking a match virtually anywhere: on a thumb, on the dumb villain's pate, on the forward chorus-girl's *derrière* and, egalitarians that they were, on the shiny seat of their own Levis as well. Thus, with the least effort and the most effrontery, they were able to light up their cheap cheroots . . . the only hitch in the yarn is that this type of match was not invented until 1890, long after the West was won.'

Never mind. Historical accuracy wasn't exactly the point. Eastwood's appearance – and the way he 'read' on screen – were. As Sergio Leone recalled, some twenty years later in June 1984, when discussing his gangster epic *Once Upon a Time in America*. 'The story is told that when Michelangelo was asked what he had seen in one particular block of marble, which he chose among hundreds of others, he replied that he saw Moses. I would offer the same answer to the question why did I choose Clint Eastwood, only backwards. When they ask me what I saw in Clint Eastwood, who was playing I don't know what kind of second-rate role in a Western television series in 1964, I reply that what I saw, simply, was a block of marble.'

He then went on to compare Clint Eastwood's approach to acting with that of his new leading character, Robert De Niro: 'It is difficult to compare Eastwood and De Niro. The first is a mask of wax. In reality, if you think about it, they don't even belong to the same profession. Robert De Niro hurls himself into this or that role, putting on a personality the way someone else might put on his coat, naturally, and with elegance; while Clint Eastwood hurls himself into a suit of armour and lowers the visor with a rusty clang. It is precisely that lowered visor which composes his character. And that creaky clang it makes as it snaps down, dry as a Martini in Harry's Bar in Venice, is also his character. Look at him carefully. Eastwood moves like a sleepwalker between explosions and hails of bullets, and he is always the same – a block of marble. Bobby, first of all, is an actor. Clint, first of all, is a star. Bobby suffers. Clint yawns . . .'

The protective shell, the impassiveness, the cool – these were what Leone saw in Rowdy Yates even through the dubbing, and, by his own account, these were what the Italian director decided to build upon like the master of Renaissance bottega (Eastwood being the model).

Eastwood himself recalls the genesis of The Man With No Name rather differently. After his agent had persuaded him, with some difficulty, to read the script of this Italian-German-Spanish co-production of a remake of a Japanese film, to be shot on a low budget in Almeria in Spain and at Cinecittà studios outside Rome, he agreed to take the role (partly because he was so fed up with *Rawhide*, and the restrictions under which CBS expected him to work), but on the strict condition that he could change the dialogue, as well as rethink the talkative central character. At least, that's how *he* remembers it.

'I went down to a wardrobe place on Santa Monica Boulevard,' he told Iain Johnstone, 'and just purchased the wardrobe and took it over there. It was very difficult because on a film you always have two or three hats of the same sort, two or three jackets of the same kind, in case you lose a piece of clothing or something gets wet and you need a change. But for this film I had only one of everything: one hat, one sort of sheepskin vest, one poncho and several pairs of pants because they were just Frisco-type jeans. If I'd lost any of it halfway through the film, I'd have really been in trouble.'

When he arrived in Spain, he said on another occasion, 'We had to change all the wardrobe because they had Davy Crockett hats and all kinds of things that didn't fit in with a Mexico situation.' Nothing too elaborate, of course, because the budget was so low: 'On *Fistful*, everybody went out behind trees, you know. There were no facilities.' But the most important priority was the script, written in a style that read like exactly what it was – poorly translated Italian ("He is buried in the hill of boots . . ."): a strange Italian version of the Western dialect.

'I knew the character. Leone knew the character. We decided together how it would be. We cut down quite a bit of the dialogue. An Italian script is usually much more descriptive and much more expository. We cut it down and made the guy more symbolic . . . I always felt that if the narrator explained everything as per the original script, he wouldn't have had any mystery at all to him.'

The contrast, valued by Leone, between the laid-back, mysterious Man With No Name and 'the blast and velocity of the gunshots' has been described by Eastwood in more down-to-earth terms: 'Italian actors come from the Hellzapoppin' school of drama. To get my effect I stayed impassive and I guess they thought I wasn't acting. All except Leone, who knew what I was doing.'

Consequently, the American actor negotiated with the Italian director about the *longueurs* of the script throughout the shooting (a tedious process which involved a lot of hand-waving, since Eastwood spoke only about two words of Italian when he arrived) and his words were gradually pared down to the minimum. Eastwood also recalls that more black humour was added after the shooting-script stage: one of the reasons he took the part, he says, was that he 'researched this director who hadn't directed but one film before that [*The Colossus of Rhodes*], and heard that he was considered talented in terms of Italian cinema, that he was a very humorous man, that he could see the humour in the story – and so one thing led to another.' When the production of *A Fistful of Dollars* was first announced in the Italian trade journals, the star of *Rawhide* was billed as both actor and 'Western consultant'.

A Fistful of Dollars, together with *For a Few Dollars More* and *The Good, The Bad and the Ugly*, introduced a new kind of hero in a new kind of setting. From the moment The Man With No Name rode into the town of San Miguel on his mule – like a mercenary version of Henry Fonda at the beginning of John Ford's *Young Mr Lincoln* – and ignored the slob in a sombrero who was roughing up a small Mexican child, it was clear to audiences all over the world that something very different was going on; that a new style of Western was being created. Actually, it was several years before American audiences got to see *A Fistful of Dollars* because the script had been based on Akira Kurosawa's Samurai film *Yojimbo* [1961] and the co-production partners had not bothered to clear the rights. Eventually, the authors of *Yojimbo* were compensated for the obvious resemblances between the two stories by being granted exclusive rights to distribute *A Fistful of Dollars* in Japan, Formosa and South Korea – a huge market – plus fifteen per cent of the worldwide box-office takings. But it took until 1967 to sort out.

Leone, for his part, argued that the author's rights for both films should be paid to the estate of the late Carlo Goldoni, who originated the idea with *Arlecchino Servo di due Padroni* (*The Servant of Two Masters*). Indeed, when *A Fistful of Dollars* and its two sequels did open in America, it infuriated him to read those newspaper criticisms which insisted on interpreting the films exclusively in terms of *American* themes, *American* traditions and even *American* visual styles: 'The critics have always accused me of trying to copy the

American Western,' he once told me. 'But that's not the point at all, for I have brought to the Western, from Italy, some strict conventions of my own. Obviously, there's a culture behind me that I can't just wish away . . .' A culture, Leone goes on, which includes not only Carlo Goldoni but the traditions of Sicilian puppet theatre, *commedia dell'arte* and the picaresque novel as well. It was, in part the (mainly Southern) Italian elements of his Westerns which helped to revitalise a dying American genre – a genre in which, as Pauline Kael had put it, the audience's interest had less to do with the characters or their supposed virtues, than with the old actors wheeled out to embody the end of the frontier.

But there were other elements, too, arising out of Leone's long experience as an assistant director working for American companies based at Cinecittà, Rome in the 1950s: by the time he made *Fistful*, he had worked with (among others) Mervyn Leroy (on *Quo Vadis*, 1952); Raoul Walsh (the second unit of Robert Wise's *Helen of Troy*, 1955); William Wyler (Andrew Marton's second unit of *Ben Hur*, 1959 – responsible for the chariot race), and Fred Zinnemann (*The Nun's Story*, 1959). He had also co-directed *The Last Days of Pompeii* (1959) and directed *The Colossus of Rhodes* [1961], as well as the second unit and the 'Italian version' of Robert Aldrich's *Sodom and Gomorrah* (1961–2) – from which he was fired. So, while Eastwood himself was observing the work of directors and guest stars on *Rawhide*, Leone was doing the same on assorted sword-and-sandal epics in Rome. And the experience was equally disillusioning: 'I was a great admirer of Raoul Walsh, one of the masters of the Western. When we were shooting *Helen of Troy*, I asked him all about this genre: he always replied, "The Western is finished." I insisted that the Western had been killed off by those who had maltreated the genre; but he still replied, "The Western is finished; the public does not want it any more." So I saw all these cinéastes, like William Wyler, sacrifice themselves to the taste of the moment . . . And I was their assistant, the victim of some curse. I was more in love with the idea of America than anyone you could imagine; I had read everything on the Conquest of the West, building up a vast archive on the subject, and I was obliged to spend my time directing Roman circuses in papier-mâché colosseums. While I organised chariot races, battles between triremes, and explosions on galleys, I was silently dreaming about Nevada and New Mexico.'

Out of this experience emerged another important element in the 'Dollars' films – the challenges to the standard visual 'grammar' of the Hollywood film. 'If the critics write that Sergio Leone resurrects the old myths and makes them even larger, that's true; but there has to be a biographical reason for that. I made fifty-eight films as an assistant – I was at the side of directors who applied all the rules: make it, for example, a close-up to show that the character is about to say something important. I reacted against all that, and so the close-ups in my films are always the expression of an emotion. I'm very careful in that area, so they call me a perfectionist and a formalist because I watch my framing. But I'm not doing it to make it pretty, I'm seeking, first and foremost, the relevant emotion. You have to frame with the emotion and the rhythm of the film in mind. It takes on a dramatic function.'

The experience of working with a variety of American directors 'from the best to the worst, from the mediocre to the talented, from the genius to the idiot', added to the Southern Italian cultural context within which Leone was operating, made for a potent combination. But an important part of Leone's strategy was to make his 'Western legend' *look* as authentic as possible, so the surface details – again – had a great significance for him. And that involved historical research into the highways and byways of American history. It also involved looking closely at the complete works of John Ford and Budd Boetticher. One piece of research which always amused Leone a great deal is in Mark Twain's tall stories about Jack Slade, a Colorado gunslinger who cut off his victims' ears and used then as 'mock payment for a drink' in *cantinas* all over the West. The stories were collected in *Roughing It*, and to Leone they said a great deal about the surreal atmosphere of the Wild West.

If audiences were 'saddle sore', bored with an exhausted Hollywood genre – 'lulled to sleep in the "pure" scenery of the West or, just for a change, clobbered by messages in "mature" Westerns', as Pauline Kael wrote in her review of *Yojimbo* – then perhaps rescue was on its way in the form of European cultural influences (which were after all, where the Western came from in the first place) combined with fresh research into the archives. Clint Eastwood disagrees: 'Sergio doesn't really know *anything* about the West. He's just a good director. I mean he has his own ideas, and I think that the fact that he doesn't know too much about the West is what works for him. He claims to have studied the West. I don't think so. I think his very open adolescent type approach to film − I don't mean this in a derogatory type of way − gave to the film a new look . . . He did things at the time that American directors would have been afraid of in a Western.'

The combination of Leone's visual flair, his iconoclasm − whether or not he did much research into the history of the West − and Eastwood's intuitive sense of what would 'work' in a contemporary hero, was clearly one of those great combinations which have not happened often in the history of cinema: Ford and Wayne, Capra and Stewart, Huston and Bogart, Scorsese and De Niro in Hollywood; Fellini and Mastroianni, Visconti and Bogarde in Italy, just might be examples of equivalent stature. But, the two protagonists tell the story of how it all came about in very different ways.

6 Eastwood on Eastwood

FRAYLING: Could we talk about the origins of the 'Eastwood style', in the Spaghetti Westerns of the mid-1960s? In retrospect, they changed both the look and the feel of the traditional Western.

EASTWOOD: Yeah, I think they changed the style, the approach to Westerns. They 'operacised' them, if there's such a word. They made the violence and the shooting aspect a little more larger than life, and they had great music and new types of scores. I wasn't involved in the music, but we used the same composer, Ennio Morricone, in *Sister Sara* and I worked with him a bit there . . . They were scores that hadn't been used in other Westerns. They just had a look and a style that was a little different at the time: I don't think the stories were any better, maybe they were less good. I don't think any of them was a classic story – like *The Searchers*, or something like that – they were more fragmented, episodic, following this central character through various little episodes.

FRAYLING: Someone once wrote that Leone's films are 'operas in which the arias aren't sung, they are stared' [*laughter*]. But when you say 'a look and a style,' do you mean that their main contribution was a technical one?

EASTWOOD: Uh-huh. I think the technical effect is the biggest – the look and the sound. A film has to have a sound of its own, and the Italians – who don't record sound while they're shooting – are very conscious of this. Sergio Leone felt that sound was very important, that a film has to have its own sound as well as its own look. And I agree . . . Leone'll get a very operatic score, a lot of trumpets, and then all of a sudden 'ka-pow!' He'll shut it off and let the horses snort and all that sort of thing. It's very effective. So, yes, I think you've hit on it when you say 'technical' – that was the star – technical changes. The lighting was different, too. It wasn't flat lit. A little more . . . style.

FRAYLING: I've read somewhere that, when you were preparing for the role of The Man With No Name, just before you left the Universal Studios set on *Rawhide* for Rome and Almeria, you brought the costume at a Santa Monica wardrobe store, and borrowed the leather gunbelt, pistol and suede boots from *Rawhide*. Yet Sergio Leone has told me that the transformation of Rowdy Yates into The Man With No Name – the basic change of 'look and style' from which everything else followed – was mostly *his* idea.

EASTWOOD: (*eyes narrowing momentarily*) He didn't accept that . . .? Well – I guess I heard that too, and I heard stories where people would say that he would lay a rope down the line on the ground where I should walk – and all that stuff – and I thought 'Funny, he's the only one who ever had to do that'. But I guess it's normal for him – all of a sudden I go off back to America, and he does several films in the same vein and then drops out for a while, and he sees me going on to do other things and maybe that affected him. Who knows why a person says different things?

FRAYLING (*not feeling lucky, not pushing it*): Whoever it was, the character's sense of visual style – the poncho in *Fistful of Dollars* (1964), the long, waisted coat in *The Good, The Bad and The Ugly* (1966) – was a world away from the fringed buckskins of Alan Ladd in *Shane*, or all those well-scrubbed army scouts in 1950s Westerns.

EASTWOOD (*visibly relaxing again*): Yeah, that was accepted at the time – sixties – and yeah, that buckskin does look a little drugstore-ish now. But we did similar things in *High Plains Drifter* and *Pale Rider*, where he's kind of a stylised character, with a little bit of a different look – the hats, the long coats, and various other things. But it was mostly the people who were *in* the clothes. Gian Maria Volonté had a good face, and all those Spanish, gypsy faces – that was just general . . . everything kind of tied together and made an interesting-looking film. You ask most people what the films were about and they can't tell you. But they tell you 'the look' [*he mimes throwing the poncho over his shoulder*] and the 'da–da–da–da–dum' [*he hums the opening bars of* The Good, The Bad and The Ugly *theme*], and the cigar and the gun and those little flash images that hit you, and we get back to 'technical' again, technical changes. Maybe I had some contribution in there, and er, maybe not . . . I remember we cut out quite a bit of dialogue together, on *Fistful*, before and during.

FRAYLING: I don't know if you recall, but in the Italian press of 1964 you were billed as 'Western consultant' on *A Fistful of Dollars*.

EASTWOOD: Uh-huh? (*laughter, and quizzical look.*)

FRAYLING: A lot of the technical lessons of the Italian films seem to me to have been carried over into your first Western as a director, *High Plains Drifter*: the sound effects, the heavy framing, the way in which the hero is presented . . .

EASTWOOD: Yeah. I don't really associate *High Plains Drifter* as closely with those films as maybe some do – other than the same actor and this mysterious drifting character who comes in, which is like the character in *A Fistful of Dollars*. But then that's sort of the classic Western – that's been done so many times before – with *Shane*, with William S. Hart, with . . . [*pause*] there's nothing really new under the sun there, it's just a question of styling. And it was the same actor playing it. Some elements that come with that character are going to come into other characters that I play, too, along the line. You adapt it to youself, you know . . . The *Fistful of Dollars* character, also – it was fun for me to do everything that was against the rules. For years in Hollywood there was a thing called the Hays Office, there were certain taboos that were put on the Western, even more so than other things. One was that you never could tie up a person shooting with a person being hit. You had to shoot separately, and then show the person fall – and that was always thought sort of stupid, but on television we always did it that way . . . We did it that way on *Rawhide* – and everybody talked about it, and it was sort of a thing that hung over there. And then, you see, Sergio never knew that, and so he was tying it up and that was great – that's terrific, tie up the shots. You see the bullet go off, you see the gun fire, you see the guy fall, and it had never been done this way before. Those things seemed to me very bad for television. Where everybody was shooting sort of standard things, the typical television filming would be where the person is in the door CUT. CUT around to other person who says some lines. CUT walks up to him. Two head close-ups. You never do see the two people together. So that was part of it.

FRAYLING: Turning to *The Outlaw Josey Wales* (1976, or twelve years after *Fistful*), which I think is one of your finest films as a director so far, there's much less emphasis on 'style', on the detached, comic-strip aspects of the Spaghetti Westerns, and much more on the kinds of things that might be on Americans' minds after the Vietnam war. It's about the rebuilding of a small community after the bloody dislocation of the American Civil War – but it could just as well be about post-Vietnam America. How conscious was that?

EASTWOOD: Right. It was inherent in the story, but I guess it made it attractive to me, but I didn't sit there and say, 'Well, I'm doing this now because this parallels some situation in history, then and now, like Vietnam'. But I think the dislocation could be the same after every war . . . *is* the same.

FRAYLING: In a way, *Josey Wales* puts the morality – the *American* morality – back into the character of 'The Man With No Name'. Josey is determined to get his revenge on the Kansas Redlegs – 'I don't want nobody belonging to me', he says – yet he's constantly being deflected from his quest by various drifters who refuse to take his macho image seriously. Even the hound-dog he picks up along the way isn't taken in by the image. The punch line is that we should choose – whatever the odds against – 'the word of life' rather than 'the word of death'. It's the gentle option, rather than the violent one . . .

EASTWOOD: Well, the thing that I liked about it was that it was a Western with a very good story and a central character, and the effects on this character and what life had done to this guy, and his search for something it would be easier to run away from – and by accident things always happen to him, which make him a better person. He starts out as a farmer, becomes a killer, and in the end, I think, becomes a farmer again – although the audience decides that. Because, like I said, the films that I did with Sergio, if they'd been done with less style, they would have been very poor shows because they weren't really good strong stories, and I like stories. It's not that we drifted apart, but I think we just became philosophically different.

I was drifting – naturally, being an actor – towards more personal, more real stories. And he wanted more production values as a director, so he was always going towards vaster and vaster scenes, with trains blowing up, and more Indians over the hill, or whatever – I'm just using examples, nothing specific . . . and I wanted more personal stories. He got into larger, epic pictures and I got into smaller pictures. In *Josey Wales*, there was a personal story that also had a large landscape to it, and that was ideal for me.

FRAYLING: It must be unique for an entire cinematic genre to depend on the fortunes of one individual, but, through the 1970s and 1980s, the future of the Western has to a large extent hinged on the box-office performance of your work. Why do you think that the Western virtually collapsed in the 1970s? Why, for example, did an Arthur Penn Western with Jack Nicholson and Marlon Brando – which must have seemed gilt-edged to those in the know – why did it go down so badly?

EASTWOOD: I don't blame all that on the Western as much as on the material . . . that Nicholson and Brando thing, *The Missouri Breaks*, for instance, was ridiculous. It wasn't a good script and they obviously felt so, too – why else would a guy dress up like his own grand-mother? Brando obviously thought there's nothing here, I might as well enjoy myself. So he's going to go off and screw off somewhere. I think that if he'd truly believed it was a great piece of material and that he was going to contribute to something that might be a fine film, he might have thought otherwise. I like to think that, anyway.

FRAYLING: So what d'you think *your* particular contribution has been to the American Western of the 1970s and 1980s?

EASTWOOD: Well, the answer maybe is just what you said. Maybe that I was lucky enough to make a few of the most successful ones of that period. I don't have any great bolt of lightning from the sky about that one. I just feel the Western is part of the American heritage; the earliest American film, as you'll know, was *The Great Train Robbery*. Americans don't have many art forms that are truly American. Most of them come from Europe or wherever. Westerns and jazz are the only two I can think of which are American art forms. But *High Plains Drifter* was great fun because I liked the irony of it, I liked the irony of doing a stylised version of what happens if the sheriff in *High Noon* is killed, and symbolically comes back as some avenging angel or something – and I think that's far more hip than doing just a straight Western, the straight old conflicts we've all seen. *Josey Wales* just had a much stronger story as far as the personal, the individual was concerned, and a good character. *Bronco Billy* wasn't really a Western at all ... More Frank Capra than Western.

Pale Rider is kind of allegorical, more in the *High Plains Drifter* mode: like that, though he isn't a reincarnation or anything, but he does ride a pale horse like the four horsemen of the apocalypse, and he could maybe be one of those guys. It's a classic story of the big guys against the little guys, little guys versus big guys, the corporate mining which ends up in hydraulic mining, they just literally mow the mountains away, you know, the trees and everything ... all that was outlawed in California some years ago, and they still do it in Montana and a few places. It was outlawed way back, even before ecological concerns were as prevalent as they are today. So we play on that in the film. It's kind of an ecological statement – the fact that this corporation is moving fast because they're afraid laws against it will come along. And so they rabble-rouse these other people and shoot 'em up – ruin their property – and a little girl prays for this figure that comes out of the mountains. He comes down, and there's a series of incidents, and he helps them ...! I like stories you can't guess the endings of. Most Westerns, you can guess the ending.

FRAYLING: So you think Westerns still have an audience, can still carry themes which are about today as well?

EASTWOOD: I think there's a market there, if somebody can make a good one – because in America, on television, Westerns do extremely well. Some of mine have been run many times – and, like the chairman of Warner Brothers, Bob Daley said, he'll be selling *Josey Wales* for ten years. So if they do well on television, maybe that means there is a more adult audience. Maybe if these people could come out to the cinema, plus maybe find a group of people who haven't seen a Western recently ...! I mean if I was taking a poll – like those studios have to do, throwing the thing in hoppers and computers, which I wouldn't – I think it would come out positive. But I'm not sure ...

FRAYLING: Certainly, country and western music, 'new' and 'old', has never been more popular – and Willie Nelson, and Kenny Rogers have both made Westerns (*Barbarosa*, *The Gambler*) on the strength of their success as singers. So maybe the way forward might be in modern Westerns. Urban cowboys. Electric horsemen . . .

EASTWOOD: Well, I think the Western *has* to be period. I don't think it can be modern. I don't think anybody's interested in a Western set today necessarily – or maybe they might be, depending on the film – I hate to say that definitely. Perhaps a picture about rodeo riding or something like that *might* help to excite somebody. Maybe. But I think a period Western is always that kind of escape – another time, times when things were more simplified . . .

7   Bringing it all back home

This dilemma – the urge to make movies about 'times when things were more simplified', in an era when the predominantly teenage audiences seemed to want movies which looked and sounded more hip, more urban, more like the experience of listening to heavily amplified rock music – was precisely the dilemma facing the generation of film-makers known as the Holywood 'movie brats' who graduated from West-Coast film schools in the late 1960s and early 1970s. Reacting against the morally ambiguous, and impeccably liberal work of a previous generation of film-makers (East-Coast people trained in television drama, such as Arthur Penn and Sidney Lumet), they turned instead to the genre films of pioneer directors John Ford and Howard Hawks, films which offered 'that kind of excape'. And in doing so, they became fascinated by the style and approach of Sergio Leone's Italian Westerns as an up-to-date 'filter' through which to view the Model T variety of film-making. Since these 'movie brats' were often concerned with making films about films (they had grown up as the images of television had grown up, in the 1950s, and had trained on film courses which had become highly self-conscious about the contribution of the director, thanks to critic Andrew Sarris and, beyond him, the Parisian cinéastes of *Cahiers du Cinema* magazine) the relationship between the Westerns of Sergio Leone and those of John Ford continued to intrigue them.

'When I saw the opening sequence of Spielberg's *Close Encounters*,' Leone once told me, 'I thought – that was made by Sergio Leone! You know, the dust, the wind, the desert, the planes, the sudden chord on the soundtrack. And it was the same with John Carpenter's films, like *Assault on Precinct 13* and *Escape from New York*: they say my 'Dollars' Westerns had an influence on him. George Lucas has told me how he kept referring to the music and the images of *Once Upon a Time in the West* when he cut *Star Wars*, which was really a Western – series B – set in space. All these younger Hollywood directors – George Lucas, Steven Spielberg, Martin Scorsese, John Carpenter – they've all said how much they owe to my work. Perhaps they admire it because it is so evidently the work of a real *director* – and they have been taught that the heroes of cinema are the 'authors'. But none of them has been tempted to make a Western which is actually a Western . . .'

Apart from the opening sequence of *Close Encounters*, the interplay of soundtrack and visuals in *Star Wars* and the script of *Assault on Precinct 13* (which quotes verbatim from Leone's Westerns), another example of this process is the 'tall story' quality of the pioneers-to-gangsters epic written by John Milius, *The Life and Times of Judge Roy Bean*. Indeed, Milius reckons that *Roy Bean* would have been a far more interesting film had it been made on location at a ghost town in Almeria with Warren Oates in the lead role (rather than attempting, unsuccessfully, to cash in on the box-office performance of *Butch Cassidy*). One could argue that the two key filmic influences on the 'movie brats' generation (in the 1970s, at least) have been Leone's Westerns and John Ford's *The Searchers* – a Western which is 'hidden' within Scorsese's *Taxi Driver*, Schrader's *Hardcore*, Milius's script for *Uncommon Valor* and, most obviously, Lucas's *Star Wars* trilogy.

But, as Leone points out, all those film-makers have recoiled from confronting the *ideology* of the Western movie head-on, preferring settings which are less concerned with 'the past', the desert, or horses, than with 'the here and now', the city and cars or spaceships. The only exception is John Milius (with his scripts for *Jeremiah Johnson* and *Roy Bean*), but he seems to be far more interested in samurais than cowboys, which might help in a roundabout way to explain his taste for spaghetti.

It was Clint Eastwood, from an earlier generation than the 'movie brats' – an actor who had appeared in those same television programmes they grew up watching in their suburban living rooms –

who successfully confronted that ideology in the 1970s when he adapted the persona of The Man With No Name for domestic consumption. But then again, he was less interested in making films about other people's films than they were; or, as he has put it, 'I don't get too misty-eyed about the past, I'm more of a go-ahead type person . . . I've never been what you might term a fan or cultist of specific directors . . . I have to admit I'm not a great film historian.'

Eastwood in fact worked with John Milius and Michael Cimino on *Magnum Force* (1973), the second of the Dirty Harry films, and with Cimino on *Thunderbolt and Lightfoot* (1974), but the two other occasions on which he might have joined 'the brats' came to nothing. The first was when he was offered the lead in *McKenna's Gold* (on which the young George Lucas worked, making 'the film of the making of the film'), but turned it down because 'I didn't understand the script'; the second was when Francis Ford Coppola offered him the Martin Sheen part in *Apocalypse Now*, but he turned *that* down because, as he informed the godfather of the movie brats, 'I know Conrad's *Heart of Darkness*, I read it in school, but I still don't understand the ending of your script'. As Eastwood cannily realised, to tell a story about Vietnam in the mid-1970s was to tell a story in which there could be no 'winners' and maybe not even an acceptable ending – so the material was not, at that stage in his career, for him.

But, considering the commercial impact of the 'Dollars' films on the American market, the domestication of The Man With No Name proved to be a surprisingly difficult thing to do. From the end of 1966, when Eastwood returned to the States after completing *The Good, The Bad and The Ugly* – and, for the first time since the autumn of 1959, did not have to rejoin the cattle drive to Sedalia even as trail boss – until the middle of 1967, he was looking for exactly the right material (or waiting for the right material to come along) with which to relaunch his American film career. 'Oh, Hollywood was suspicious for a long time. So few actors had come out of television series to go into cinema, that they were very, very suspicious. It wasn't after all until after *three* of those Leone films that I did one or two American films.'

Apparently the fact that he was a 'tv actor' was considered more significant, by the front-office people, than his experience of working in Europe as the star of a trio of cult successes (budgets $200,000, $600,000 and $1,200,000 respectively) – for, in Hollywood terms, 'once a tv actor, always a tv actor', and it would take a great deal more than a fistful of 'ersatz Westerns' (as most American critics dubbed them) to prove the market analysts wrong. As Eastwood later remembered, 'There was a feeling that an American actor making an Italian movie was sort of taking a step backward', like all those ageing Hollywood stars who hung around the Via Veneto, relying on the lifetime brand-loyalty of European audiences. When Sophia Loren visited America in 1967, she was amazed to discover that the name 'Clint Eastwood' simply meant to her hosts the lead actor in a failing tv series: she had expected a more up-to-date reaction. Of his contemporaries or near-contemporaries, who featured in small-screen Westerns and who tried at one time or another to gain promotion to large-screen, Clint Walker, Robert Horton, Hugh O'Brian, James Arness, Dale Robertson, Michael Landon and Will Hutchins were all to remain penned in the tv corral. Only Steve McQueen (*Wanted: Dead or Alive*), and, later, Burt Reynolds (*Riverboat, Gunsmoke*) and James Garner (*Maverick*) successfully made the transition. Eric Fleming, having been dropped from the cast of *Rawhide* after the disappointing 1964 season, died on location in the Amazon, after appearing as a CIA man in an indifferent comedy film opposite Doris Day.

But the causes for suspicion perhaps went deeper than that. Eastwood had come to the attention of Hollywood, via the publicity departments of the studios' European subsidiaries, as the enigmatic central character in a series of surreal Westerns which satirised (and questioned) the very bases of the American Western myth. And this was at a time when significant numbers of cinema-goers in the minimum age group recommended for those films were asking, with Norman Mailer's deerslayers in the American wilderness, 'Why are we in Vietnam?' I can remember going to a 'Dollars' triple bill, an all-nighter, at a cinema in San Francisco – July 1968 – which caused much hilarity among the audience of (mainly) eighteen to twenty-five-olds until Clint Eastwood's line after the inconclusive battle of the bridge in *The Good, the Bad and the Ugly*, 'I've never seen so many men wasted so badly'. At which point the entire audience cheered. Right on, brother! I can also remember seeing posters for *Et pour quelques dollars de plus* in Paris – March 1969 – with the words *Viva Leone* printed across them, in imitation of the student graffiti (painted rather than spray-gunned in those days) of the previous May. Viva Danny le Rouge! Viva Guevara! Viva il Cigarillo!

The personal style of The Man With No Name – an impassive mixture of silence, exile and cunning (the portrait of the bounty hunter as a young man, perhaps, or was it Zen and the art of gunfighting?) – exactly fitted him for the late 1960s pantheon of cultural heroes: posters of Clint Eastwood, clutching a rifle and a pocket-watch, from the final duel in *For A Few Dollars More*, would appear side-by-side with a countrified Bob Dylan (in his *John Wesley Harding* sepia-tinted incarnation), and a Warhol-style two-colour image of Che Guevara – the three unshaven gods, and bandits, of the counterculture. Ten years after, the silence, and the exile from society, would come in for some fairly heavy criticism from feminist critics such as Joan Mellen in *Big Bad Wolves*: ' . . . Eastwood even responded to that alienation of the sixties in which the most radical among the young refused on principle to accept any established values as sacred. Like Eastwood, they distrusted everything but their own effectiveness. The anger masked by Eastwood's face in dissociated impassiveness found in the deeply alienated a perverse echo. Eastwood too felt that the world had betrayed him, and was outraged. He, however, handled his fear of weakness by suppressing rather than expressing all feeling. Hence, he held that weakness deep within him . . . Eastwood's silence itself duplicated the spiritual mood of the sixties.' A season of Eastwood's films, intended to illustrate the thesis that the characters he played were really Big (and Scared) Bad Wolves, toured British arts centres in 1977: the poster showed the scowling Stranger, complete with his rawhide whip, from *High Plains Drifter*, with the added punchline *Machismo in peril: a loss of male confidence*.

So back in 1966 – 7, The Man With No Name was a long way away from the mainstream of Hollywood cinema, and the problem facing Clint Eastwood was how to find a script which could repatriate him. Not, of course, a John Wayne-style vehicle, for Eastwood himself had signalled his arrival back in the States by saying, 'Everybody knows nobody ever stood in the street and let the heavy draw first. It's me or him. To me that's practical, and that's where I disagree with the Wayne concept ... I do all the stuff John Wayne would never do. I play bigger-than-life characters, but I'll shoot a guy in the back. I go by the expediency of the moment.' But he did need a vehicle which would at least put him back in the same ballpark, or landscape, as John Wayne. It was, after all, John Wayne who, looking at the results of Eastwood's researches, was to say, 'Of all the actors of the new generation, it is Clint Eastwood who gives me the most hope ... he is the best cowboy of modern cinema.' Wayne couldn't adapt. He was too old for that, and in any case he wouldn't want to; it was more sensible for him to appear in loosely-put-together films directed by Hollywood pros who were in sympathy with his image and his views.

But Eastwood could adapt. His first American film as a name above the title was thought by United Artists (the studio which had distributed the 'Dollars' trilogy in America) to be simply a home-grown continuation of the Italian saga, and the opportunity to make armfuls of dollars. In fact, although it *looked* like a Spaghetti – Las Cruces, New Mexico and White Sands National Park standing in for the adobe villages and sand dunes of Almeria – and although director Ted Post (personally selected by Eastwood) was evidently aiming for the latest line in Leone styling, *Hang 'em High* was really a traditional American revenge Western, with a more-brutal-than-usual hero: its alternative title could well have been *For More Than Money*. Deputy Marshal Jed Cooper (son of Gary?) was clean shaven, he had a name, he talked – occasionally in paragraphs – he had a girlfriend, he seemed to have no sense of humour, but perhaps above all he had a *motive*: the opening of the film showed nine hoodlums beating him up and lynching him, and the rest of the story, give or take a few digressions, showed Cooper making up his mind whether or not to take the law into his own hands and have his revenge. Eastwood has called *Hang 'em High* 'a picture that analysed the pros and cons of capital punishment' – and it *does* contrast the razzamatazz of a mass public hanging with Jed Cooper's personal crusade. But, in the end, it seems to want both ends of the rope. The film clearly prefers due process of law to vigilante 'justice' (and seems, therefore, to be echoing

William Wellman's 1943 classic *Ox-Bow Incident* (one of Eastwood's favourite films), but it also celebrates Jed Cooper's wish to cut through the bureaucracy and kill the entire lynch-mob himself (and seems, therefore, to be questioning the morality of *Ox Bow*). The muddle becomes explicit when vigilante Cooper agrees to hold on to his badge of office rather than resign and is described by hanging-Judge Fenton as a good American. No matter. *Hang 'em High* broke even in one weekend, indeed went on to make more money – for Eastwood personally and for the studio – than any of the 'Dollars' films. The *New York Times* said of it that it at least 'had a *point* . . . unlike the previous sado-masochistic exercises on foreign prairies'.

By that time, the relationship between Eastwood and the director of those 'sado-masochistic exercises' was not as friendly as once it had been. During post-production on *The Good, the Bad and the Ugly*, there had been some public confrontations and Leone started bad-mouthing Eastwood (at first in a fairly genial way) soon afterwards. The two versions of how *A Fistful of Dollars* came about began to go in quite separate directions. Eastwood refused to appear in the credits sequence of *Once Upon a Time in the West* with Eli Wallach and Lee Van Cleef as part of a jokey '*arrivederci*' to the 'Dollars' trilogy, so the idea was abandoned and Leone was forced to wipe out three other guest stars instead. Yet, shortly before he died, Leone informed me that Eastwood had, in fact, offered him the direction of *Hang 'em High*, even though the film was intended to move the actor's career into a fresh direction: 'He went back to his own country a great star. Very soon, he offered me the project of directing his first American Western. I refused. Later, he arranged for me to see the script of *Two Mules for Sister Sara*. After the first five pages, I knew that the nun was a prostitute. So it wasn't really worth making the film.'

Evidently, at one stage Clint Eastwood had considered 'importing' the 'Dollars' package lock, stock and barrel. But Leone was not interested, and in any case Eastwood must have realised that at this stage in his career such a multinational solution would not work. The two were eventually to be reconciled, but they couldn't possibly have ever made a film together again. 'I didn't see Clint for years,' Leone recalled. 'Then, when I was making *Once Upon a Time in*

America, he came to see me in my hotel room. We reminisced about the past. He seemed to have a great respect for me, which was nice. I've often been asked if I could make another film with him. I always refuse. It is impossible.' Both men still tended to bristle when discussing each others' work (with me), even after the passage of some twenty years.

With *Hang 'em High*, Eastwood had superimposed a crusading element, and even a hint of vulnerability, on the Spaghetti Western prototype: the result was still a Western, and a brutal one, and it looked on the surface like 'more of the same', another not-very-respectable product in a marginal career. Eastwood was evidently thinking along these lines as well, for he took much more trouble hammering his next project, *Coogan's Bluff*, into shape, and custom-ising it. By now he was in charge of his own limited liability company, Malpaso, and the deal with Universal was that he would have final approval on script and director. This led to a protracted period of negotiation. First of all the allotted director, Alex Segal, walked away from the project when he was unable to agree on a storyline which 'fitted'. Then Eastwood suggested Don Taylor, then the studio suggested Mark Rydell, who in turn suggested Don Siegel who only agreed to direct when he had seen Leone's three Italian Westerns: he thought they were 'fun' and 'imaginative', and so agreed to take on *Coogan's Bluff*.

'It wasn't all great pleasantries when we first met,' Eastwood recalls. 'In the first place, Don had replaced another director . . . and I had seen only two of his films at the time – *The Killers*, which he had made with Lee Marvin, and another one for tv with Henry Fonda. I liked his work, but I didn't know much about it, and we had some discrepancies, some arguments over the script. He had sort of tailored it one way, and I wanted it another way, so finally after shouting at each other for four or five minutes, in his office, one of the studio executives said – he saw everything crumbling before him, so he said – "Why don't you two fellows just talk about it to see if you can come up with something", and he excused himself. So Don and I sat there for a few minutes in silence, and pretty soon we started saying, "What *is* the best way of telling this story? Supposing we did this, supposing we did that" – and pretty soon we were getting on rather well. So we called in a contract writer from Universal and next thing we were all handshakes and everything was going OK. It took a little time and quite a few meetings, but finally we had a script and said "Let's go make it". After we did the film, we became very much in sync on philosophy.'

Actually, the process seems to have been a great deal less good humoured than this memory would suggest. When Don Siegel took over, the script was on its ninth separate version. A tenth version appealed to both Jennings Lang (the 'studio executive' mentioned by Eastwood , actually vice-president in charge of Features) and Siegel, who had developed it – but Clint Eastwood said *he* would pull out if it was used. So, back to square one, and back to the earliest drafts, which were compiled into the final version with help from Dean Reisner (the 'contract writer', actually another old friend, who wrote some of the early episodes of *Rawhide*). Eastwood clearly liked working with people he knew and trusted, and he had a very strong sense of the story, and the character, which would suit his first major American film. The film Don Siegel had made for tv with Henry Fonda was called *Stranger on the Run*, and that same Dean Reisner had written it.

For a Few Dollars More opened with a Techniscope image of the desert and in the middle distance a rider on a horse: just off-screen right, a bounty hunter is whistling to himself (the whistling was provided by Leone) and cocking his rifle. There is a shot, and the rider falls off his horse; another, and the horse bolts away into the desert. 'Where life had no value,' says the prologue, 'Death, sometimes had its price. That is why the bounty hunters arrived.'

Coogan's Bluff opens with a wide-angle image of the Mojave desert. Up among the parched rocks, an Indian has pitched his camp. Then, in the middle distance, the man in the cowboy hat, Deputy Sheriff Walt Coogan appears – in a modern-day jeep. The Indian, who is clearly on the run, cocks his ultra-modern high velocity rifle with telescopic sight, and waits. Meanwhile, the soundtrack mixes country and western with Lalo Schifrin big city jazz.

Not only has the visual arrangement of the sequence been reversed (the bounty hunter waiting 'above' becomes the Indian), and the period updated, but the world to which we have been introduced is, quite literally, oceans apart from the world 'where life had no value'. The Italian critic Franco Ferrini wrote of Leone's West, 'It is a world irredeemably condemned to immobility, somnolence, to the lack of all resource and development'. By contrast, after Walt Coogan from Arizona has reached New York to extradite a prisoner named Ringerman and take him back to the West for trial, he looks down on the hustle and bustle of Manhattan, and says, 'I'm trying to picture it the way it was – trees, rivers – before people came along and screwed it up.'

In *Coogan's Bluff*, Eastwood has come to represent the rugged individualist of frontier mythology, and his behaviour is forever contrasted with the pen-pushers, the social workers, the time-servers and even the taxi-drivers of present-day civilisation. This was the theme which Eastwood was searching for. Country virtues and city vices. Individual action versus the reaction of mass society. Or, as President Ronald Reagan liked to put it, 'There is nothing so good for a man's insides as the outsides of a horse'.

When first he arrives in New York, Coogan – decked out in suit, bootlace tie, cowboy hat and tooled leather boots – travels by yellow cab rather than by horse. But we are immediately alerted to the fact that he ain't gonna take no horseshit from anyone when he has the following exchange with the driver:

'How many stores are there in this town named Bloomingdales?'
'One.'
'We passed it twice.'
'It's still $2.95, including the luggage.'
'Here's $3.00, including the tip.'

Later, during one of the many altercations between New York City Police Detective McElroy (Lee J. Cobb), the theme which had been hammered out by Eastwood and Siegel really gets into its stride. McElroy, who insists on calling Coogan 'Tex' or 'Wyatt' throughout, and who at one point has to remind our hero that Manahattan 'isn't the OK Corral', of course ends up having a great deal of respect for him. Maybe there's something to be said for the slogan 'order before law', after all. Especially if the rogue cop can think of as many good one-liners as the remorselessly honest deputy from Arizona. 'You better drop that blade,' he says at one point to a degenerate in the Pigeon-Toed Orange Peel discotheque, 'or you won't *believe* what happens next.'

There is a key moment in *Coogan's Bluff*:

MCELROY: We're asking your co-operation. Because what you remember on the plane going home isn't going to help us find Ringerman right now.

COOGAN: I'm not going any place. Not without my prisoner.

MCELROY: Didn't that whack on the skull teach you anything? This is a whole other kind of ball game. You're out of your league. We got 28,000 cops in this city. You leave Ringerman to us.

COOGAN: It's got kinda personal now.

MCELROY: And a man's gotta do what a man's gotta do. That it, Wyatt?

COOGAN: That's one way of putting it.

MCELROY: Here's another. Forget it, understand? Forget it. This isn't just me talking. This comes direct from the DA's office. You are not a policeman in the city of New York. Am I getting through?

COOGAN: Still got a badge.

MCELROY: In Arizona you're a Deputy Sheriff. Here you're just another private citizen with a sore head.

This exchange is also a key moment in Clint Eastwood's American film career. Its fusion of Wild West morality ('A man's gotta do . . .') with the rogue cop of today ('Still got a badge') and its fusion of populism (the inefficient bureaucracy surrounding those 28,000 cops needs a thorough overhaul) and conservatism ('I'm trying to picture it the way it was') directly paves the way for the *Dirty Harry* cycle of the 1970s and 1980s. Coogan even has a Harry-style punchline (instead of 'Do you feel lucky?' – 'Okay, Chief, put your pants on'). The two major differences are that in *Coogan's Bluff* the deputy eventually comes to understand his adversary Ringerman (with whom he has more in common than with McElroy), and – the most unre-solved aspect of the script – Coogan seems to be uncharacteristically interested in sex: with his own girlfriend in Arizona (while the hapless Indian is chained up, on the porch outside), with the social worker Julie, and with Ringerman's acid-head girlfriend in New York.

Coogan's Bluff was the first of Eastwood's films to make feminist critics really angry. Harry Callahan, still bitter about the death of his wife, is much more of a lone wolf. Unlike Coogan, he manages to suppress nearly *all* his feelings.

Don Siegel had recently directed *Madigan*, which also contrasted the street-cop methods of policeman Dan Madigan (Richard Widmark) with the rule-book methods of his Commissioner (Henry Fonda): the setting, a modern city which has become a threatening jungle, was similar to *Coogan's Bluff*; but in *Madigan* the conclusion is for more ambiguous. For a start, Henry Fonda is more sympathetic than Lee J. Cobb. But the big difference is that Madigan's vigilante methods lead directly to his own death. You have to be tough (Widmark was perfect casting as a punk-turned-cop), but it doesn't begin to solve the bigger problems. By the time Eastwood and Siegel collaborated again on a cop film – *Dirty Harry* – this gloomy ending had subtly turned into Harry Callahan throwing away his badge: so you could be a rogue cop and *still* be in the right, but you couldn't expect to keep your job when others were more concerned with their promotion prospects than with the enforcement of justice (rather than the law).

Coogan's Bluff made explicit the relationship between the new-style cop and the new-style Western hero: this winning formula was to turn into the television series *McCloud*, with Dennis Weaver of *Gunsmoke* fame as the Coogan figure: ironically, the name McCloud originated in William Wyler's *Detective Story*, one of the great police procedural/rogue cop films of the early 1950s. What was never explained in *Dirty Harry* was how Inspector Harry Callahan had managed to grow up, and be trained, in the modern city of San Francisco and still retain the values of a deputy sheriff from Arizona. He must have grown up watching Clint Eastwood movies.

8   The Clint Eastwood Corporation . . .

When his own first film as a director, *Play Misty for Me*, was released, a film in which Don Siegel made a guest appearance playing a bartender, Eastwood wrote of his enormous debt to Siegel's working methods as a filmmaker: 'I have admired many directors individually for specific films: William Wellman for his classic *Ox Bow Incident* [though not for *Lafayette Escadrille*], Gillo Pontecorvo for *Battle of Algiers*, and Akira Kurosawa for *Seven Samurai* and *Red Beard*. But there are others, many others . . . I think I've learned most about direction from working with Don Siegel, whom I respect very much as a director. His special qualities include the organised way he prepares for production and his economy in shooting. I don't mean dollars-and-cents economy (although it amounts to that), but his sure knowledge of what he's doing and of the shots he wants to put down on film – and not merely shooting massive footage, nine-tenths of which will be thrown away. This really boils down to editing while shooting. It seems to me that in the past, accolades have been bestowed unfairly primarily on the motion picture directors who have spent the most time and money on their pictures. There are all too many directors, like Don Siegel, who were never given the credit they deserved.'

Don Siegel, returning the compliment, had some nicer things to say about Eastwood the actor than Sergio Leone, although on close inspection their comments do have much in common. 'Clint,' Siegel said at the time of *Two Mules*, 'has an absolute fixation with being an anti-hero. It's his credo in life and in all the films he's done so far . . . I've never worked with an actor who was less conscious of his good image.'

And when *The Beguiled* was released he added: 'From the beginning of our relationship, I found Clint very knowledgeable about making pictures, very good at knowing what to do with the camera. He knows his craft. I also found that he is inclined to underestimate his range as an actor. I think he's a very underrated actor, partly because he is so successful . . . Clint is a very strong individual, on and off the screen. He doesn't require, and I don't give him, too much direction. A good rule with Clint is that when you give him a direction, be sure you're right about it. If you don't think you're right, don't say it. Clint knows what he's doing when he acts and when he picks material. His character is usually bigger than life. In spite of the current mode, I think people don't really want to see pictures about mundane things and ordinary people. Clint's character is far from mundane or ordinary. He is a tarnished super-hero, actually an anti-hero. You can poke at a character like that. He makes mistakes, does things in questionable taste, is vulnerable. He's not a white knight rescuing the girl . . .'

Ten years later, Siegel replied to a question about whether Eastwood is a good actor by saying, 'From one standpoint, looking at his bank account, I'd say he was brilliant.'

Siegel's working methods on the set were, according to Eastwood, an influence on the evolution of his own production company Malpaso: 'When I stress the importance of an organisation, I don't mean to imply that the old concept of dozens of people hanging around assists the director. On the contrary, when I went into directing, I brought to it the philosophy that a director needs a lean, creative, hand-picked crew, large enough to do the job but small enough so everyone has a sense of participation and constant involvement . . . One of the first lessons I learned, and I learned it very quickly – during the shooting of *Misty* – was that by keeping everybody involved in what you, the director, are doing, crews will work twice as hard and develop a tremendous *esprit de corps*. Movie-making is no longer a ride that everyone goes along for. It is a serious job, one that can be fun, but nonetheless a job seriously dedicated to making a profit. That means bringing the film in for a reasonable price, and the only reasonable price is the lowest possible cost consistent with telling your story well. The twenty-week schedule seems to me to be an anomaly today. It is saddling a dinosaur.'

Although Clint Eastwood is clearly pleased that his work as a director is at last being given a second look, he has always been generous about sharing the credit for his films. A press still issued at the time of *High Plains Drifter* showed him on the set of the town cemetery of Lago, leaning on two gravestones bearing the names 'Sergio Leone' and 'Don Siegel' – a nice in-joke, and a stylish acknowledgement of his debt to the two directors who had the most influence on him during his long apprenticeship in the 1960s and 1970s. As he has recalled, the lessons he learned were very different. 'Siegel shoots fast, thinner than I do. Leone, because of the European influence, shoots lots of the same shot, but they're always having problems, the lab scratches one and maybe three others . . .' Siegel was more disciplined, Leone more imaginative – and in any case, Eastwood believes that the role of the director in the creative process of film-making can easily be overrated. 'That *auteur* crap is exactly that – it's an ensemble: fifty, forty, twenty – or however big your crew is – guys all working together'.

He also believes that the ensemble works far better on location than in the studio. 'I think once you get into a studio, a major studio, you can get bogged down. Everyone gets wrapped up in who's supposed to pick up what. When you're on natural sets, everybody chips in and goes. You're on a sound stage – the other day, everybody was looking for their canvas chair!'

Play Misty for Me, which was shot in 'my own backyard', the Carmel-Monterey area, was budgeted at $950,000: it was brought in four days ahead of schedule and $50,000 under budget. *High Plains Drifter*, Eastwood's second film as a director, had to be shot in continuity (partly because the entire wooden town, on the shore of Mono Lake in the Sierras, had to be destroyed in the last reel), but was still delivered within two days of the six-week schedule. And ever since then, his own productions have tended to be delivered cost-effectively, quickly and efficiently, involving a small and friendly repertory company of actors, technicians and managers, some of whom go all the way back to pre-*Rawhide* days. Three of the stalwarts of the Malpaso Company were schoolfriend Fritz Manes, who became associate producer with a special interest in publicity;

Robert Daley, who as a Universal accountant and a neighbour had met Eastwood in 1954 and who became producer of all his films; and Sonia Chernus who from being a junior in the script department at CBS, became a script reader at Malpaso. The story and script of *Play Misty for Me*, the first Eastwood-directed Malpaso production, were written by Jo Heims, an old friend who had been a legal secretary with writing ambitions when Eastwood was an apprentice actor at Universal.

John Milius has said of Eastwood, 'He's very practical. When you deal with him it's not like dealing with an actor, it's like dealing with the chairman of the board of the Clint Eastwood Corporation'. Writer-director Richard Tuggle has added, 'He doesn't like a lot of intellectual mumbo-jumbo' – a preference (and a determination to enforce it) which must have helped him bring in *The Outlaw Josey Wales* for $3.7 million in 1976 and *Pale Rider* for $6.9 million nearly ten inflationary years later, in an era when Michael Cimino (who cut his teeth writing and directing for Malpaso, but evidently didn't get the message) was spending over $40 million on *Heaven's Gate*. When you meet him, Clint Eastwood is far more at ease talking about such logistics than what he calls 'analysing your shots and your motivations for a film'. He gives no evidence of the temperament which he is known occasionally to display on set or on location in his efforts to keep the home team organised. One of his colleagues from Malpaso said to *Newsweek* in 1985, 'As a leader, he doesn't want to look over his shoulder to see if the troops are following. He *knows* they're following – or God help them!' To which Eastwood has added, 'I'm always appalled, just knocked out, by disloyalty. I never think it's coming.'

David Lees and Stan Berkowitz, in their book *The Movie Business*, have referred to the Malpaso Company as one of the tiniest in the business, and they explain its financial structure and operations like this: 'Since Eastwood is a sought-after star, the other two ingredients needed to get a film off the ground – a literary property and financing – both gravitate toward him. A studio that wants Eastwood's services will first give Eastwood the money to buy a screenplay or have one written. Then the studio will give Eastwood the financing to make his film and the assurance that it won't be looking over his shoulder.

Since Eastwood and his company (just one or two other individuals) decide which movie to make and spend the money as they see fit, it's legitimate to see the Malpaso name on his films. It would also be legitimate to see Eastwood's name listed as producer or executive producer, but he tends to decline those credits.'

From the time Malpaso was set up in 1967 for *Hang 'em High* (although its close involvement dates from two years later with *Two Mules*), Eastwood himself owned the controlling stock, but held no post in the company: this meant he could be 'hired out', to the advantage of Malpaso. He retained script control and choice of creative crew, while his circle of 'one or two other individuals' dealt with the administrative side. In the mid-1970s Robert Daley explained the kinds of budgetary considerations for which Malpaso was already becoming well known: 'Only accurately and tightly budgeted screenplays would be bought. "Pre-sold" packages would be avoided, as would screenplays which included too much spectacle and special effects. Location filming would be favoured over studio work.' Daley agreed on this with his boss: 'There's an *esprit de corps* that develops on location, and your crews work harder and faster.' The company would aim to use the same key technical staff (as it turned out, most of Malpaso's productions were to be photographed by Bruce Surtees or, after the mid-1980s, his ex-camera operator Jack Green; many of the 1970s projects were edited by Ferris Webster). 'New technological developments would be encouraged, if they led to ease of production. Technology for its own sake was out.'

At the time when Hollywood budgets were just beginning to spiral out of control and the agents and packagers were beginning to take over, *Variety* was suitably impressed by this policy. It could never be said of Malpaso that the most creative aspect of film-making was 'the deal'.

The reasons why Eastwood decided to turn himself into 'the Clint Eastwood Corporation' in the first place had a lot to do with three unfortunate experiences he had while turning himself into an international household name in the late 1960s. In *Where Eagles Dare* (1968, directed by Brian G. Hutton), he had seemed to be in a different movie than everyone else: the vehicle simply didn't fit the star. As a cold-blooded professional assassin (1960s style) who found

himself in the Second World War (Alistair MacLean-style), he had
to say lines like, 'I'm an American. I don't even know why the hell
I'm here'. In the much-too-big-budget musical *Paint Your Wagon*
(1969, directed by Joshua Logan), he had played a sympathetic love-
sick young man name Pardner, and watched the studio, Paramount,
re-cut the director's version of the film. In Eastwood's view, 'The
director's was actually the best one [of the *four* which were doing
the rounds]. But that wasn't the one that was released.' In retrospect,
he may well have agreed with the rewrite of Pardner's big stage show
number which Spike Milligan did for the radio *Goon Show*: 'I talk
to the trees, that's why they put me away . . .' Acting Lee Marvin's
rival for the hand of Jean Seberg, and wearing a gathered floral shirt
while breathlessly singing romantic lyrics about finding the words
to say all the things she means to him must have seemed like a big
mistake. In fact his big song was issued as the B side to Lee Marvin's
'Wand'rin' Star.' In *Kelly's Heroes*, the most interesting of the three
(1970, directed again by Brian G. Hutton), he had led an
anachronistic platoon of oddballs – a hippy actually named Oddball,
a hustler named Crap Game and a made-for-Telly Savalas character
named Big Joe – towards several million dollars' worth of gold,
behind enemy lines. It was all supposed to be happening just after
D-Day in France and it included a parody of the final duel in *The
Good*, *The Bad and The Ugly* (which was of course parodic in the
first place), an alarming sign that Eastwood might be writing *finis*
too early to a story and a style which had a lot of mileage left in them.
He reckoned that *Kelly's Heroes* could have been a classic – school
of *Catch 22* – if only the director had been left alone by MGM.

The lessons were much the same in each case; Eastwood was at
his best playing characters who were variations on The Man With
No Name (in manner) and Walt Coogan (in ideology); and if his
career was to develop satisfactorily, studio interference was to be
avoided at all times. Hence Malpaso, which at first had a special
relationship with Universal Studios, then Warner Brothers.

Eastwood's career, since the early 1970s, has been synonymous
with Malpaso, which helps explain why it has been so unusually
consistent and self-contained – a very different approach from the
eclecticism of the 'movie brats' who succeeded him, as we have seen.

As Jeffrey Ryder perceptively wrote during Ronald Reagan's second term of office: 'Machismo may be in this month, along with don't-think-twice-it's-all-right action on the international political front, but Clint Eastwood has never been one to change direction with the prevailing winds. Like the composer of a baroque fugue, Eastwood stated his themes – the self-sufficient man as cop or cowboy; the cop or cowboy as a vehicle for Supreme Justice – at the very start, shading them with variations as he went along, with no concern (well, almost no concern, anyway) for outside opinion. *Pale Rider*, in 1985, is a plot twist on 1973's *High Plains Drifter*, which of course tips its dusty hat to 1967's *A Fistful of Dollars*. The four *Dirty Harry* movies to date – *Dirty Harry* (1971), *Magnum Force* (1973), *The Enforcer* (1975) and *Sudden Impact* (1983) – answer each other more than they do their critics ... Two of Eastwood's personal favourites, *The Beguiled* (1971) and *Honkytonk Man* (1982), play against expectations because of endings fatal to our hero, and some of the public's favourites – the ribald comedies *Every Which Way But Loose* (1977) and *Any Which Way You Can* (1980) – play against the studio's predictions by being two of Clint's top-grossing films (the former made $48 million to *Dirty Harry*'s paltry $17.9 million). But Eastwood is the single most consistent – and the most consistently successful – movie star alive.'

As early as 1971, *Life* magazine featured Clint Eastwood as their cover story, accompanied by the amazed, and amazing, headline, 'The world's favourite movie star is – no kidding – Clint Eastwood'. That was the year after he took a risk on his first major film project which didn't have an upbeat ending – Don Siegel's elegant piece of Southern Gothic, *The Beguiled*. Eastwood had enjoyed the lengthy novel by Thomas Cullinan, during lulls in the shooting of *Two Mules for Sister Sara*, and passed it on to Siegel, who felt it provided an excellent, and timely, opportunity for the actor to adapt his public image.

By the time Eastwood was available (after completing *Kelly's Heroes*), he was no longer so sure. Apart from anything else, he *died* at the end of the story. One theme of *Two Mules* had been that The Man With No Name (American-style) was more vulnerable than he realised, that he was probably right to look upon all close relationships with either sex – but especially the opposite one – as potentially diminishing. But *The Beguiled* was to be something else again, a wild parable about an enclosed gynaecocracy which succeeds in first castrating (actually, it's his leg but the symbolism is clear) then poisoning our super-hero. With *Two Mules* and *Play Misty for Me* (which was made immediately after), *The Beguiled* belongs to the most misogynist phase in the development of the Eastwood persona. Critic David Thomson attributes this phase to 'the good humour of a happily married man lusted after by so many strangers' and implies that Clint was showing himself the victim of women (a prostitute, an entire girls' seminary and a psychopath respectively) as a kind of joke about the behaviour of his fans. Maybe.

Eventually, Don Siegel persuaded him to continue with the role – and still reckons that if *The Beguiled* had been more of a box-office hit, Clint Eastwood's career 'might have taken a very different turn'. Eastwood, for his part, interpreted the story as a tale about 'the frustration and the degeneration, the effects that war can have on people on the periphery', a theme to which he would return, with *The Outlaw Josey Wales*. It gave him the chance to act opposite some fine actresses – especially Elizabeth Hartman and Geraldine Page – who tended, unlike himself, to 'play large', and he compares the results with the two different acting styles which worked so well together in Billy Wilder's *Sunset Boulevard*, William Holden's and Gloria Swanson's. It gave cinematographer Bruce Surtees his first big break as principal photographer on a film and he responded by giving *The Beguiled* a suitably Gothic, other-worldly look – one of its most distinctive features. (Surtees was to photograph all Eastwood's major films as a director, until the mid-1980s.) But the film was initially marketed as a Clint-Eastwood-takes-on-the-entire-Confederacy movie, and his audience felt short-changed, with the result that 'Maybe people expected a certain type of thing from me. They didn't like the film' and it wasn't targetted properly at 'others who might like that particular project'. In London, it quietly opened as an 'art film' in St Martin's Lane. I went on the second night, and the cinema was almost empty. Perhaps Jennings Lang, of Universal, was right when he said, 'Maybe a lot of people just don't want to see Clint Eastwood's leg cut off.'

9 'Do I feel lucky . . .?'

The next collaboration between Clint Eastwood and Don Siegel – and their first to hit the headlines on the news pages – was *Dirty Harry*, the first Eastwood film with which it became really problematic for liberals to identify; which was, on the contrary, associated by many American critics with the hard law-and-order line of Richard Nixon.

In the forties, Hollywood had specialised in stories about private detectives, and just occasionally working policemen, about whom it could be written (as it was, by Raymond Chandler), 'Down these mean streets a man must go who is himself not mean, who is neither tarnished nor afraid . . . He must be a complete man and a common man and yet an unusual man. He must be, to use a rather weathered phrase, a man of honor.' This 'man of honor' tended to have a healthy cynicism about the capability of your average working cop: as Philip Marlowe says in *The Long Goodbye*, 'Cops are like a doctor that gives you aspirin for a brain tumor, except that the cop would rather cure it with a blackjack.' But, even if the private eye can only manage what one critic has described as 'his hopeless little moral gestures' in such a world, he still attempts to function as some kind of a St George with 'a coat, a hat and a gun', fighting the dragons of inner-city corruption. In the fifties, it was the turn of 'police procedurals' such as *Naked City* and the *Dragnet* series on television ('Just the facts, ma'am'), which showed ordinary policemen rather than the more glamorous special agents and G-Men, going through their everyday routines of enquiry. Don Siegel, for example, made a cop film in 1958 called *The Lineup*, a big screen version of tv's *San Francisco Beat*, which combined the 'police procedural' with the *film*

Above: Publicity shot of Clint Eastwood
during his apprenticeship at Universal
Studios in the mid 1950s
Above right: As dashing Lieutenant Jack
Rice, playing opposite Carol Channing in
The First Traveling Saleslady
Right: As Rowdy Yates in an episode from
the long-running CBS tv series *Rawhide*

Above: As The Man With No Name in Sergio Leone's *For a Few Dollars More*, the second of the Italian 'Dollars' trilogy
Below: As the 'Good' in the final sequence of Leone's *The Good, the Bad and the Ugly*

Above: On active service as Lieutenant Morris Schaffer in the British epic, *Where Eagles Dare*
Below: Lee Marvin as Ben Rumson discusses gold fever with his Pardner in *Paint Your Wagon*

Above: Director Don Siegel sets up the opening sequence of *Two Mules for Sister Sara*
Below: As John McBurney, about to undergo some serious surgery at the hands of Geraldine Page, in Don Siegel's *The Beguiled*

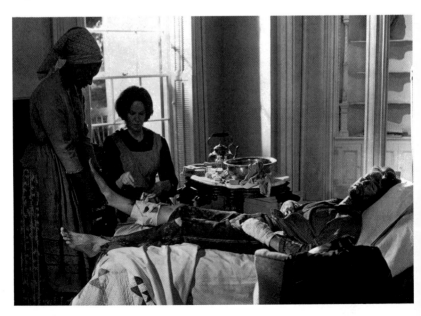

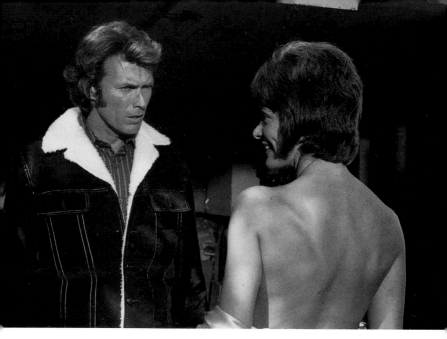

Above: Disc jockey Dave Garland is fatally attracted to Evelyn Draper, played by Jessica Walter, in *Play Misty for Me*
Below: Washed-up cop Ben Shockley brings in key witness Gus Mally, played by Sondra Locke, in *The Gauntlet*

Left: The mysterious stranger, known only as the Preacher, dispenses rough justice in *Pale Rider*
Below: Author Christopher Frayling (second from left) meets Clint Eastwood at London's National Film Theatre shortly after completion of *Pale Rider*
Opposite, top: Wearing a different hat – opposite rival superhero Burt Reynolds in the gangster film send-up, *City Heat*
Opposite, bottom: Dirty Harry returns, in *Sudden Impact*, the only one of the series to be directed by Clint Eastwood

Above: In costume as Hollywood director John Wilson (based on real-life director John Huston), Eastwood directs his own *White Hunter, Black Heart*
Below: Jazz-fan Clint Eastwood directs Forest Whitaker as jazz-man Charlie Parker in *Bird*

noir, in a Bay Area setting. The film was dedicated (rather solemnly in the circumstances) to the San Francisco Police Department.

But in the early 1970s, it was *Dirty Harry* which decisively challenged both species of blue film. For a start, the look on Harry Callahan's face as he finally blows away the villainous Scorpio belonged less to a St George than to a Mickey Spillane character who was still nostalgic about the certainties of the McCarthy era.

'Just how *did* you kill a dragon?' wrote Spillane in *The Girl Hunters*. 'I could bury the axe in his belly. That would be fun, all right. Stick it right in the middle of his skull and it would look a lot better. They wouldn't come fooling around after seeing pictures of that. How about the neck? One whack and his head would roll like the Japs used to do. But nuts, why be that kind?

'This guy was *really* going to die . . .'

Secondly, those very procedures which had been the subject of the 1950s cycle of cop movies, had now become the *enemy*. Eastwood himself reckons that films concerned with 'paperwork' or 'details of routine' tend to be 'very, very boring'.

DISTRICT ATTORNEY: You're lucky I'm not indicting you for assault with intent to commit murder. Where the hell does it say that you have the right to kick down doors, torture subjects, deny medical attention and legal counsel? *Where have you been*? What I'm saying is that man had rights.

INSPECTOR CALLAHAN: Well, I'm all broken up about that man's rights.

In short, Callahan (like his predecessor Madigan) seemed to have more in common with the Irish-American gangsters played by James Cagney in the 1930s than with your traditional Hollywood police-man. Cagney is, as it happens, one of Eastwood's favourite actors.

As criminologist Robert Reiner has written: '*Dirty Harry*, with its explicit condemnation of the due process requirements laid down by the Supreme Court, clearly supports the reactionary demands of police organisations and right-wing politicians who saw the law as "hand-cuffing" the cops. The film chimes in with the grass-roots "police rebellion" against liberal chiefs, lawyers and politicians which exploded in the late 1960s. But it is important to note that the message works within the context of the movie in such a way as to win the support of audience groups who would normally support civil liberties. The film achieves this by postulating that the law primarily protects the rights of an insane psychopath, whereas in reality the majority of suspects are poor, inarticulate and ignorant petty criminals open to police bamboozlement. Dirty Harry, like most policemen, justifies his contempt for civil liberties by a "victim-oriented" perspective.'

The result was that when *Dirty Harry* was released, it was seized upon – for political capital – by both pro- and anti-Nixonites. As Jeffrey Ryder recalls: 'Speaking for the right, *Commentary*'s Richard Grenier remembered it this way: "Kent State had been in 1970. The campuses were alive with peace demonstrations. Students carried the Vietcong flag, called their own country fascist. Policemen were known as pigs. But Clint Eastwood and director Dan Siegel thought that there was another America out there. Warner Bros, which put up the money, agreed with them. And, judging by the forty-nine states that went for Nixon in 1972 and the success of their film, they were right". Meanwhile, though, Pauline Kael of *The New Yorker* led the hue and cry from the left. She may not have ever called her country "fascist", but that *is* what she called *Dirty Harry*. She was offended by Harry's disregard for civil liberties, but she was even more upset by what she saw as his automatic resort to violence and the glee she felt he took in killing.'

Eastwood himself, as we have seen, prefers to interpret the film as a classic 'individual versus red tape' story, a sort of *Mr Deeds Gets a .44 Magnum* – just as *Coogan's Bluff* was a variation on the middle-Westerner-goes-East stories of Frank Capra. He now says that Pauline Kael 'didn't bother me because I knew she was full of shit the whole time. She was writing to be controversial'. But he was still sufficiently bugged by Miss Kael to include a character who bears a marked resemblance to her – a television film critic called Molly Fisher – and to have her stabbed to death by a psychopath, as one of the many in-jokes which punctuate (literally at times) the fifth *Dirty Harry* movie, *The Dead Pool* (1988). You don't call Dirty Harry a 'psychopathic personality . . . a machine for killing, and expect to get away with it in the movies: nor do you say of Eastwood in real life 'he isn't an actor . . . so one could hardly call him a bad actor. He'd have to *do* something before we could consider him bad at it', and expect him to forget all about it.

Eastwood also responds by saying that cinema audiences are a great deal more intelligent than critics would allow, since *they* know very well when a fantasy figure is merely a fantasy figure: if that wasn't so, 'then every guy on Death Row would have reason to be released because Tom Mix or James Cagney shot guys on the screen'. His own view seems to be more close to that of a more subdued Harry Callahan, in the second *Harry* film *Magnum Force* (1973): 'When the police start becoming their own executioners, where's it going to end, eh? Pretty soon you start executing people for jaywalking, and executing people for traffic violations. Then you end up executing your neighbour because his dog pisses on your lawn.'

Certainly, Eastwood liked to quote that last sentence when he was interviewed by the press about his attitude to the real-life New York subway vigilante Bernhard Goetz in 1984.

Above all, he views *Dirty Harry* as well put together, fast paced, action-packed, in short a very *effective* crime drama. If it had been lacking in any one of these departments, it might well have created less of a stir: 'I'd never seen a crime drama quite like it. When he was given six hours to solve a case, and it was an impossible deal, and really he never *does* solve it. In the course of all that, he has to fight the bureaucracy and the political régime of the inner-city workings and the justice system – which was quite slow-moving and ponderous, like it is in real life. And that was fun to tell. But then as we went on to subsequent films, we had to put him in different situations, we couldn't just go back each time and bring another homicidal maniac out of the woodwork and have the exact same arguments – even though in all these films he is always fighting to speed up and streamline things, and the bureaucrats don't ever agree with him.'

The 'fun' in the early *Dirty Harry* films arises in sequences where Harry is rudely interrupted while grabbing a meal: in *Dirty Harry*, a hot-dog lunch is spoiled by a bank robbery; in *Magnum Force*, a hamburger lunch is spoiled by a hijacking (only this time he hangs on to the burger); in *The Enforcer*, the equivalent moment occurs

when Harry promises some terrorists that he will deliver a car –
and then proceeds to drive it straight through the plate-glass window.
On each occasion, Harry Callahan has the chance to demonstrate
his cool, to behave like a modern-day cowboy, to create mayhem
in the street, to deliver a great one-liner, and to walk away in one
piece:

> 'You've got to ask yourself one question: "Do I feel lucky?" Well,
> *do you, punk*?'

> 'How can you be hungry after seeing that?'
> 'Seeing what?'

> 'This is my best sports jacket.'

Such sequences wouldn't be out of place in a Warner-style cartoon
– *Tom and Harry*, perhaps.

The really serious bit, though, came in the final sequence when
Harry Callahan completely lost his cool, repeated the question '*Do
you, punk*?' through clenched teeth, and proceeded to blow the
terrified Scorpio to kingdom come. He then threw the badge of the
San Francisco police force, an organisation to which the film (just
like *The Lineup*) was dedicated, into the muddy water where Scorpio's
corpse was floating. The gesture implied that a man like Harry –
the rugged individualist, the frontiersman, the Westerner – could
never be able to play his part among the 'bureaucrats': the 'bureaucrats' would never let him, and in any case he wouldn't want to work
with people like *them*. Like Gary Cooper throwing his star into the
dust at the end of *High Noon*, the gesture implied a rejection of –
even a disgust with – the modern community. And, just as John
Wayne publicly criticised that sequence as 'unAmerican', and made
Rio Bravo as a reply to it, so Don Siegel and Clint Eastwood had
a row about the ending of *Dirty Harry*. Apparently, Eastwood refused
to shoot the sequence for three days.

At London's National Film Theatre, in 1984, he played down this
difference of opinion:

'We had discussed the pros and cons of throwing the badge away.

The original screenplay had all kinds of situations at the end – an airport, marine snipers, all kinds of people were included. We kept it much more simple with the antagonist. But the only thing we disagreed on was the badge – whether he dumped it à la *High Noon* in the dust, or continued to wear it . . . Then he said, "Try throwing away the badge": after I took one pitch with this badge I said, "Yeah, this feels good" . . . For *Magnum Force*, he must have gone skin-diving; he got the badge and just put it back on! Harry is a fantasy police officer who gets to do a few things that most police officers don't ever get to do . . . Maybe you shouldn't say "Hold on, what's involved here?" Maybe you should walk out and say "Did I enjoy that?", and *afterwards* you should maybe say he shouldn't have done this or that.'

Don Siegel, at the time when *Dirty Harry* was released, tended to distance himself more from the character – recalling, perhaps the liberal tendency in his little 1950s thrillers (which had implied that prison conditions stank, McCarthyism was pernicious, and 'the silent majority' could be misguided):

'In *Dirty Harry*, Clint was a hard-nosed cop who believed that what he was doing was right. It doesn't mean that Clint and I agree with the character one hundred per cent. Harry is a racist, a reactionary. Yet policemen *do* lose their lives protecting us, and it has nothing to do with politics. Some policemen are like Harry, genuine heroes whose attitudes I abhor . . . ' The discussion about the badge must have been interesting.

Anyway, Harry Callahan remained an unrepentant vigilante, a private individual who sees himself as above the law, in a sequence whose setting (a disused quarry in San Anselmo, Marin County) and atmosphere resembled the last reel of a classic Western. John Wayne replied to the equivalent sequence in *High Noon* by showing how in a similar situation the sheriff could rely on the support of his colleagues – and of 'people of honor' in the community – when the chips were down. Clint Eastwood's 'reply' to critics of *Dirty Harry*, which came in *Magnum Force* two years after the original movie, showed how Harry Callahan's attitudes were as nothing compared with those of a group of extreme, almost neo-Nazi, vigilantes operating from within the force.

Wayne had tried to show that the whole premise of *High Noon* was mistaken: Eastwood simply upped the ante, in order to demonstrate that Harry wasn't quite as dirty as some of his colleagues. But Pauline Kael reckoned this was a step in the right direction, and argued that scriptwriter John Milius had taken 'his plot gimmick from those of us who attacked *Dirty Harry* for its fascist medievalism'. She was particularly delighted when Harry Callahan says to one of the vigilantes, 'I'm afraid you've misjudged me'. Whether or not *Magnum Force* was intended as such a 'reply' (unlikely, given John Milius's political views), there is no doubt that the controversy surrounding the first film had fuelled the plot of the second.

LIEUTENANT BRIGGS *(the secret, apparently liberal, leader of the death squad):* What the hell do you know about the law? You're a great cop, Harry. You've got a chance to join the team but you'd rather stick with the system.
HARRY CALLAHAN: When the police start becoming their own executioners, where's it going to end, eh? . . . Briggs, I hate the goddamned system, but until someone comes along with some changes that make sense I'll stick with it.

As Robert Reiner has observed of this key exchange, 'What is perplexing is why Harry objects to behaviour not unlike his own in *Dirty Harry*. His explanation clearly points to the "professional" versus "organisation" dichotomy . . . Harry argues that vigilantism, the pursuit of order at the cost of law, is acceptable but only if it is organisationally sanctioned (the *system*) not maverick action (the *team*).'

So Wild West behaviour within the system is fine: death-squad-style executions by a team of mavericks are not, especially when they are carried out by *ubermensch* David Soul (later of tv's *Hutch* fame). The distinction is at best a fine one.

Magnum Force was criticised at the time less for its confused ideology than for its treatment of the women characters. In one particularly nasty sequence, a prostitute has a lavatory cleaner forced down her throat; in a more lyrical moment, a Chinese-American woman from Harry's apartment block (so *that's* where he lives) throws herself at him with words, 'What does a girl have to do to go to bed with you?' (Answer: 'Knock on the door'); when she later confesses that he is 'her first cop', Harry replies, 'I guess that'll be two firsts tonight, won't it?' As if to make amends for all this, Eastwood made *The Enforcer* in 1976 and *Sudden Impact* in 1983, both of which featured independently minded and physically courageous women in the important roles. *The Enforcer* introduced Tyne Daly (later of tv's *Cagney and Lacey*) to a police uniform for the first time: she played Harry Callahan's partner (appointed because the SFPD wants to enhance 'the areas of participation for women'), and as the story progressed, she gradually succeeded in putting a dent in his stereotypical view of female cops by becoming more and more self-reliant. When first they meet, he immediately asks her, 'How fast can you run the one hundred?' But when she dies, in the last reel, Harry turns his back on the mayor (in a variation on the badge-pitching sequence of *Dirty Harry*) to pay his respects to her corpse. Maybe Harry is capable of an adult relationship, after all. Maybe. But the partners – by now, two per film – never seem to live long enough to find out. And why do they have to become honorary 'Dirty Harriets' to qualify for the accolade, 'You did all right'?

In *Sudden Impact*, things get a great deal more complicated when his chosen partner (Sondra Locke) turns out to be a serial killer who is going around blowing the genitals off the men who gang-raped her ten years before: instantly attracted to one another, Harry and this diminutive blonde avenger tend to discuss areas of common interest, such as the perennial 'Everybody wants results, but nobody wants to do what they have to do to get them'.

In the end, Harry (complete with a back-lit halo) has a Western-style showdown with the rapists on a fairground boardwalk while his beloved vigilantette gets off scot free: the punchline seems to be that, with such similar outlooks on life, they could make sweet music together. As she says to him with all-too-evident admiration, 'You're an endangered species.' The world is going soft on the sorts of people who are responsible for 'old ladies getting bashed on the head for Social Security checks', and only Harry has what it takes to do something about it. *Sudden Impact* was the first time Eastwood had directed himself as Dirty Harry, and he celebrated by blowing to kingdom come all the ironies and ambiguities of the original.

The Dead Pool (1988), the latest and weakest of the series – Harry's inevitable tagline 'You're shit out of luck' isn't a patch on 'Go ahead, make my day' – recoils from such heady (well, relatively) themes, and gets its simple kicks by watching what happens when a meaner-than-ever Harry Callahan is let loose in the world of rock videos and splatter movies: the answer is that his adventures begin to resemble more and more the very movies they are intended to be satirising. By the time he was 58, John Wayne was beginning to play cattle barons and grandfathers and crusty old senior citizens: but in *The Dead Pool*, Eastwood seems for the first time to be hanging on to the part he had made his own eighteen years before. Comments to the press about 'going back to see how Dirty Harry feels about things now', 'how is he existing eighteen years later?' are not borne out by a film which shows little or no interest in Harry himself (unlike the original).

But, as Eastwood recalls, the Harry films do have one important thing in common. In all of them, Harry 'is always fighting to speed up and streamline things, and the bureaucrats don't ever agree with him'. So the films are all variations on the theme of 'order before law' and it is this aspect of them – together with their vision of the inner city as Inferno – which has continued to intrigue and infuriate East Coast critics. But they are also among the most commercially successful films Clint Eastwood has ever made (*The Enforcer*, for example, made $23.9 million and *Sudden Impact* $75 million, as compared with *Dirty Harry*'s $17.9 million: all of them shot on tight, Malpaso-sized budgets). So perhaps a more characteristic response, from a card-carrying redneck who prefers to see his movies 'out under the stars like God intended', is contained in *Joe Bob Briggs Goes to the Drive-in*. Joe Bob's considered judgement on *Sudden Impact* first appeared in the *Dallas Times Herald*:

'Dirty Harry is p.o.ed. There's a gazebo mangler out there, and that bothers him. Dirty Harry's in a bad mood anyway. First this lady bimbo judge tells Dirty Harry he "conducted an illegal search", and so these goon jerkolas he picked up can go free . . . Next thing, Dirty Harry's cop boss tells him he didn't have probable cause to pick the goons up, even though he found stolen goods in their car. "Psychic don't count", he tells Harry.

'I think we all know what time it is. I think we all know it's .44 Magnum time. I think we all know it's time for Harry to say "Go ahead. Make my day."

'So Dirty Harry goes to a diner for coffee, and while he's there he blows away four black guys in the middle of a robbery, and then he feels a *lot* better.

'Then the police commissioner calls Dirty Harry in and says, "What the *hell* did you think you were doing?"

'And Dirty Harry looks at him and moves his sunglasses a little bit and just says, "My job."

'And the commissioner says, "You're a dinosaur, Callahan. Don't you know who I am?"

'And Harry says, "Yeah, you're a legend in your own mind."

'We're talking some serious heavy load that Dirty Harry is carrying around now. We're talking a man who's getting *concerned* about the state of the world. We're talking a guy who's *sick and tired* of "a society where teachers are being thrown out of fourth-floor windows because they don't give As".

'We're talking the scene where Harry gets out his .44 Magnum *Automag* . . .

Joe Bob's conclusion is that *Sudden Impact* should go straight in at number nine in his Final Best of '83 Drive-in Movie List, just above Chuck Bronson in *10 to Midnight* 'blowing scum off the streets and saying lines like, "I hate quiche".

'I don't want to give away the ending, but I'll just say that Harry gets to say "Go ahead, make my day" two more times, and he puts the .44 Magnum Automag to good use. We're talking five beasts. We're talking one beast named Mick the Spic. We're talking two pints blood. Three motor vehicle chases, one motor vehicle explosion, one motor vehicle dumped in the bay. Gazebos roll. Body count: twenty-one. Some kung-fu . . . Drive-in Academy Award nominations for Clint, Sondra Locke as the bimbo gazebo killer, and Paul Drake as Mick the Spic.'

With the *Dirty Harry* series, Clint Eastwood had finally succeeded in bringing it all back home, with a vengeance. As Joe Bob liked to say when signing off his column, *check it out*.

Or, as a colleague of Harry Callahan says in *Dirty Harry*, 'He hates *everyone*: Limeys, Micks, Heebs, Dagos, Niggers, Honkies, Chinks – you name it'. Or perhaps the sheer length of the list was meant to be ironic (Harry Callahan as Alf Garnett?). Or perhaps, like Don Siegel, we were meant to think of Harry as one of those 'genuine heroes whose attitudes I abhor'. Or . . . or. One of the unnerving things about Dirty Harry, as director John Boorman has pointed out, is that he is so clean. He isn't the unshaven lout of *The French Connection*. He isn't, as Eastwood put it, 'a dirty unbathed person, walking about the streets of San Francisco'. He doesn't have the bearded, sunburnt look of the bounty hunter. Sure, he gets some of the dirty jobs; and sure, he plays dirty to get them done. But he is so damn clean and well turned out. Maybe Joe Bob was on to something.

10 This thing of darkness . . .

hroughout the 1970s and early 1980s, Eastwood continued to add to the *Dirty Harry* series, just as he continued to make one Western to match each 'Harry' film at that time. He also continued to make bland international-style action movies (school of Alastair Maclean) such as *The Eiger Sanction* (1975) and *Firefox* (1982). But, in between these sure-fire box-office hits, he took some interesting chances – exploring what *really* made the super-cop tick, in *The Gauntlet* (1977) and especially *Tightrope* (1984); examining what might happen to The Man With No Name if he began to collect responsibilities, in *The Outlaw Josey Wales* (1976); showing how the American Dream is really 'about a dreamy bunch of losers getting their act together' in *Bronco Billy* (1980); and touching on his own upbringing in the depression years, in *Honky-tonk Man* (1982).

It may be significant that all of these films were made in a period when Eastwood's own son Kyle was growing up from seven to sixteen years old, and his daughter Alison from three to eleven years old. Alison appears in *Tightrope*, Kyle in *Honkytonk Man*. *The Outlaw Josey Wales* opens by showing how Josey is turned into an embittered, obsessive loner when his wife and child are butchered by the Kansas Redlegs: the rest of the movie tells the story of how Josey becomes human again, by gathering a new family around him. It may also be significant that all of these films were made during Eastwood's close relationship with Sondra Locke, who had auditioned for *Breezy* (1973) – the story of a middle-aged man who, in the words of the director, 'rediscovers life through the eyes of this young girl' – before appearing in, among other works, *The Outlaw Josey Wales* (as a hippie waif called Laura Lee who falls for Josey); *The Gauntlet* (as a hooker called 'Gus' Mally who can easily outguess the slow-witted, hard-drinking macho cop Ben Shockley with her wisdom and her wisecracks); *Bronco Billy* (as an heiress called Antoinette, who prefers Bronco Billy's Wild West show to her swish apartment on Park Avenue); and *Sudden Impact* (as the 'bimbo gazebo killer' who so impresses lone wolf Harry Callahan). Whatever the reasons, and whether they are biographical or not, there is certainly a new mellowness, and a humanity, about Clint Eastwood's best films of this period, and the characters he plays within them tend to be capable of an uncharacteristic gentleness and sociability (uncharacteristic, that is, of Eastwood's Americanised star persona in the late 1960s and the early 1970s; very characteristic of the man himself, by all accounts).

As Jeffrey Ryder has written of these attempts to question Eastwood's own hard-won image as a magnum star: 'Clint would spend the fifteen years following the explosive success of *Dirty Harry*, by carefully testing the contradictions between his screen image and personal life . . . He managed to maintain his popularity in the midst of such variations by skilful balancing and interweaving of his roles. He would return to a *Harry* or a cowboy often enough to make it seem that they had continued to live while we weren't watching them. The boundary-testing sprinkled in and around these standbys would therefore have the freedom to give us glimpses of Clint Eastwood, the man, a gradual sculpting of new features that would only add to our affection for him, to our identification with him, and to his heroic stature.'

At one level, *The Gauntlet* – with its traditional theme of cop-with-integrity-versus-corrupt-bosses-at-City-Hall – resembled the *Dirty Harry* films. But at another level, the *development* of the lone cop figure within the story – in particular, the stages through which he recovers his self-respect – *The Gauntlet* showed Eastwood (as actor and director) to be extending his range. As he said when the film was first released, 'All of a sudden this man finds himself in a situation that he has to fight himself out of – he may be thicker than the girl but his determination is the same'. *The Gauntlet* opens with policeman Ben Shockley falling out of his car clutching a bottle of whisky: the car's interior looks like the morning after a works party. It appears that Shockley's disillusionment with 'the bureaucrats' has had the effect, over the years, of turning him into one of the standing jokes of the Phoenix, Arizona, police department; of turning him in on himself. As the story progresses, it transpires that he has been chosen to escort a witness from Las Vegas, a prostitute, just *because* he is thought to be so inept at his job, and because he is such a damaged person. But Shockley learns a lot from his charge – indeed, he comes to depend upon her – and by the final reel, he manages to regain the respect of his colleagues as well (a process which is mirrored by the prostitute's attempts to prove herself worthy of Shockley's attentions).

The Gauntlet had an unusually free-wheeling structure: some critics even dubbed it as Clint Eastwood's *Annie Hall*. Within this structure, it set out to make some changes by debunking the Eastwood mythology: first, by taking the macho-man image down a peg or two, and second, by showing that firepower isn't necessarily the best way to solve a problem. This latter theme was illustrated by two extremely elaborate set-pieces, sequences which Eastwood himself reckoned 'You just have to accept on an outrageous level . . . the overkill is part of the entertainment'. In one, a house is literally shot to pieces (until it completely collapses), but Eastwood and Locke walk out of it unharmed. And a steel-plated Greyhound Bus runs the gauntlet of an entire police department firing small-arms at it (8,000 rounds in all): but finally reaches the steps of City Hall (in a variation on the old *Stagecoach* gag – why didn't they shoot at the tyres?), and Eastwood and Locke, with slightly dirty faces, exit from it holding hands.

Tightrope takes this debunking process several stages further. The title refers (as we are helpfully told by a psychiatrist in the film) to the thin line which separates 'the darkness inside all of us and the darkness outside', and in this story, the Eastwood character has to face up to both. The series of sex murders which take place in the brothels of Bourbon Street, New Orleans, seem to chime with the darkest fantasies of the cop, Wes Block, himself. Indeed, there are moments in the film when we think that the cop may even be the killer – an identification which begins with the opening chase sequence, where Eastwood's voice is dubbed over the predator's *before* we have met Eastwood the cop (which may be cheating, but certainly adds to the excitement).

'I liked the parallel,' he said when *Tightrope* opened. 'And I liked the *not knowing*. And I felt the more we could lead the audience to think that maybe this was it, the more it gives them somewhere to go.' Somewhere a great deal more interesting than *Dirty Harry's* San Francisco. Wes Block takes a pair of handcuffs with him as he goes out for a long night interrogating the prostitutes, and we sympathise with the girl who asks him point-blank, 'Who knows? Maybe it was *you*'. Only when Block has the courage to say to himself, like Prospero in *The Tempest*, 'This thing of darkness I acknowledge mine' – with counselling from rape specialist Beryl Thibodeaux (Genevieve Bujold) along the way – can we be sure that he is the hunter rather than the hunted: and only when we have actually *seen* the killer peeping at the cop, as he engages in a spot of tension relief (with the aid of an electric vibrator) can we be absolutely sure. Meanwhile, there's been much talk of Block's 'stereotyped' view of women (especially 'women from rape centres'), of 'the front he puts on' to keep his distance from personal relationships, and of obnoxious 'cops with a chip on their shoulder'. In the *Dirty Harry* series, by contrast, there had been at least one gag about sociologists per film.

But above all, *Tightrope* emphasises the contrast between Block's home life (like Eastwood at the time, he is divorced with two children – one of them played by his daughter Alison – and he likes pet dogs) and his life after dark. The two worlds even *look* different: light, softness and domesticity versus dark, garishness and casual sex, like a version of *Night of the Hunter* updated to the mid-1980s. *Tightrope* presented a cop-figure who was far more complex than any of the lone wolves who developed out of the Walt Coogan character, by showing that he was capable of tenderness (his family), of dark fantasies (his night work), emotional development (his relationship with social worker Beryl Thibodeaux and of co-operating with his colleagues (his reliance on, and trust of, the forensic office in the police department). He still had to fight it out with the bureaucracy, of course – but he did so with his words and his wits. He still began by resenting the feminine character, of course (he meets her at a Rape Crisis Centre, where in an over-literal moment he picks up a tennis ball representing a rapist's testicles), but she was a more credible character than ever before. 'First thing I asked Genevieve Bujold,' said Eastwood, 'was would she play the part with no make-up because I felt the character has to go for this woman because of everything she stands for, rather than the usual Hollywood glamour – picture-perfect, with a pony-tail'. In the final sequence, a riot of Gothic imagery – a graveyard, tombstones, thunder and lightning, a dismembered arm clutching at a throat – the cop doesn't even get the satisfaction of killing his prey. As an East Coast reviewer observed, 'I've resisted Clint Eastwood for years, but it's time to stop making jokes.'

If the two *policiers*, *The Gauntlet* and *Tightrope*, played significant variations on the *Dirty Harry* theme whilst taking the domestic audience with them, to judge by box-office returns – *The Outlaw Josey Wales* gave the same treatment to the Spaghetti Western hero. Eastwood had, in fact, been exploring connections between the two genres since *Coogan's Bluff*, and it was a piece of contemporary criminology which first inspired his own Western *High Plains Drifter* (eighteen months after *Dirty Harry*): 'It was a nine-page treatment that the writer, Ernest Tidyman sent over to one of the executives at Universal. And they sent it down, I'm sure thinking I wouldn't like it, but I was kind of attracted to it . . . It was the allegorical aspect and the whole entertainment aspect of that; that complacent thing which allows 32 people to witness a crime, and nobody goes to a telephone and they all shut the windows – which happened in a famous case, the Kitty Genovese case in New York. It happens periodically, and the film kind of explores that . . .'

High Plains Drifter fused The Man With No Name with an up-front version of the rogue cop: because it was set in 'another time, times when things were more simplified', it could, within the conventions of the Western genre, confront the *Dirty Harry* dilemmas in a more direct way. In the process, it attempted (literally) to exorcise the enigmatic persona of The Man With No Name. Indeed, the whole project comes over as a medieval morality play (each of the townsfolk seems to represent one of the seven deadly sins, and the Drifter himself, Marshal Jim Duncan, is the ultimate *deus ex machina*) reinterpreted through the early 1970s cinematic image of Clint Eastwood: the dwarf Mordecai, standing in for Little Joey in *Shane*, acts as the chorus. Instead of throwing his badge away, the law-enforcer (the emphasis being, as ever, on *enforcement*) is resurrected to haunt the townsfolk who made his job impossible before watching him get killed in the street.

The Outlaw Josey Wales represented another exorcism of The Man With No Name, only this time, it shed the simple-minded morality of the mystery play in favour of an epic story about the impossibility of going through life as a macho loner. Josey Wales rides through Missouri, Kansas, the Indian Nations and Texas just after the American Civil War, bent on personal revenge ('I don't want *nobody* belonging to me'). But he is constantly being deflected from his quest by various people from on the margins of history (an elderly Comanche Indian, a hippie girl, an old lady from Kansas) who refuse to take his macho image seriously. Even a hound dog he picks up along the way seems to see through his tough exterior: Josey Wales spits a wad of tobacco in the direction of the dog (hitting it right between the eyes) but the dog simply growls, then comes back for more, wagging its tail. Eventually, the 'lone avenger' is persuaded by these perceptive characters to give up his quest, to choose 'the word of life', and to settle down in a log cabin in the prairies.

The interpretation of the Civil War in *Josey Wales* may be cynical (a ferryman sings 'Dixie' or the 'Battle Hymn of the Republic' according to whether he is ferrying Union or Confederate troops) but the conclusion to the film – for once – is not: there is hope for the post-Vietnam generation after all.

The social world of *Josey Wales* at first sight resembles that of the Spaghetti Western, a world, as we have seen, 'irredeemably con-demned to immobility, somnolence, to the lack of all resource and development'. It is just after the Civil War, and there are drifters and uprooted persons everywhere: bounty hunters ('There's no other way to make a living'), carpetbaggers, con men, redlegs, vigilantes, unemployed saloon folk. But, by the end of the story, Josey Wales has travelled a long way away from his distant cousin, The Man With No Name. It is not that his revenge is unjustified: on the contrary, it is made clear at the outset that the death of Josey's wife and child is more than enough justification for his transformation from farmer to outlaw (in Hollywood terms, this resembles the argument of Henry King's *Jesse James* and most cinematic versions of the Billy the Kid legend). But that he cannot go through life after the war is over with revenge as his prime mover. As film writer David Thomson has said: 'Eastwood's anti-hero has mellowed to become a more relaxed, more amused and marginally less robust observer. That was the process of tolerance that worked so well in *Josey Wales*, in which a righteous moral anger softens with time to become aware of foibles, frailty and humour. In many ways it is his most adventurous picture, a sign of the kindness he is often too shy or laid back to reveal.'

And as critic Stephanie McKnight has added: 'By calling upon both the traditional and the alternative images of Clint Eastwood, the film is able to present a character of considerable complexity in a very economical way since the audience's knowledge of the traditional image can be counted upon to support or modify the play of any contradiction in the alternative image.' Or as the film itself expresses it – in its lateral way – at various stages in the saga: a tree grows by the graveside . . . 'Dying ain't hard for people like you and me, it's the living that's hard . . . Governments don't live together, people live together' . . . 'It shall be life' . . . 'I guess we all died a little in that damned war'; 'What do you say to the war being over?' . . . 'I reckon so'. In a script which also included its fair share of Harry-style one-liners – like the immortal 'Don't piss down my back and tell me its raining' – such lines represented quite a risk. As did Eastwood's own generosity as an actor, in allowing Chief Dan George and assorted members of the Malpaso repertory company to sneak up on him and steal his scenes.

Although he was the name above the title, he spent a surprising amount of the film in the shadows created by cinematographer Bruce Surtees. 'I like that. First place, I'm not that enamoured of my face that I think it should be absolutely plastered in front of the camera every minute. And I think that a person's going to get tired of that sort of thing. So I feel that if you ration the amount of . . . , if you come in at the right moments, you dramatically highlight what's going on. But if you want to be seen with a lot of light in the eyes – in the old school style, John Wayne, John Ford, those guys did that

– the protagonist was there, he was the money, blast him in – well, I feel that if the presence is there, when you want to, you pump the light in, but it's got to be at the right moment.'

Evidently the presence *was* still there: *The Outlaw Josey Wales* made $13.5 million at the box-office as compared to *High Plains Drifter*'s $7.5 million. Respectable profits, although considerably below those of his cop movies set in the contemporary world.

The Outlaw Josey Wales coheres as a film in the light of Clint Eastwood's development as a director and an actor. But one feature of it which remains an enigma is its politics. While it was being filmed, Eastwood spoke of the author of the original book, Forrest Carter, as a 46-year-old 'half Cherokee Indian with no formal education', an 'Indian poet and teller of stories' who had never written a novel before, and who had been persuaded to commit his yarn-spinning skills to print by a few friends. The resulting publication, called *The Rebel Outlaw*, then *Gone to Texas*, was dedicated 'for Ten Bears'.

This was a romantic piece of production background and, at a time when a growing number of writings about or commentaries on the American West were reappraising the history of the native Americans and stressing the region's ecological significance, it struck a distinct chord. But a little while after the film's first release, the *New York Times* delightedly revealed that several people had identified Forrest Carter not with an obscure Storyteller-in-Council to the Cherokee Nations, but with Asa Carter, a former speechwriter for Governor George Wallace and the very same person who had penned Wallace's notorious 1963 inaugural speech in which the Governor-elect had intoned the words 'Segregation now! Segregation tomorrow! Segregation forever!'

So, although the reviews of the *The Outlaw Josey Wales* (unlike those of *Dirty Harry*) did not make disapproving noises about the film's politics – rather to the contrary – the story later went around that it was *really* a covert political allegory. Joan Mellen, for example, made much of this in her 1977 book *Big Bad Wolves*: 'The romanticism attached to the renegade Southerner battling the brutal Yankees who kill women and children is pure Confederate propaganda. The *New York Times* has in fact noted that Asa Carter's particular hero was the Confederate general Bedford Forrest, the first

Imperial Wizard of the Ku Klux Klan, and Forrest Carter's first copyright was appropriately enough recorded in the name of Bedford Forrest Carter. Southern populism and nostalgia for the racist, feudal past fuel this softening of the Eastwood male persona.'

When Forrest Carter went on to write *The Education of Little Tree* – using his own Indian name of Little Tree and dedicating this autobiography to 'The Cherokee', in 1976 – and *The Vengeance Trail of Josey Wales* (also in 1976, a brutal sequel which Eastwood reckoned 'wasn't a bad story, but I didn't feel there could be a sequel to *The Outlaw Josey Wales*: I liked the picture so much that I just wanted to leave it alone') – the identification of Forrest with Asa Carter became more and more mysterious. And when Asa Carter subsequently died, the identification died with him (as, apparently, did the writing career of Forrest Carter).

Philip Kaufman – director of *The Great Northfield Minnesota Raid* (1972), originator of *Raiders of the Lost Ark* and (after the preparation of *Josey Wales*) director of *The Right Stuff* (1983) – was commissioned to make the original adaptation of the book into a screenplay, and also to direct. He seemed the best person to ask about the politics of the film – although he is notoriously reluctant to discuss his involvement in the project. He told me: 'My script changed the political thing of the original book. Somewhere along the line I read, I think it was in the *New York Times*, that Forrest Carter had even run for some governorship – that he was to the *right* of George Wallace! Well, it was something to me to step into that, and turn all that around. But I've never seen the film. I just didn't want to see it. I shot a couple of weeks of it on location and left under unhappy circumstances and disagreements . . . It was a bad time: when you cast the movie, you've done the sets, you've done the wardrobe and you've done the *look* of the movie and you've got all that stuff going – and then you don't finish the movie, for whatever reason.'

The novel *Gone to Texas* lacks the humour, the clear characterisation and the larger-than-life violence of the film – and it also has a pronounced mystical streak running through it, notably at the end when, as Forrest Carter wrote: 'The firstborn to Josey and Laura Lee was a boy, blue-eyed and blond, and now Grandma Sarah relaxed to grow old in the contentment that the seed was replenished in the land.'

The film, on the other hand, ends with a badly wounded Josey riding away into the geology of America: we don't even know if he will survive. 'Yes, the script was different. It was about this band of innocents with one capable man in their midst – pursued, surrounded by a world that was hostile to them, and trying for the survival of some human values. How will these people – caught in history, being pursued – how will they work out their relationships? To look back into it all is a bit painful, but my memory of the book is that it was *really* trying to prove which side was right in the American Civil War . . . I saw that thing about Forrest Carter in the *New York Times*. It *felt* true. There were some complicating things about the Cherokee Nation in general, about what role they played: I downplayed all that. So many people in Western American say they're part Indian. Many very right-wing people.'

But what of the theme of post-war dislocation (Civil War/ Vietnam), which is much stronger in the movie that in the book? 'Right. Again, it was a tough thing to deal with. My sympathies had always been to the Union side. To go into this and deal with it – the injustices of the Union side – seemed like an interesting thing. To go in, and to explore, which in a way was the Vietnam revelation in America – that we've *had* to deal with the other side, the loser's side, the people who history had passed by, where do they run to? It was a time when American consciousness *was* changing. Maybe America was more isolationist in a way, running away from confrontations, being pulled away from them.'

Certainly, the final version of the movie (with Eastwood now at the helm, 'listening to myself a lot' as he put it) transformed the nostalgic romanticism of the book into a vehicle for the most positive and forward-looking character he had ever played. Joan Mellen's remarks apply to *Gone to Texas* much more than they do to *The Outlaw Josey Wales*.

11 Small-town art

To shift this new, more positive character into the modern era – the era of Harry Callahan's ubiquitous 'punks', of twentieth-century frontier towns such as San Francisco – and still to take his audience with him, was the next challenge and Eastwood met it by moving towards the category which video shops sometimes call 'comedy action'. In *Every Which Way But Loose* (1978) he plays a Los Angeles truck driver and bare-knuckle fighter with a sidekick who is an orang-utan (School of Mr Ed) and a sweet girlfriend who is a country-and-western singer who can't actually sing. *Newsweek*'s view was that 'it could not possibly have been made by human hands'. Clint Eastwood said: 'I didn't know it would go over as well as it did [to the tune of $48 million dollars, one of the greatest hits in the history of Warner Brothers] but there was something in the back of my mind that told me to do something like that. Also, there were an awful lot of films I'd done that were 'R' rated – I thought this would be a reaching out to maybe more of a family audience. To the *next* generation.'

Again, Eastwood allowed himself to be upstaged – this time by Clyde, the eleven-year-old orang-utan whom he'd discovered using the name of Manis and acting in cabaret at Las Vegas. Clyde does everything dead on cue: gets drunk, sticks his hands in the air when a gun is pointed at him, and listens to Clint explaining in traditional male bonding style that 'It takes me a long time to get to know a girl, even longer for her to know me'. Eastwood recalls, 'You had to get Clyde on one take, because his boredom threshold was low.' Eastwood also let himself be upstaged by the slapstick we-don't-mean-it-really Hell's Angels, renamed the Black Indians (who seem to have taken over from the more realistic ones inhabiting the Nevada desert in *The Gauntlet* of the previous year). *Every Which Way* (and its sequel) may have been relaxing – in a lazy way – into some of those old-fashioned, hick-town mannerisms and values which Eastwood's self-directed films were seriously beginning to question or parody, but at least he was continuing his transformation from invulnerable professional into vulnerable drifter, a transformation of which Norman Mailer was to write: 'One was encountering a homegrown philosophy, a hardworking everyday subtle American philosophy in film . . . A protagonist in each of these films stands near to his creator. Eastwood has made five cinematic relatives. They are spread over more than 100 years, from the Civil War to the present, and the action is in different places west of the Mississippi, from Missouri to California. They are Okies and outlaws, truckers, rodeo entertainers, and country and western singers, but they come out of the old, wild, hard, dry, sad, sour redneck wisdom of small-town life in the Southwest. All of Eastwood's knowledge is in them, a sardonic, unsentimental set of values that is equal to art, for it would grapple with the roots of life itself . . . One has to think of the Depression years of Eastwood's childhood when his father was looking for work and taking the family up and down the San Joaquin and Sacramento Valleys, out there with a respectable family in a mix of Okies also wandering up and down California searching for work . . . [and when] "You've got to outlast yourself" was the only way to talk of overcoming fatigue. The words happen to be Eastwood's, but the language was shared with his characters, brothers in the same family, ready to share a family humour.

'It is that a proper orang-utan will not miss a good opportunity to defecate on the front seat of a police cruiser, as indeed it did in *Every Which Way But Loose*. Small-town humour, but in *Honkytonk Man* . . . it became art.'

For Norman Mailer, *Bronco Billy* and *Honkytonk Man* were Eastwood's masterpieces, because they seemed to be his most autobiographical films, and thus owed the least to considerations of genre ('to manipulate audiences and satisfy producers'): 'The harsh, yearning belly of rural America is there, used to making out with next to nothing but hard concerns and the spark of a dream that will never give up.' Eastwood concedes that there was a certain autobiographical interest in these projects, although as we have seen he reckons that Mailer was being over-sentimental about the 'mix of Okies' angle. Whether he accepts the implication, though, that genre films can never in the end be as interesting as autobiographical ones must be a moot point: his own career tends to prove otherwise.

Characteristically, he has always been careful about making that career seem too schematic, too self-consciously manipulative of his own screen image. He prefers to talk about interesting stories which just happen to land on his table. He has recently said about the transformation in his persona noted by Mailer: 'I could go around pointing guns all the time, but that doesn't get too difficult after a while. Both *Honkytonk Man* and *Tightrope* were very dramatic roles for me but there was nothing deliberate about choosing them outside the fact that I found the stories and the characters interesting. In *Honkytonk Man* it was the self-destructive nature of the character which interested me. I've known people like him who were on the way to being something and then purposely destroyed themselves. *Tightrope* was about a man who had deep questions about himself due to the pressures of his work — it was taking a detective, not a super-detective who was out shooting all the time, and he had seen so much of the sordid life it was beginning to affect him.'

Not so much genre versus art as a career built on keeping life interesting, and keeping companies like Warner Brothers interested in keeping it interesting — mainly a financial consideration, of course, but also to do with work 'they'd be happy to have their logo on'.

In *Bronco Billy*, the 'spark of a dream' is symbolised by an 'out-of-date Wild West show' in which 'a dreamy bunch of losers' have the chance to act out their fantasies. You can become what you believe you are, so long as you remain under the Big Top — with the spirit of Frank Capra and Jiminy Cricket presiding over you. As Clint Eastwood wisely warned his audience: 'It's not *Dirty Bronco Billy*'. And it certainly wasn't. The pivotal sequence in the film showed Billy McCoy (on a horse) and friends (in a red convertible, with Colt pistols as door handles), armed with the weapons of the old Wild West, planning to solve their chronic economic problems by doing the traditional Hollywood thing and holding up a train. The train hurtles by, Billy is forced to get off the line at the last minute, and the circus people hurl harmless arrows at the passenger cars – at which point a small child tells his mother 'It's cowboys and Indians!' and she doesn't take a blind bit of notice. Billy – who, it turns out, is a shoe salesman from New Jersey rather than a high plains drifter – continues to dream his dreams ('Are you *for real*', asks his more sophisticated girlfriend, before herself joining the circus in time for the fade-out) even though he has a lot of hard evidence of everyday reality. But audiences, it seemed, wanted Eastwood to rob that train.

In *Honkytonk Man*, the dream is that of a drunk, over-the-hill country singer with tuberculosis who wants to reach Nashville (in the 1930s), in time to have 'a try-out at the Grand Ole Opry'. Eastwood, as Red Stovall, is accompanied on the journey by his real-life son – the thirteen-year-old Kyle playing his nephew Whit or 'Hoss' – who tries to keep him on the straight and narrow as 'side kick and chauffeur', and by a brand-new Gibson guitar.

STOVALL: Just honkytonks and flophouses – that's the life of a country singer, Hoss. Sound good to you?
WHIT: Don't sound too hot when you say it like that, but it sure beats pickin' cotton and living in a sharecropper's shack.
STOVALL (smiling) Maybe you're right, boy.

At one point, they drive past the old Cherokee Strip – scene of the famous land-race, when the Strip was opened up to white settlers in September 1893 – and Grandpa (a grizzled John McIntyre) muses on the changes which have come with the passage of time: 'That was the greatest horse race in the history of the world, boy, and for the greatest prize ... but it wasn't just the land, just the dirt itself, I was a-racing for, it was the *promised land*, that's what you gotta understand. It wasn't just the land, it was the dream. Just look at it now – all turned to dust.'

At another point, young Whit gets an idea of how to spring Uncle Red from jail, by looking at a Buck Jones movie poster, for *When a Man Sees Red*, outside the Tallapoosa Theatre: another kind of dream, which on this occasion comes true, for a brief time. The reality is that in order to finance his trip to the Grand Ole Opry, Red has had to rustle chickens, to collect debts in gambling dens and to play piano and guitar in cathouses across several States.

When finally they reach Nashville, Red Stovall collapses on the stage of the Opry, coughing his life away in the middle of the chorus he has written with his nephew:

> But I've still got my guitar and I've got a plan
> Throw your arms round this honkytonk man
> Throw your arms round this honkytonk man
> And we'll get through this night the best way we can.

Before he dies, he manages to record the best of his songs (for 'twenty dollars per song flat fee'), so he does at least have 'a chance to be somebody'. And a film which begins (like *The Outlaw Josey Wales*) with a hand-plough cutting into the wilderness, ends with young Hoss walking away with his late uncle's Gibson guitar as the title song is heard on a car radio.

It sounds sentimental, and it is, but the real revelation of *Honkytonk Man* is Eastwood's low-key performance: Norman Mailer's phrase 'a subtle man full of memories of old cunning deeds and weary shows' captures it well. And although there are, as ever, some smart one-liners ('I got money ten miles up a bull's ass – 'course I got to find that bull first'; 'When was the last time you saw chicken shit? When you was shaving this morning?') even these are delivered as if they are as tired as the sad character who is spitting them out. The trouble (from the commercial point of view) was that Clint Eastwood's audience in 1982, just as a decade earlier with *The Beguiled*, did not want to watch a sad character, least of all a sad character who died on screen. Warner Brothers had tried hard to get him to substitute an upbeat ending but, as Eastwood laconically put it, 'I resisted that'. *Honkytonk Man* was his least successful film at the box-office so far. He immediately followed it with *Sudden Impact*, a surprise return to the character of Harry Callahan after a seven-year gap. Some critics were dismayed by this apparent regression. One of them had even compared *Honkytonk*, favourably, with *The Grapes of Wrath*. About which Eastwood had sensibly observed, 'My God!'

12 Charlie Parker and John Huston

I n one important respect, *Honkytonk Man* was characteristic of its actor/director's entire career, and that was its distinct emphasis on American music: the film's odyssey takes us from rotgut country music at the Pair A Dice café, to a radio recording session with Bob Wills and his Texas Playboys, to a jam session at the all-black Top Hat Club on Beal Street, Memphis (where Eastwood plays blues piano), to the Grand Ole Opry itself.

This, also, may have had some autobiography in it, for Eastwood himself has had a passionate interest in music ever since his schooldays at Oakland Technical High School in the 1940s and his national service during the Korean War at Fort Ord, California: not just going to concerts, such as the famous 1946 'Jazz at the Philharmonic' evening when Coleman Hawkins, Lester Young and Charlie Parker jammed together, or collecting books and magazines about his heroes Bix Beiderbecke and King Oliver, but regularly playing jazz piano at the Omar Club in Oakland for pocket money. At one time, it was touch and go whether he would study on the undergraduate music programme at Seattle University, but he was drafted instead. After two years as a swimming instructor in the army (during which he joined a weekend jazz band, with Lennie Niehaus, later to join the Malpaso team as orchestrator on *The Enforcer, The Outlaw Josey Wales* and *The Gauntlet,* composer on *Tightrope, City Heat* and *Pale Rider* and technical whizz-kid on the soundtack of *Bird*) he decided to study business administration at Los Angeles City College. A suitable choice, in the light of later developments.

After that, Eastwood's film career and his musical interests often tended to overlap, sometimes in bizarre ways. There was that record of 'Unknown Girl', originally sung by Rowdy Yates. And his attempt to revive the Pat Boone sound in the late sixties, with 'I Talk to the Trees' in *Paint Your Wagon*. For his debut film as a director – *Play Misty for Me* (1971) – he played a jazz-loving Carmel disc jockey who is terrorised by a psychopathic woman, obsessed with Errol Garner's version of 'Misty': eventually, things get so out of control that Eastwood has to punch her straight through a window and into the Pacific Ocean. The more lyrical moments in the film, which gave the audience a well-earned rest from the knife attacks, turned Roberta Flack's version of 'The first time ever I saw your face' into a hit. Eastwood's contributions to the soundtracks of his films after that included singing a boozy duet entitled 'Bar-Room Buddies', with country and western superstar Merle Haggard (for *Bronco Billy*); writing a musical theme for his daughter Alison in *Tightrope*; playing piano with Mike Lang and Pete Jolly, for a three-keyboard boogie-woogie number in *City Heat*; writing one of the main themes for *Pale Rider*; and playing that blues piano in *Honkytonk Man*. Plus, of course, helping to transpose Ennio Morricone from Cinecittà to Hollywood. In the light of Eastwood's belief that, to be distinctive, a film should have 'its own sound as well as its own look', such snippets of information reveal, once again, how deeply and at what level of detail he is involved in the construction of all aspects of his own Malpaso productions.

So when he came to direct *Bird* (1988), he liked to call it 'a very personal story – I think I understand the time-frame and I *love* the music'. It was only the second film he'd made in which he does not appear (not counting the episode of the tv series *Amazing Stories* which he directed for Steven Spielberg in 1985). The first had been *Breezy* (1973), the romantic tale of a middle-aged executive in California whose life is transformed by a blonde Californian girl half his age. At the time, it was hinted that part of the attraction of this uncharacteristic project – in which the hero wears his heart on his sleeve, in a *very* uncool way – may have been autobiographical.

Bird – which is dedicated 'to musicians everywhere' – tells the story of the life and times of Charlie Parker, the great be-bop saxophone player who, in Adrian Mitchell's words, 'breathed in air and breathed out light' when Clint Eastwood was in his teens and early twenties, and who died of an overdose of 'bird-seed' (heroin) at the age of 34 in 1955. The doctor who diagnosed the cause of death thought Bird must have been all of 65 years of age. The film is full of period reconstructions – from the sound of Charlie Parker (part pastiche, part remixing of original and little-known tapes) to the big sets of New York's 52nd Street and Birdland on Broadway – and Eastwood even managed to find the actual television programme (a juggling turn from a variety show) which Parker was watching when he died. It's shot in *film noir* style – nearly all at night, in the rain, on mean streets lit by neon, with a complex series of narrative flashbacks.

So what on earth could be 'very personal' to Eastwood about a $9.5 million historical reconstruction apart from the music itself ('The central fact is that he revolutionised the way everyone plays the saxophone') and the collaboration on the soundtrack with his old bar-room buddy Lennie Niehaus? The key moment in Parker's life as shown here (which is repeated several times, in slow motion) is when the drummer Jo Jones, later of the Count Basie outfit, throws one of his cymbals across the stage of a Kansas City jazz club to force the young Charlie to stop playing. As Parker's girlfriend Chan Richardson says in the script, 'It took a little while to get used to the sound', at a time when most big band music was 'so corny' and there was at first 'a disappointing public reaction, bordering on hostility'.

Like his contemporary, Jackson Pollock, Charlie Parker spent his short life pushing forward the frontiers of his art, and he became a cultural hero by constantly living on the edge, before self-destructing: the very word 'be-bop' is said to derive from the New York patois for 'knife-fight'. In *Bird*, these frontiers are represented at the beginning by the big band sound, and at the end by rock-'n-roll – and, in case we might miss the point, they are both embodied in the same fictional character, named Buster. So Charlie Parker is presented as fighting against the music of mere genre, the music of the commonplace – and one of his tragedies is (as he says in the film) 'I made the records, but someone else done sold 'em'. Echoes of *Honkytonk Man*. Could it be that Clint Eastwood, who seems to be just beginning his third act (as director, not actor), was also attracted to *Bird* by fellow-feeling? Since founding Malpaso Productions, of course, he both makes the films *and* sells 'em. But it has taken all his box-office firepower in Hollywood to resist the pressure to stand still, over the last twenty-odd years. It may seem far-fetched – and of course Clint Eastwood would be the last to admit it – but *Bird* could well be one of his more autobiographical films. Unlike Charlie Parker, he has created a large number of genre works in the form of Westerns, cop films, action adventures. But he has then gone on to use his strong position *within* the industry (a position Parker was never fortunate enough to occupy) to create a smaller number of works which push forward the frontiers of popular art and which 'it took a little while' for his fans to accept. As head of Malpaso, he has had a lot of persuading to do.

His next non-genre project, which again may have had an autobiographical or at least a personal motivation behind it – one critic wrote that it was his 'best since *Bird* and maybe his best since *Josey Wales*' – was released two years later: *White Hunter, Black Heart*.

Eastwood was first introduced to the book of *White Hunter* by 'a fellow I'd known years ago; actually I'd had a bit part in a picture he'd produced'. It turned out that various scripts of it had been floating around for some time. Other films-makers might have been put off by that fact – sensing that the script was jinxed in some way, or out of date – but Eastwood felt that its moment had finally arrived. In any case, the scripts of *A Fistful of Dollars*, *Play Misty for Me*, *Pale Rider* and *Bird* had also been floating around for some time when he picked them up. And someone he trusted had recommended this latest one. Peter Viertel, the author of the novel – loosely based on his own experiences working with director John Huston on the script of *The African Queen* in Kenya, Uganda and the Belgian Congo, 1950 – had himself written the first draft script shortly after the novel was published in 1953. As he has recalled: 'I sold the motion picture rights prematurely, and the "property" changed hands several times without ever being seriously prepared for production. I suppose that while John Huston was alive people in the industry were naturally hesitant about bringing the novel to the screen.'

If *White Hunter had* been made into a movie in the mid-1950s, it would probably have come out looking like a mixture of *Mogambo* and *Where No Vultures Fly* – as Eastwood puts it, 'with cockamamie ideas combining it with other African stories'. Certainly the ecological theme (about endangered species and the poaching of elephants), the political theme (in Viertel's words 'the race hatred which was a part of the picture of crumbling empires, the British as well as the Belgian'), and the portrait of a larger-than-life Hollywood 'character' (with its implied contrast with the youthful film school graduates of today), would have been handled very differently. Jeff Chandler as an unrecognisable John Huston, perhaps? Eventually, the book was optioned by Burt Kennedy, the same Burt Kennedy who had written all those Randolph Scott/Budd Boetticher Westerns from the mid-1950s onwards. He purchased it in the mid-1980s, but had been chasing it since Boetticher days. 'For years – like twenty-five years,' he told me shortly before Eastwood was at last to make the film, 'I'd been after *White Hunter, Black Heart*, and I finally optioned it from Columbia and did a script from the book. There had been many, many scripts. And none of them had really done the book. Even Peter Viertel had done a version of it, which wasn't the book – even his book. So Clint picked it up, and bought us all out. Because that's what he does. He wants to be the complete boss – which I can understand, I really can. Anyway, the book is very much *in*, you know. Doing John Huston, that's kind of exciting. *Out of Africa* maybe. And the fact that Huston died. It's a good book: some wonderful scenes in it.'

In the end, the screenplay credit reads 'Peter Viertel and James Bridges and Burt Kennedy' (director James Bridges had prepared *his* version at some stage as well). It is clear what had attracted Burt Kennedy: the Huston character in the book – 'a violent man' with an obsessive temperament, but also a very talented man with an 'almost divine ability to land on his feet' – bore a certain family resemblance to those flawed Western heroes called Stride, Brennan, Brigade and Cody. Eastwood's interest appears to have been in the ecological themes – 'If someone *now* wanted to kill elephants, it'd be a much more consciously evil thing than it was then . . . I guess I wanted to suggest how backward we still are'; in a central character who lives on the edge – 'most of the characters I've played have been flawed, or anti-heroes as they used to call them back in the 1960s' – and, again, in the theme of a creative artist who has to cope with the pressures of a voracious industry.

JOHN WILSON (*the renamed Huston character*): You know something, Pete? You're never going to be a great screenwriter and you know why? . . . Because you let eighty-five million popcorn eaters pull you this way and that way. To write a movie, you've got to forget anyone's going to see it . . . I figure there's two ways to live in this world: one is to crawl and kiss ass and write their happy endings . . . the other way is to let the chips fall where they may.

This speech, taken almost verbatim from one of the key confrontations in the novel and filmed straight on, may well have been part of the attraction. It mirrors the basic theme (and, indeed, the period) of *Bird*, albeit in a very different cultural setting. And yet, it is a long speech, and it is spoken in the Huston-style – breathy, over-enunciated, condescending, with a touch of Irish in the vowels – that one might expect from a character actor. Maybe this was part of it, for Eastwood, as well: 'It seemed a very good part, and an actor always has to look out for himself. I never met John Huston but when I was a substitute projectionist in the army, I used to run *The Battle of San Pietro*, the documentary Huston made in 1945, all the time. He narrated it as well, so when I began preparing I ran that documentary many times and listened to it over and over. And there's so much documentary footage of him that I was able to get a good perception of what he was like. The main pitfall would have been to do a nightclub impersonation. What I tried to do was think like he did, to catch the kind of delivery he had, slightly condescending at times and yet deliberate. He was kind of commanding people to listen to him. I just took on that kind of attitude . . . it all came out quite naturally.'

Certainly, his first speech in the film, delivered to the Peter Viertel character, Pete Verrill (Jeff Fahey), contains two surprises: first, he is wearing jodphurs and hunting scarlet (after some hard galloping around the English countryside) and second, the accent is almost convincing.

JOHN WILSON (*getting up from reading his newspaper*): *Pete*, for God's sake . . . How the hell *are* you, kid . . . You're *looking good* . . . Care for some *cawfie*?

It's the first Eastwood accent since he put on a Texan drawl for the last two reels of *Two Mules for Sister Sara*. Later, there will be further surprises: discussions of Stendhal, Flaubert and Tolstoy (in an *Eastwood* movie?); elaborate put-downs of obnoxious, racist Brits ('You, my dear, are the ugliest god-damned bitch I've ever dined with'), and a fist-fight, which our hero roundly loses, with an equally racist manager at the Victoria Falls Hotel ('We fought the preliminary for the kikes,' says Wilson with a mischievous Irish twinkle in his eye, for the benefit of the up-tight dinner guests, 'now we're going to fight the main event for the niggers'); Eastwood acting a (deliberately phoney) upper-crust English great white hunter ('Do come in, chaps, do come in'); a restrained 'world-music' soundtrack from Lennie Niehaus, consisting almost entirely of drumbeats; and a splendidly judged ending (added to the original novel by Burt Kennedy) which has John Wilson just *beginning* to get down to the business of directing *The African Queen* at the fade-out. Eastwood was keen to establish that this is 'a what-if story *based upon* Peter Viertel's experience with Huston' rather than 'some movie about Bogart and Bacall' (during the shooting, he was quoted as saying that the elephant proved more difficult to cast than the Bogart part), and the film ends just where people would probably have expected it to begin:

ASSISTANT: Ready, Mr Wilson.
JOHN WILSON (*in close-up, trembling, with a choked voice*): Action.

Wilson has found his precious bull elephant but at the last moment is unable to commit the 'sin' – 'It's more than a crime' – of shooting it. Tragically, his hesitation leads directly to the death of Kivu, the local guide. So he begins the other shooting – of the film – full of remorse, self-hatred and self-pity. As Wilson says to Verrill, 'You were right, Pete, the ending's all *wrong*, it *should* be a happy one.' And as Eastwood has added, 'When he says "Action", you feel his life has definitely been affected and he's going to be different in his approach'. The long-term result is one of the great movies of the 1950s.

Eastwood has often said how disappointed he remains never to have worked with the veteran action directors (action films *and* people of action) who were just entering their twilight years or retiring when he got going in the business – Ford, Hawks, Walsh. Maybe he associated Huston with that bygone era of movie-making and its attendant mythologies. As story material – and in retrospect – the monster-director's antics seem bizarre and entertaining, although Eastwood's own working methods couldn't be further removed from them. Wilson thrives on chaos, he always seems to have his mind on something more interesting, and in time-honoured fashion he enjoys needling the people around him (especially producers and writers). Like John Ford tearing pages out of the scripts, when told by his executive producer to economise. Eastwood is very well organised, his shoots are highly concentrated, and he works best on a calm set with people he knows well. He has nothing but scorn for the profligate sons of John Wilson, working today:

'Huston couldn't have been more careless about the whole project, and yet he came up with a terrific movie. If you read his autobiography *An Open Book*, you realise that he was always directing himself away from matters in hand. He'd go off horse-racing or gambling or maybe he'd spend some time with a lady friend . . . I'm not too sure about his psychology but I guess that he needed to get himself into other things to get away from his own anxieties . . . I'm not at all like that myself. I figure that if a company has trusted me with the money to make a film, it's my job to do the best I can.'

As to Wilson/Huston's well-known tendency to destabilise people, on and off the set: 'Well, once in a while you're bound to get annoyed with something, but you *have* to keep calm because if you fly off the handle, it becomes like a disease which infects the whole company. Pretty soon everyone's walking on eggshells and people don't give their best that way. I know people who work like that – they get nervous and they let it rub off on everyone else, but that's the wrong way. It's self-defeating in the end.'

So *White Hunter, Black Heart* may have 'all gelled together' for Eastwood (his words) for autobiographical, as well as topical reasons:

the movie world we have lost, when directors went out and shot elephants instead of poring all day over spread-sheets. It certainly has its faults: the dialogue is often anachronistic (Verrill refers at one point to 'mental callisthenics' – in *1950*?) and sometimes crass (Pilot Hodkins to Verrill, after an over-written and slightly embarrassing speech about prehistoric elephants versus 'little creatures without any dignity', in other words human beings: 'You certainly have a way with words, Pete, no wonder you're a writer'). Eastwood seems too light, vocally and physically, for the part, and in a strange way never convinces us that he is the sort of man who would *really* shoot animals (which rather undercuts the climactic scene with the elephant). Strange that an actor who normally has so much charisma or presence on screen (even when he is directing himself) should somehow lack it here. But, that said, it is a fascinating project for him to have undertaken at this late stage in his career. At the time it was released, he said he hoped the Eastwood audience, or some of them at least, would go with it – as, presumably did Warner Brothers. He told critic Tony Rayns: 'I can only say that the film seemed like it was worth doing. Maybe that's the way that I do, finally, resemble the character of John Wilson. I'm not afraid of the risk. But hopefully once in a while you can do an off-beat project like this and find an audience that appreciates being taken on this kind of journey. It might not be the *Dirty Harry* audience, although I hope that some of them would also enjoy it, but perhaps there's another audience.'

But, in the event, despite a poster which featured a grizzled, steely-eyed Clint Eastwood smoking a cigar, *White Hunter, Black Heart* did very badly at the box-office: even worse, relatively, than *Bird*, which also had difficulty finding an audience. *White Hunter* cost $24 million, and returned one million at the domestic box-office. Sure, neither of them were 'obviously commercial projects', says Eastwood of both films, but in any case, they'll probably have a long shelf life in other forms of distribution.

13 'A couple of grey hairs don't hurt . . .'

Meanwhile, Clint Eastwood has continued to make more 'obviously commercial projects' which have presumably justified Warner Brothers in backing his maverick streak. In 1986 it was *Heatbreak Ridge*, a film made 'with the special co-operation of the Marine Corps' (until the Corps became upset – seriously! – by the stream of bad language in the finished film). Eastwood plays Gunnery Sergeant Tom Highway, veteran of Korea *and* Vietnam, who whips the formula platoon into shape (a black rock singer, a bookish lieutenant, a Hispanic recruit, and a huge prize fighter called Swede), while proving to his battalion commander that rule of thumb is better than military academy: all this, plus the invasion of the island of Grenada presented as a post-Rambo rematch for Vietnam, and Eastwood reading magazines about New Age relationships to try and cope with his ex-wife Aggie (Marsha Mason). At the fadeout, Aggie sheepishly waves an American flag, to greet the returning heroes – with military music blaring on the soundtrack – as she realises that she isn't so New Age after all.

It's like those old, pre-*Dirty Dozen*, melting-pot platoon movies, where O'Leary, Kowalksi, Schwarz, Mancini, Ellington and Wayne are welded into a fighting unit, and a nation, in time for the storming of the citadel. Like them, only *Sands of Iwo Jima* and *Fort Apache* could never hope to 'click' again after the experience of Vietnam, as Michael Herr's *Dispatches* so eloquently showed. And in any case, Clint Eastwood was supposed to have superseded Duke Wayne, wasn't he? The incessant swearing, the 'Missing In Action' type story, even the shape of Eastwood's torso (he seems to have been going to the same gymnasium as Sylvester Stallone) may have been of the

1980s. But little else was.

Then, in 1989, it was *Pink Cadillac*, in which Eastwood played Tom Nowack, a latter-day bounty hunter − a 'track 'em and snatch 'em' man, or skip tracer − who makes his job a little more interesting by dressing up in outlandish disguises and adopting different personae (a chauffeur, a rodeo clown, a gold-lamé-jacketed swinger, a W.C. Fields soundalike) and who teams up with Bernadette Peters in her precious car − with the loot in the boot − against a group of neo-Nazi survivalists who train on a mock-up of Main Street USA in the forest and call themselves Birthright. The new idea here is that Nowack is a gentle, nice, vulnerable man who only pretends to be macho because it is expected of him in his job − a development of the *Every Which Way But Loose* formula. In fact, the repartee between him and Mrs Lou Ann McGuinn (who turns out to be every bit as tough as he is) is considerably sharper than the redneck bawdy and over-the-top country-and-western vulgarity of the *Every Which Way* films:

'Where are the handcuffs . . . aren't you into the bondage part of the job?'
'Lady, I don't even like starch on my collars.'

'How can you run that fast in heels?'
'Tina Turner taught me.'

(*a man exposes himself to her*)
'What do you think?'
'Looks like a penis, only smaller . . .'

'Let me guess, you're not really the type to settle down. You're an American wildcat. Your kind can't breed in captivity. The *road* is your only home, huh?'
He laughs. 'Well now . . .'

'I've got a firm policy on gun control. If there's a gun around, I want to control it.'
'Well, change your policy.'

The trouble is that the film is *so* loose and rambling in its structure – a kind of craggy dog story, which periodically stops to listen to some new country records – that only the energy of Bernadette Peters keeps it moving. *Pink Cadillac* is Eastwood's first American film since *Star in the Dust* (1956) not to get any distribution at all in British cinemas.

If *Heartbreak Ridge* tried to update John Ford, and *Pink Cadillac* to fuse the bounty hunter image with the vulnerable drifter, *The Rookie*, made in 1990, revisited *Dirty Harry* territory – the twist here being that Eastwood plays an older cop who hands on his wisdom, if not his dead-behind-the-eyes values, to a younger rich kid partner (Charlie Sheen of the brat pack) who at first rejects both. 'I hate the way you drive,' says Sheen, 'and I hate your stinkin' whisky breath.' But in the end, they cross the class and age barriers to become buddies, as the rookie at last manages to light the older cop's cigar.

Eastwood refers to *The Rookie* as 'a good shoot-'em-up', and adds, 'The older cop isn't so much embittered, like Harry, as callous. Obviously I'm beyond the age of playing the rookie, so I'm playing the senior cop who teaches him the ropes . . . the rookie is a man from a wealthy family, who has no reason to join the profession of law enforcement; my character can't understand why he does it – unless he has to.' The action sequences, shot and edited in post-*Die Hard* 'flying glass movie' style, are terrific: in particular, a chase involving a car transporter which hurls luxury limos at Nick Pulovski's pursuing car as if they were four-wheeled arrows; and a car driven through the window of a building's *upper* storey. But, in the end, the film turns out to be just a tuppence-coloured 'shoot-'em-up', and a rather old-fashioned one at that. It made $10.5 million at the domestic box-office, in one month flat.

In *Heartbreak Ridge*, one of the characters says to Eastwood when he happens to use the word 'hippy', 'Are you freeze-dried or been doing time?' In *Pink Cadillac*, the dialogue is chock full of 1960s idioms (such as 'That's a major bummer' or 'You don't know diddly shit', or countless jokes – again – about ageing hippies) which go unchallenged. In *The Rookie*, the older cop is presented as a dinosaur or endangered species but at the sentimental fadeout, the 1980s boy comes round to his way of thinking. In the age of 'Tom films', in the immortal phrase of Mel Brooks – films starring aggressively youthful heroes such as Tom Cruise, Tom Berenger or Tom Hanks – Eastwood's mainstream action films have begun to appear, for the first time since the 1960s, out of date, and if the average age of the audience for action films is late teens, perhaps very out of date.

In the age when most of the major action film genres have been reinterpreted from a feminist point of view – Kathryn Bigelow's *Blue Steel* (1990) reclaiming *Dirty Harry*, while Ridley Scott's *Thelma and Louise* (1991) reclaims the road movie (especially the 'Smokey and the Bandit' type), the Western and the Hitchcock journey films all at the same time – Eastwood's use of 'strong women' to offset his larger-than-life persona no longer seems quite enough. In the age of cartoon-style action films (or 'no brainers') starring bodybuilders – who are directly related to The Man With No Name, indeed who were made possible by him – and co-starring the special effects team, Eastwood's emphasis on down-home values, the 'politics of resent-ment', and well-made stories, begins to seem unhip:

'There are a lot of pictures out now,' he says, in a faintly bemused way, 'where the pyrotechnics and the effects are the star and you can't really remember what the story was. If anyone asked you the story you couldn't really care less because you didn't go to it for that reason. If that is the way the world is going maybe we are on the wrong track. But I can't believe that there aren't cases out there where people are interested in scripts and so forth.' In the age when John Wayne's catchphrase from *The Searchers* – 'That'll be the day' – is kept alive, if at all, by increasingly anodine versions of Buddy Holly's song of the same name, Eastwood's inheritance of the John Wayne mantle has left him with less and less room to manoeuvre. As Richard Combs wrote in his *Monthly Film Bulletin* review of *Heartbreak Ridge*:

'For a while it seemed that parody and self-criticism would open up the films in interesting ways. Not much has been opened up recently; the self-mockery itself has become institutionalised and strangely inexpressive . . . Eastwood's recent films have closed around him with a stylistic heaviness, a sombreness, that reflects the influence not so much of his first mentors, Sergio Leone and Don Siegel, as of his regular cinematographer Bruce Surtees, who has given to many of Eastwood's films a peculiarly penumbral look, even in broad daylight, suggestive of a twilight of the gods.'

Although this is not entirely fair – we have seen how Eastwood's less commercial projects (some of which have in fact proved to be commercially successful) have remained a consistently important, and still developing, body of work – it is a pretty apt description of his mainstream films since *Pale Rider* in the mid-1980s. Ironically, his more personal projects have themselves sometimes inspired younger mainstream film-makers: 'They admit to stealing *Fatal Attraction* from *Play Misty for Me*,' Eastwood says genially, and recalls that he told Sherry Lansing, one of *Fatal Attraction*'s producers, that she owes him a beer.

At the same time, Eastwood's well-guarded private life has become more and more public property. He and Maggie had separated in 1979, and new partner Sondra Locke featured in six films plus one Eastwood-directed television show between 1976 and 1985 (the last big screen partnership was *Sudden Impact*). The divorce from Maggie was finalised in 1984, after 31 years of marriage, with a much-publicised settlement of $25 million for her. Then, in spring 1989, he split from Sondra Locke – and the acrimonious palimony scandal which ensued involved worldwide press speculation (school of *National Enquirer*) about their relationship, about the attitude of Locke's husband of twenty years, Gordon (with whom Eastwood had apparently 'shared' her), and about Locke's opinion of Eastwood's children Kyle and Alison. Photographs of a very strained-looking Eastwood began to appear all over the world. 'His story,' crowed the *Enquirer*, 'She spent my money on her husband and split her time between us. Her story: Clint cheated on me and forced me to have two abortions,' etc.

The remarkable thing is that Eastwood has remained so productive for so long ('I enjoy working . . . and I follow a regular regime of fitness') – and in recent years has become so open and talkative about his work as well, especially in Europe. Whatever the sense of formula work, of narrative closure in some of his action films, he has certainly continued to adapt to changing circumstances, as cult heroes must, and to show that he has indeed far 'more than one good idea'. He has also continued to struggle – in Robert Mazzocco's words – against 'absorption into mere genre, mere style, even while appearing, with his long-boned casualness and hypnotic presence, to be *nothing but style* . . .' His transformation of the hero into the outsider, and his subsequent explorations of what makes the outsider tick by 'picking things up that work for me', have been a major force within popular culture: a hero about heroes. His journey from the ironic to the mythic and back again has provided a map for the fantasies and projections of filmgoers all over the world for over a quarter of a century. And those films as a director over which he has had total control have been both consistent and consistently self-contained: they have built on to one another, often surprisingly, sometimes predictably. Only Woody Allen, among today's mainstream film-makers, can claim as much for so long, but his palette has always been more limited by geography and by the instincts of a stand-up comic. As Orson Welles said of Clint Eastwood, 'He is the most underrated director in America today'. Underrated because he is such big box-office, because Eastwood the actor grabs all the attention, and because his output is, with one or two exceptions, so seamless.

Throughout his quarter century at the top of his profession, he has managed stubbornly to resist the pigeon-holing which most actors (and, indeed, directors) of his stature have eventually come to accept. A 'fascist'? Don't be absurd. A 'liberal behind the Magnum image'? as *The Guardian* once headlined. Of course not. A 'reactionary antidote to the liberal young lions, Hoffman and Redford', as a French newspaper once dubbed him? Are you kidding? What then? Something rather less ambitious, it seems:

'Well, I guess I revere the individual, which is why I've been attracted to playing individualist kind of characters on screen, but I think people who are really dogmatic in political philosophy are sometimes very boring. I'd rather have strong feelings on certain subjects, and then approach them individually, and if you change your mind as you grow and mature in life, then that's fine too. I know, because there's certain things you feel at one point in life that you don't feel in another.'

Now that the critics are being so much nicer to him (at least, to his more thoughtful works), is it because *he* has changed, or his audiences, or the critics, or who?

'I don't have an explanation other than the fact that maybe there were certain prejudices in the times of *Dirty Harry* in 1971 that don't exist now, or are changing now, or times are changing. Maybe I'm older, more mature; maybe the audiences are changing and I'm changing. It's just circumstances.' Are his own *political* views changing? And does he still have those friendly little telephone chats with ex-President Reagan?

'I find as I get older I get more libertarian in my outlook. I get more "Hey, I just want to be left alone" . . . In this last election I surprised even me. You go through each issue and you vote in an individual way. I found myself voting for a *Democrat* on certain issues.'

Any political ambitions?

'Well, I think there's a line in *Magnum Force*, "A good man knows his limitations . . ." '

But what about his term of office as Mayor of Carmel?

'I think we achieved quite a bit. We got rid of quite a lot of punitive attitudes on the council and helped people get things done. We got things built – beach walkways, a library annexe which had been waiting twenty-five years, and so on. I approached it from a business point of view, not a political one. We once had a council composed entirely of schoolteachers. There's nothing wrong with school-teachers, but they've never had to meet payrolls or anything like that.'

But what about his new-found respectability as a film artist? The retrospective at the Museum of Modern Art, the macho accolades from Norman Mailer, the Chevalier des Arts et Lettres in Paris, this book, even? 'Well I guess a couple of grey hairs don't hurt.'

And the close attention he continues to pay to the details of all aspects of his work – script, budgeting, performance, music, visuals and marketing? That must take a lot of energy. 'My dad's dream was to have a hardware store. I'm his son.'

Somehow you can never imagine Eastwood in psychoanalysis. And that may be what is so damn reassuring and impressive about him.

F. Scott Fitzgerald coined the phrase 'There are no second acts in American lives' – the words which open the film *Bird*. But, in the special case of Clint Eastwood at least, he was most definitely wrong. The man is on his third act, and there may well be more to come.

Filmography

I. APPRENTICESHIP, 1955–58

'To look at some of the billings in *TV Guide* these days, you'd think I co-starred in those films ...'

Revenge of the Creature

USA, 1955   **Director: Jack Arnold**

P.c.: Universal-International. *p*: William Alland. *sc*: Martin Berkley. *ph*: Charles S. Welbourne. *ed*: Paul Weatherwax. *a.d*: Alexander Golitzen, Alfred Sweeney. *m.sup*: Joseph Gersenshon. *sd*: Leslie I. Carey, Jack Bolger. *l.p.*: John Agar *(Clete Ferguson)*, Lori Nelson *(Helen Dobson)*, John Bromfield *(Joe Hayes)*, Robert B. Williams *(George Johnson)*, Nestor Paiva *(Lucas)*, Grandon Rhodes *(Foster)*, Dave Willock *(Gibson)*, Charles Crane *(Police Captain)*. (Clint Eastwood, uncredited, as *Jennings,* a lab technician.) 82 mins.

Tarantula

USA, 1955   **Director: Jack Arnold**

P.c.: Universal-International. *p*: William Alland. *sc*: Robert M. Fresco and Martin Berkeley. *ph*: George Robinson. *ed*: William M. Morgan. *a.d*: Alexander Golitzen, Alfred Sweeney. *m.sup*: Joseph Gershenson. *sd*: Leslie I. Carey, Frank Wilkinson. *l.p.*: John Agar *(Dr. Matt Hastings)*, Mara Corday *(Stephanie Clayton)*, Leo G. Carroll *(Prof. Deemer)*, Nestor Paiva *(Sheriff)*, Ross Elliott *(John Burch)*, Edwin Rand *(Lt. John Nolan)*, Raymond Bailey *(Townsend)*. (Clint Eastwood, uncredited, as a bomber pilot.) 80 mins.

Lady Godiva of Coventry

USA, 1955   Director: Arthur Lubin

P.c.: Universal-International. *p*: Robert Arthur. *sc*: Oscar Brodney and Harry
Ruskin. *ph*: Carl Guthrie. *col.p*: Print by Technicolor. *ed*: Paul Weatherwax.
a.d: Alexander Golitzen, Robert Boyle. *m.sup*: Joseph Gershenson. *sd*: Leslie
I. Carey, Joe Lapis. *l.p.*: Maureen O'Hara (*Lady Godiva*), George Nader
(*Lord Leofric*), Eduard Franz (*King Edward*), Leslie Bradley (*Count Eustace*),
Victor McLaglen (*Grimald*), Torin Thatcher (*Lord Godwin*), Rex Reason
(*Harold*), Grant Withers (Pendar), Clint Eastwood (First Saxon). 88 mins.

Francis in the Navy

USA, 1955   Director: Arthur Lubin

P.c.: Universal-International. *p*: Stanley Rubin. *sc*: Devery Freeman, based
on the character "Francis" created by David Stern. *ph*: Carl Guthrie. *eds*:
Milton Carruth, Ray Snyder. *a.d*: Alexander Golitzen, Bill Newberry, *m.sup*:
Joseph Gershenson. *sd:* Leslie I. Carey, Frank H. Wilkinson. *l.p.*: Donald
O'Connor (*Lt. Peter Stirling* and *Bosun's Mate Slicker Donevan*), Martha
Hyer (*Betsy Donevan*), Richard Erdman (*Murph*), Jim Backus (*Commander
Hutch*), Myrna Hansen (*Helen*), David Janssen (*Lt. Anders*), Leigh Snowden
(*Appleby*), Martin Milner (*Rick*), Paul Burke (*Tate*), Phil Garris (*Stover*),
Clint Eastwood (*Jonesy*) and Chill Wills (*voice of Francis*). 80 mins.

Never Say Goodbye

USA, 1955   Director: Jerry Hopper

P.c.: Universal-International. *p*: Albert J. Cohen. *sc*: Charles Hoffman. Based
on a screenplay by Bruce Manning, John Klorer and Leonard Lee, from the
play *Come Prima Meglio di Prima* by Luigi Pirandello. *ph*: Maury Gertsman.
col: Print by Technicolor. *ed*: Paul Weatherwax *a.d*: Alexander Golitzen,
Robert Boyle, *m*: Frank Skinner, *m.sup*: Joseph Gershenson. *sd*: Leslie I.
Carey, Frank H. Wilkinson. *l.p.*: Rock Hudson (*Dr Michael Parker*), Cornell
Borchers (*Lisa*), George Sanders (*Victor*), Ray Collins (*Dr Bailey*), David
Janssen (*Dave*), Shelley Fabares (*Suzy Parker*), Raymond Greenleaf (*Dr Kelly
Andrews*), Clint Eastwood (Will), and Gia Scala. 96 mins.

The First Traveling Saleslady

USA, 1956   Director: Arthur Lubin

P.c.: RKO-Radio. *sc*: Devery Freeman and Stephen Longstreet. *ph*: William Snyder. *col*: Print by Technicolor. *ed*: Otto Ludwig. *ad*: Albert S. D'Agostino. *m*: Irving Gertz. *sd*: Stanford Houghton and Terry Kellum. *cos*: Edward Stevenson. *songs*: 'The First Traveling Saleslady' sung by The Lancers, 'The Corset Can Do For A Lady' sung by Carol Channing (*m*: Irving Getz, *l*: Hal Levy). *l.p.*: Ginger Rogers (*Rose Gillray*), Barry Nelson (*Charles Masters*), Carol Channing (*Molly Wade*), David Brian (*James Carter*), James Arness (*Joel Kingdom*), Clint Eastwood (*Jack Rice*), Robert Simon (*Cal*), Frank Wilcox (*Marshal Duncan*) with John Eldredge, Kate Lawson, Lane Chandler. 92 mins.

Star in the Dust

USA, 1956   Director: Charles Haas

P.c.: Universal-International. *p*: Albert Zugsmith. *sc*: Oscar Brodney, based on the novel *Lawman* by Lee Leighton. *ph*: John L. Russell, Jr. *col*: Print by Technicolor. *m*: Frank Skinner. *l.p.*: John Agar (*Bill Jordan*), Mamie van Doren (*Ellen Ballard*), Richard Boone (*Sam Hall*), Leif Erikson (*George Ballard*), Paul Fix (*Mike MacNamara*), Harry Morgan (*Lew Hogan*), James Gleason (*Orval Jones*), Coleen Gray (*Nellie Mason*), (Clint Eastwood, uncredited, in a very small part as a ranch hand). 80 mins.

Escapade in Japan

USA, 1957   Director: Arthur Lubin

P.c.: RKO-Radio. *p*: Arthur Lubin. *sc*: Winston Miller. *ph*: William Snyder. Technirama. *col*: Technicolor. *ed*: Otto Ludwig. *a.d*: George W. Davis, Walter Holscher. *m*: Max Steiner. *sd*: Francis J. Scheid, Terry Kellum. *l.p.*: Teresa Wright (*Mary Saunders*), Cameron Mitchell (*Dick Saunders*), John Provost (*Tony Saunders*), Roger Nakagawa (*Hiko*), Philip Ober (*Lieut.-Col. Hargrave*), Kuniko Miyake (*Michiko*), Susumu Fujita (*Kei Tanaka*), Tatsuo Saito (*Mr. Fushimi*), (Clint Eastwood, uncredited, as rescue pilot One Dumbo). 93 mins.

Lafayette Escadrille

USA, 1957   Director: William A. Wellman

P.c.: Warner Bros. *p.*: William A. Wellman. *sc*: A.S. Fleischman, from a
story by William A Welman. *ph*: William Clothier. *ed*: Owen Marks. *a.d*:
John Beckman. *m*: Leonard Rosenman. *sd:* John Kean. *l.p.*: Tab Hunter
(*Thad Walker*), Etchika Choureau (*Renée*), Marcel Dalio (*Drillmaster*), David
Janssen (*Duke Sinclaire*), Paul Fix (*U.S. General*), Veola Vonn (*Madame
Olga*), Will Hutchins (*Dave Putnam*), Clint Eastwood (*George Moseley*),
Bill Wellman Jr. (*Bill Wellman*), Jody McCrea (*Tom Hitchcock*), Dennis
Devine (*Red Scanlon*). British title: Hell Bent for Glory. 93 mins.

Ambush at Cimarron Pass

USA, 1957   Director: Jodie Copelan

dist: 20th Century-Fox. *p.c.*: Regal. *p*: Herbert E. Mendelson. *sc*: Richard
G. Taylor, John K. Butler, from a story by Robert A. Reeds and Robert
W. Woods. *ph*: John M. Nickolaus Jr., RegalScope. *ed*: Carl L. Pierson.
a.d: John Mansbridge. *m*: Paul Sawtell, Bert Shefter. *sd*: Harold Hanks,
Harry M. Leonard. *l.p.*: Scott Brady (*Sgt. Matt Blake*), Margia Dean (*Teresa*),
Clint Eastwood (*Keith Williams*), Irving Bacon (*Stanfield*), Frank Gerstle (*Sam
Prescott*), Dirk London (*Johnny Willows*), Baynes Barron (*Corbin*), William
Vaughan (*Henry*), Ken Mayer (*Corporal Schwitzer*), John Manier (*Private
Zach*), Keith Richards (*Private Lasky*), John Merrick (*Private Nathan*),
Desmond Slattery (Cobb). 73 mins.

II. THE RAWHIDE YEARS, 1958 – 66

'When you've done a couple of hundred shows in seven or eight years, you
can pick up a lot.'

The CBS series *Rawhide* was aired on American television from 9 January
1959 ('Incident of the Tumbleweed Wagon') to 4 January 1966 (repeat of
'Crossing at White Feather'), five days short of a seven-year run. It was created
by Charles Marquis Warren, produced by Warren from 1958 to 1961, then
– in one- or two-year intervals – by Endre Bohem, Vincent Fenelly, Bernard
Kowalski and Robert Thompson. The famous theme song was written by
Dmitri Tiomkin and Ned Washington, and sung by Frankie Laine (who
appeared in episode 60). Clint Eastwood, who had appeared in most – but
not all – of episodes 1 – 204, took over as trail boss for the last thirteen
episodes, after which the series was cancelled mid-season, in Christmas 1965.

Clint Eastwood

By the beginning of its final season, *Rawhide* had dropped to fifteenth *from the bottom* of the Neilsen rating. But it had achieved the fourth longest run of any TV series, and it is still repeated from time to time.

The regular cast members were Eric Fleming (Gil Favour, the trail boss until 1965), Clint Eastwood (Rowdy Yates, the ramrod), Sheb Wooley (Pete Nolan, the scout from 1958 – 62, then 1964 – 5), Paul Brinegar (Wishbone, the cook), James Murdock (Mushy Mushgrove, the cook's helper until 1965), Steve Raines (Jim Quince, drover), Rocky Shahan (Joe Scarlett, drover, until 1965), Robert Cabal (Hey Soos Patines, the wrangler, until 1965), John Cole (Bailey, a drover, 1959 – 61), Don Harvey (Collins, a drover, 1959 – 62) and sometimes John Erwin (Teddy, a drover, 1959 – 62, 1969 – 5). Charles Gray played Clay Forrester in various individual episodes from 1961 – 4.

The final season introduces three new regulars (as well as dropping at least five others): John Ireland as deputy trail boss Jed Colby (but *not* as replacement ramrod), Raymond St Jacques as drover Simon Blake (the first major black character in a tv Western) and David Watson as hotheaded youngster Ian Cabot (the Yates replacement in the plots). The following teleography includes the date of first airing, number and title of each episode, director, writer and guest star.

Season 1958 – 59

1 (9 Jan) *Incident of the Tumbleweed Wagon*
D: Richard Whorf. *sc*: Fred Freiberger. *Guest star*: Terry Moore (*Dallas Storm*).

2 (16 Jan) *Incident at Alabaster Plain*
D: Richard Whorf. *sc*: David Swift. *Guest star*: Troy Donahue (*Buzz Travis*).

3 (23 Jan) *Incident with an Executioner*
D: Charles Marquis Warren. *sc*: James Edmiston. *Guest star*: Dan Duryea (*Jardin*).

4 (30 Jan) *Incident of the Widowed Dove*
D: Ted Post. *sc*: David Lang. *Guest star:* Sally Forrest (*Clovis*).

5 (6 Feb) *Incident on the Edge of Madness*
D: Andrew V. McLaglen. *sc*: David Victor and Herbert Little, Jr. *Guest star*: Marie Windsor (*Narcie*).

6 (13 Feb) *Incident of the Power and the Plow*
D: Andrew V. McLaglen. *sc*: Fred Freiberger. *Guest star*: Brian Donlevy (*Jed Reston*).

7 (20 Feb) *Incident at Barker Springs*
D: Charles Marquis Warren. *sc*: Les Crutchfield. *Guest star*: June Lockhart
(*Rainy Dawson*).

8 (27 Feb) *Incident West of Lano*
D: Charles Marquis Warren. *sc*: Buckley Angell. *Guest star*: Martha Hyer
(*Hannah Haley*).

9 (6 Mar) *Incident of the Town in Terror*
D: Ted Post. *sc*: Oliver Crawford. *Guest star*: Margaret O'Brien (*Betsy
Stauffer*).

10 (13 Mar) *Incident of the Golden Calf*
D: Charles Marquis Warren. *sc*: Endre Bohem. *Guest star:* MacDonald Carey
(*Brother Bent*).

11 (20 Mar) *Incident of the Coyote Weed*
D: Jesse Hibbs. *sc*: David Lang. *Guest star*: Buzz Martin (*Roy Evans*).

12 (3 April) *Incident of the Chubasco*
D: Buzz Kulik. *sc*: Al C. Ward. *Guest star*: George Brent (*Jefferson Dever-
eaux*).

13 (10 April) *Incident of the Curious Street*
D: Ted Post. *sc*: Earl Baldwin. *Guest star*: Mercedes McCambridge (*Mrs
Miller*).

14 (17 April) *Incident of the Dog Days*
D: George Sherman. *sc*: Samuel A. Peeples. *Guest star*: Den Debbins (*Johnny
Camber*).

15 (24 April) *Incident of the Calico Gun*
D: Jesse Hibbs. *sc*: Winston Miller. *Guest star*: Gloria Talbott (*Jenny*).

16 (1 May) *Incident of the Misplaced Indians*
D: Jesse Hibbs. *sc*: David Victor and Herbert Little, Jr. *Guest star*: Kim
Hunter (*Amelia Spaulding*).

17 (8 May) *Incident of Fear in the Streets*
D: Andrew V. McLaglen. *sc*: Fred Freiberger. *Guest star*: Gary Merrill (*Jed*).

18 (15 May) *Incident Below the Brazos*
D: Jack Arnold. *sc*: Herb Purdom. *Guest star*: Leslie Nielsen (*Eli Becker*).

19 (22 May) *Incident of the Dry Drive*
D: Andrew V. McLaglen. *sc*: John Dunkel. *Guest star*: Victor Jory (*Jess
Hode*).

20 (5 June) *Incident of the Judas Trap*
D: Jesse Hibbs. *sc*: David Lang. *Guest star*: Nina Foch (*Medrina Wilcox*).

21 (12 June) *Incident in No Man's Land*
D: Jack Arnold. *sc*: Buckley Angell. *Guest star*: Brian Keith (*Tod MacCauley*).

22 (26 June) *Incident of the Burst of Evil*
D: George Sherman. *sc*: Buckley Angell. *Guest star*: Linda Cristal (*Louise*).

23 (10 July) *Incident of the Roman Candles*
D: Stuart Heisler. *sc*: Jan Winters. *Guest star*: Richard Eyer (*Davey Colby*).

Season 1959 – 60

24 (18 Sept) *Incident of the Day of the Dead*
D: Stuart Heisler. *sc*: David Victor and Herb Little, Jr. *Guest star*: Viveca Lindfors (*Luisa Hadley*).

25 (2 Oct) *Incident at Dangerfield Dip*
D: Charles Marquis Warren. *sc*: Herbert Purdom. *Guest star*: Philip Pine (*Reese Dangerfield*).

26 (9 Oct) *Incident of the Shambling Man*
D: Andrew V. McLaglen. *sc*: Charles Larson. *Guest star*: Victor McLaglen (*Harry Wittman*).

27 (16 Oct) *Incident at Jacob's Well*
D: Jack Arnold. *sc*: Robert Sherman. *Guest star*: Patricia Medina (*Illora Calvin*).

28 (23 Oct) *Incident of the Thirteenth Man*
D: Charles Marquis Warren. *Guest star*: Robert Anderson (*Gene Matson*).

29 (30 Oct) *Incident at the Buffalo Smokehouse*
sc: Louis Vittes. *Guest star*: Vera Miles (*Helen Walsh*).

30 (6 Nov) *Incident of the Haunted Hills*
D: Jesse Hibbs. *sc*: Louis Vittes. *Guest star*: John Drew Barrymore (*Tasunka*).

31 (13 Nov) *Incident of the Stalking Death*
D: Harmon Jones. *sc*: Louis Vittes. *Guest star*: Cesar Romero (*Ben Teagle*).

32 (20 Nov) *Incident of the Valley in Shadow*
Guest star: Fay Spain (*Winoka*).

33 (11 Dec) *Incident of the Blue Fire*
Guest star: Skip Homeier (*Lucky Markley*).

34 (18 Dec) *Incident at Spanish Rock*
D: Harmon Jones. *sc*: Claire Huffaker. *Guest star*: Elena Verdugo (*Maria Carroyo*).

35 (8 Jan) *Incident of the Druid Curse*
D: Jesse Hibbs. *sc*: Alva Hudson. *Guest star*: Luana Patten (*Naeve Lismore*).

36 (15 Jan) *Incident at Red River Station*
D: Gene Fowler Jr. *sc*: Charles Larson. *Guest star*: James Dunn (*Dr Solomon Flood*).

37 (22 Jan) *Incident of the Devil and his Due*
Guest star: Neville Brand (*Gaff*).

38 (29 Jan) *Incident of the Wanted Painter*
Guest star: Arthur Franz (*Charles Fredericks*).

39 (5 Feb) *Incident of the Tinkers Dam*
D: Gene Fowler, Jr. *sc*: Jan Winter. *Guest star*: Regis Toomey (*T.J. Wishbone*).

40 (19 Feb) *Incident of the Night Horse*
D: Joseph Kane. *sc*: John Dunkel. *Guest star*: George Wallace (*Jed Carst*).

41 (26 Feb) *Incident of the Sharpshooter*
D: Jesse Hibbs. *sc*: Winston Miller. *Guest star*: Jock Mahoney (*Vance*).

42 (4 Mar) *Incident of the Dust Flower*
D: Ted Post. *sc*: Winston Miller. *Guest star*: Arthur Shields (*Sam*).

43 (11 Mar) *Incident at Sulphur Creek*
Guest star: John Dehner (*Arvid Lacey*).

44 (18 Mar) *Incident of the Champagne Bottles*
D: Joseph Kane. *sc*: Louis Vittes and Curtis Kenyon. *Guest star*: Lane Bradford (*Matt Holden*).

45 (1 April) *Incident of the stargazer*
Guest star: Buddy Ebsen (*Will Kinch*).

46 (8 April) *Incident of the Dancing Death*
D: William Claxton, Joseph Kane. *sc*: Dallas Gaultois and James Edmiston. *Guest star*: Kipp Hamilton (*Shezoe*).

47 (22 April) *Incident of the Arana Sacar*
Guest star: Chris Alcaide (*The Pagan*).

48 (29 April) *Incident of the Deserter*
Guest star: Sheila Bromley (*Mrs Spencer*).

49 (6 May) *Incident of the 100 Amulets*
D: Stuart Heisler.*sc*: Louis Vittes and Fred Freiberger. *Guest star*: Argentina Brunetti (*Rose Patines*).

50 (13 May) *Incident of the Murder Steer*
D: Joseph Kane. *sc*: John Dunkel. *Guest star*: James Franciscus (*Andy Nye*).

51 (20 May) *Incident of the Music Maker*
D: Bud Springsteen. *sc*: Rik Vollaerts. *Guest star*: Peter Whitney (*Anton Zwahlen*).

52 (3 June) *Incident of the Silent Web*
D: Joseph Kane. *sc*: Winston Miller and Charles B Smith. *Guest star*: Don Haggerty (*Chaney*).

53 (10 June) *Incident of the Last Chance*
D: Ted Post. *sc*: Winston Miller. *Guest star*: John Kerr (*Bert Eaton*).

54 (17 June) *Incident of the Garden of Eden*
Guest star: Robert Coote (*Sir Richard Ashley*).

Season 1960 – 61

55 (30 Sept) *Incident at Roja Canyon*
D: Ted Post. *sc*: Budd Bankson and Steve Raines. *Guest star*: Julie London (*Anne Danvers*).

56 (14 Oct) *Incident of the Challenge*
sc: Charles Marquis Warren. *Guest star*: Michael Pate (*Mitla*).

57 (21 Oct) *Incident at Dragoon Crossing*
D: Ted Post. *sc*: John Dunkel. *Guest star*: Dan O'Herlihy (*John Cord*).

58 (4 Nov) *Incident of the Night Visitor*
D: Bud Springsteen. *sc*: John Dunkel. *Guest star*: Dane Clark (*Jeff Barkley*).

59 (11 Nov) *Incident of the Slavemaster*
D: Ted Post. *sc*: Clayton Fox. *Guest star*: Peter Lorre (*Victor Laurier*).

60 (18 Nov) *Incident on the Road to Yesterday*
D: Bud Springsteen. *sc*: Winston Miller and Jan Winters. *Guest star*: Frankie Laine (*Ralph Bartlett*).

61 (2 Dec) *Incident at Superstition Prairie*
D: Stuart Heisler. *sc*: Wilton Shiller. *Guest star*: Michael Pate (*Sankeno*).

62 (9 Dec) *Incident at Poco Tiempo*
D: Ted Post. *sc*: Buckley Angell. *Guest star*: Agnes Moorehead (*Sister Francis*).

63 (16 Dec) *Incident of the Captive*
D: Stuart Heisler. *sc*: Ted Gardner. *Guest star*: Mercedes McCambridge (*Martha Mushgrove*).

64 (6 Jan) *Incident of the Buffalo Soldier*
D: Ted Post. *sc*: John Dunkel. *Guest star*: Woody Strode (*Corp. Gabe Washington*).

65 (20 Jan) *Incident of the Broken Sword*
D: Bud Springsteen. *sc*: Louis Vittes. *Guest star*: E.G. Marshall (*Ben Foley*).

66 (27 Jan) *Incident at the Top of the World*
D: Ted Post. *sc*: Peggy and Lou Shaw. *Guest star*: Robert Culp (*Craig Kern*).

67 (3 Feb) *Incident of the Promised Land*
D: Ted Post. *sc*: Wilton Schiller. *Guest star*: Mary Astor (*Emma Cardwell*).

68 (10 Feb) *Incident of the Big Blowout*
D: George Templeton. *Guest star*: Mari Blanchard (*Laura Carter*).

69 (17 Feb) *Incident of the Fish out of Water*
D: Ted Post. *sc*: Albert Aley. *Guest star*: Dorothy Green (*Eleanor Bradley*).

70 (24 Feb) *Incident on the Road Back*
D: Dick Templeton. *sc*: Louis Vittes. *Guest star*: Gene Evans (*Sheriff Tom Wilson*).

71 (3 Mar) *Incident of the New start*
D: Justus Addiss. *sc*: Endre Bohem. *Guest star*: John Dehner (*Jubal Wade*).

72 (10 Mar) *Incident of the Running Iron*
D: Harmon Jones. *sc*: John Dunkel. *Guest star*: Frank Wilcox (*Marshal Cox*).

73 (17 Mar) *Incident Near Gloomy River*
D: Bud Springsteen. *sc*: John Dunkel. *Guest star*: John Cassavetes (*Cal Fletcher*).

74 (24 Mar) *Incident of the Boomerang*
D: Allen Reisner. *sc*: Michael Pate. *Guest star*: Patricia Medina (*Ruthanne Harper*).

75 (31 Mar) *Incident of his Brother's Keeper*
sc: Charles Marquis Warren. *Guest star*: Jack Lord (*Paul Evans*).

76 (7 April) *Incident in the Middle of Nowhere*
D: Bud Springsteen. *sc*: Howard Rigsby and Louis Vittes. *Guest star*: Cecil Kellaway (*Mackay*).

77 (14 April) *Incident of the Phantom Bugler*
D: George B. Templeton. *sc*: Louis Vittes and Buckley Angell. *Guest star*: Jock Mahoney (*Capt. Donahue*).

78 (28 April) *Incident of the Lost Idol*
D: Ted Post. *sc*: Albert Aley. *Guest star*: Dan Duryea (*Vic Slade*).

79 (5 May) *Incident of the Running Man*
Guest star: Robert Donner (*Toland*).

80 (12 May) *Incident of the Painted Lady*
D: Harmon Jones. *sc*: John Dunkel. *Guest star*: Mary Windsor (*Miss Katie*).

81 (19 May) *Incident before Black Pass*
sc: Arthur Rowe & Don Moore. *Guest star*: Zachary Scott (*Chief Grey Eyes*).

82 (26 May) *Incident of the Blackstorms*
D: Bud Springsteen. *sc*: Tony Habeed and Sheb Wooley. *Guest star*: Stephen McNally (*Sky Blackstorm*).

83 (2 June) *Incident of the Night on the Town*
D: Antony Leader. *sc*: Louis Vittes. *Guest star*: Harry Townes (*Lewis Lewis*).

84 (16 June) *Incident of the Wager on Payday*
sc: Endre Bohem. *Guest star*: Stephen Joyce (*Sidney Porter*).

Season 1961 – 62

85 (29 Sept) *Incident at Rio Salado*
D: Ted Post. *sc*: John Dunkel. *Guest star*: Tom Tully (*Jake Yates*).

86 (6 Oct) *Incident of the Sendoff*
D: George B. Templeton. *sc*: John Dunkel. *Guest star*: Darren McGavin (*Jed Hadley*).

87 (13 Oct) *Incident of the Long Shakedown*
D: Justus Addiss. *sc*: Albert Aley. *Guest star*: Skip Homeier (*Jess Clayton*).

88 (20 Oct) *Incident at Hondo Seco*
D: Perry Lafferty. *sc*: Louis Vittes. *Guest star*: Ralph Bellamy (*Judge Quince*).

89 (27 Oct) *Incident of the Lost Tribe*
D: George B. Templeton. *sc*: John Dunkel. *Guest star*: Sonya Wilde (*White Deer*).

90 (3 Nov) *Incident of the Inside Man*
D: George B. Templeton. *sc*: Albert Aley. *Guest star*: Charles Gray (*Clay Forrester*).

91 (10 Nov) *Incident of the Black Sheep*
D: Tony Leader. *sc*: Charles Larson. *Guest star*: Richard Basehart (*Tod Stone*).

92 (17 Nov) *Incident of the Prairie Elephant*
D: Robert L. Friend. *sc*: Louis Vittes. *Guest star*: Gloria Talbott (*Jenny*).

93 (24 Nov) *Incident of the Little Fishes*
D: Justus Addiss. *sc*: Charles Larson. *Guest star*: Burgess Meredith (*Tom Gwynn*).

94 (8 Dec) *Incident of the Blue Spy*
D: Sobey Martin. *sc*: Tom Seller. *Guest star*: Phyllis Thaxter (*Pauline Cushman*).

95 (15 Dec) *Incident of the Gentleman's Gentleman*
D: Sobey Martin. *sc*: J.E. Selby. *Guest star*: Brian Aherne (*Woolsey*).

96 (22 Dec) *Twenty-Five Santa Clauses*
D: Robert L. Friend. *sc*: Charles Larson. *Guest star*: Ed Wynn (*Bateman*).

97 (5 Jan) *Incident of the Long Count*
D: Jesse Hibbs. *sc*: Albert Aley. *Guest star*: Charles Gray (*Clay Forrester*).

98 (12 Jan) *The Captain's Wife*
D: Tay Garnett. *sc*: John Dunkel. *Guest star*: Barbara Stanwyck (*Nora Holloway*).

99 (19 Jan) *The Peddler*
D: Laslo Benedek. *sc*: Charles Larson. *Guest star*: Shelley Berman (*Mendel J. Sorkin*).

100 (26 Jan) *Incident of the Woman Trap*
D: George B. Templeton. *sc*: Buckley Angell. *Guest star*: Alan Hale (*the Wagon Master*).

101 (2 Feb) *Boss's Daughters*
D: Sobey Martin. *sc*: Albert Aley. *Guest star*: Paul Richards (*Vance Caldwell*).

102 (9 Feb) *Deserters' Patrol*
D: Andrew V. McLaglen. *sc*: Louis Vittes. *Guest star*: Russ Conway (*Col. Hiller*).

103 (16 Feb) *The Greedy Town*
D: Murray Golden. *sc*: Tom Seller. *Guest star*: Mercedes McCambridge (*Ada Randolph*).

104 (23 Feb) *Grandma's Money*
D: Sobey Martin. *sc*: J.E. Selby. *story*: Sonia Chernus. *Guest star*: Josephine Hutchinson (*Grandma Abigail Briggs*).

105 (2 Mar) *The Pitchwagon*
D: Marc Lawrence. *sc*: Wilton Schiller. *Guest star*: Buddy Ebsen (*George Stimson*).

106 (9 Mar) *Hostage Child*
D: Harmon Jones. *sc*: Ric Hardman. *Guest star*: James Coburn (*Col. Mathew Briscoe*).

107 (16 Mar) *The Immigrants*
D: Tay Garnett. *sc*: Elliott Arnold. *Guest star*: John Van Dreelen (*Count Ulrich*).

108 (23 Mar) *The Child-Woman*
D: Murray Golden. *sc*: Elliott Arnold. *Guest star*: Cesar Romero (*Big Tim Sloan*).

109 (30 Mar) *A Woman's Place*
D: Justus Addiss. *sc*: Eric Fleming and Chris Miller. *Guest star*: Gail Kobe (*Dr Louise Amadon*).

110 (6 April) *The Reunion*
D: Sobey Martin. *sc*: Elliott Arnold. *Guest star*: Walter Pidgeon (*Gen. Augustus Perry*).

111 (20 April) *The House of the Hunter*
D: Tay Garnett. *sc*: Louis Vittes. *Guest star*: Robert F. Simon (*Mackie*).

112 (4 May) *Gold Fever*
D: James P. Yarborough. *sc*: J.E. Selby. *Guest star*: Victor Jory (*Josea Brewer*).

113 (11 May) *The Devil and the Deep Blue*
D: George B. Templeton. *sc*: Louis Vittes. *Guest star*: Ted De Corsia (*Ben Wade*).

114 (18 May) *Abilene*
D: Tony Leader. *sc*: Charles Larson. *Guest star*: Vada Nordquist (*Audrey Totter*).

Season 1962 – 63

115 (28 Sept) *Incident of the Hunter*
D: Thomas Carr. *sc*: Charles Larson. *Guest star*: Mark Stephens (*Rankin*).

116 (5 Oct) *Incident of the Portrait*
D: Ted Post. *sc*: Michael Gleason and William Blinn. *Guest star*: John Ireland (*Frank Trask*).

117 (12 Oct) *Incident at Cactus Wells*
D: Christian Nyby. *sc*: Albert Aley. *Guest star*: Keenan Wynn (*Simon Royce*).

118 (19 Oct) *Incident of the Prodigal Son*
D: Christian Nyby. *sc*: Richard Fielder. *Guest star*: Carl Reindel (*Benjamin*).

119 (26 Oct) *Incident of the Four Horsemen*
D: Thomas Carr. *sc*: Charles Larson. *Guest star*: Robert J. Wilke (*Tom Gault*).

120 (2 Nov) *Incident of the Lost Woman*
D: Thomas Carr. *Guest star*: Fay Spain (*Lissa Hobson*).

121 (9 Nov) *Incident of the Dogfaces*
D: Don McDougall. *sc*: Gene L. Coon. *Guest star*: James Whitmore (*Sergeant Duclos*).

122 (16 Nov) *Incident of the Wolves*
D: Thomas Carr. *sc*: William L. Stuart. *Guest star*: Dan Duryea (*Cannon*).

123 (23 Nov) *Incident at Sugar Creek*
D: Christian Nyby. *sc*: Fred Freiberger. *Guest star*: John Larch (*Sam Garrett*).

124 (30 Nov) *Incident of the Reluctant Bridegroom*
D: Don McDougall. *sc*: Winston Miller. *Guest star*: Ruta Lee (*Sheila Delancey*).

125 (7 Dec) *Incident of the Querencias*
D: Thomas Carr. *sc*: Joseph Petracca. *Guest star*: Edward Andrews (*Lije Crowning*).

126 (14 Dec) *Incident at Quiriva*
D: Christian Nyby. *sc*: Raphael Hayes. *Guest star*: Royal Dano (*Monty Fox*).

127 (28 Dec) *Incident of Decision*
D: Don McDougall. *sc*: John Dunkel. *Guest star*: Doug Lambert (*Johnny Calvin*).

128 (4 Jan) *Incident of the Buryin' Man*
D: Thomas Carr. *sc*: Jack Turley. *Guest star*: King Donovan (*Poke Tolliver*).

129 (11 Jan) *Incident of the Trail's End*
D: Don McDougall. *sc*: Ed Adamson. *Guest star*: Harold J. Stone (*Harry Maxton*).

130 (18 Jan) *Incident at Spider Rock*
D: Thomas Carr. *sc*: Al C. Ward. *Guest star*: Susan Oliver (*Judy Hall*).

131 (25 Jan) *Incident of the Mountain Man*
D: Don McDougall. *sc*: Richard Fielder. *Guest star*: Robert Middleton (*Josh Green*).

132 (1 Feb) *Incident at Crooked Hat*
D: Don McDougall. *sc*: Joseph Petracca and Paul King. *Guest star*: James Gregory (*Jack Jennings*).

133 (8 Feb) *Incident of Judgment Day*
D: Thomas Carr. *sc*: Richard Landau. *Guest star*: Claude Rains (*Judge Alexander Langford*).

134 (22 Feb) *Incident of the Gallows Tree*
D: Christian Nyby. *sc*: Albert Aley. *Guest star*: Beverly Garland (*Della Locke*).

135 (1 Mar) *Incident of the Married Widow*
D: Thomas Carr. *sc*: Paul King. *Guest star*: Patricia Barry (*Miss Abigail*).

136 (15 Mar) *Incident of the Pale Rider*
D: Christian Nyby. *sc*: Dean Reisner. *Guest star*: Albert Salmi (*John Day*).

137 (22 Mar) *Incident of the Comancheros*
D: Thomas Carr. *sc*: Al C. Ward. *Guest star*: Robert Loggia (*Maria Jose Chappala*).

138 (29 Mar) *Incidendent of the Clown*
D: Don McDougall. *sc*: Charles Larson. *Guest star*: Eddie Bracken (*Morris G. Stevens*).

139 (12 April) *Incident of the Black Ace*
D: Thomas Carr. *sc*: Dean Reisner. *Guest star*: Walter Slezak (*Lazio Tzgorni*).

140 (19 April) *Incident of the Hostages*
D: Don McDougall. *sc*: Paul King. *Guest star*: Leslie Wales (*Yellow Sky*).

141 (3 May) *Incident of White Eyes*
D: Christian Nyby. *sc*: Paul King. *Guest star*: Nehemiah Persoff (*Domingo*).

142 (10 May) *Incident at Rio Doloroso*
D: Thomas Carr. *sc*: Paul King. *Guest star*: Cesar Romero (*Don Francisco Maldenado*).

143 (24 May) *Incident at Alkali Sink*
D: Don McDougall. *sc*: Thomas Thompson. *Guest star*: Ruta Lee (*Lorraine Stanton*).

Season 1963 – 64

144 (26 Sept) *Incident of the Red Wind*
D: Thomas Carr. *sc*: Dean Reisner. *Guest star*: Neville Brand (*Lou Bowdark*).

145 (3 Oct) *Incident of Iron Bull*
D: Christian Nyby. *sc*: Carey Wilber. *Guest star*: James Whitmore (*Col. John Macklin*).

146 (10 Oct) *Incident at El Crucero*
D: Earl Bellamy. *sc*: Charles Larson. *Guest star*: Elizabeth Montgomery (*Rose Cornelius*).

147 (17 Oct) *Incident of the Travelin' Man*
D: Ted Post. *sc*: Paul King. *Guest star*: Simon Oakland (*Bolivar Jagger*).

148 (24 Oct) *Incident at Paradise*
D: Thomas Carr. *sc*: Charles Larson. *Guest star*: Burgess Meredith (*Matthew Higgins*).

149 (31 Oct) *Incident at Farragut Pass*
D: Thomas Carr. *sc*: Jack Turley. *Guest star*: Frankie Avalon (*Billy Farragut*).

150 (7 Nov) *Incident at Two Graves*
D: Harry Harris. *sc*: Al C. Ward. *Guest star*: Bill Travers (*Jeremiah O'Neal*).

151 (14 Nov) *Incident of the Rawhiders*
D: Ted Post. *sc*: Jay Simms. *Guest star*: Denver Pyle (*Daddy Quade*).

152 (21 Nov) *Incident of the Prophecy*
D: Thomas Carr. *Guest star*: Dan Duryea (*Brother William*).

153 (28 Nov) *Incident at Confidence Creek*
D: Harry Harris. *sc*: Jack Turley. *Guest star*: Dick York (*Elwood P. Gilroy*).

154 (5 Dec) *Incident of the Death Dancer*
D: Thomas Carr. *sc*: Dean Reisner. *Guest star*: Forrest Tucker (*Dan Carlock*).

155 (12 Dec) *Incident of the Wild Deuces*
D: Harry Harris. *sc*: Jack Turley and Preston Wood. *Guest star*: Barbara Stuart (*Lorelie Mears*).

156 (19 Dec) *Incident of the Geisha*
D: Ted Post. *sc*: Charles Larson. *Guest star*: Miyoshi Umeki (*Nami*).

157 (2 Jan) *Incident at Ten Trees*
D: Ted Post. *sc*: Carey Wilber. *Guest star*: Susan Kohner (*Abbie Bartlett*).

158 (9 Jan) *Incident of the Rusty Shotgun*
D: Ted Post. *sc*: Paul King. *Guest star*: Marie Windsor (*Amy Claybank*).

159 (16 Jan) *Incident of the Midnight Cave*
D: Thomas Carr. *sc*: Sam Roeca and Barry Trivers. *Guest star*: Edward Kemmer (*Dr Jethro Manning*).

160 (23 Jan) *Incident of the Dowry Dundee*
D: Ted Post. *sc*: Sam Roeca. *Guest star*: Hazel Court (*Kathleen Dundee*).

161 (30 Jan) *Incident at Gila Flats*
D: Thomas Carr. *sc*: Sam Roeca. *Guest star*: Rodolfo Acosta (*Del Latigo*).

162 (6 Feb) *Incident of the Pied Piper*
D: Harry Harris. *sc*: Albert Aley. *Guest star*: Eddie Bracken (*Edgar Allan Smithers*).

163 (20 Feb) *Incident of the Swindler*
D: Thomas Carr. *sc*: Jack Turley. *Guest star*: John Dehner (*Straw Coleman*).

164 (27 Feb) *Incident of the Wanderer*
D: Christian Nyby. *sc*: Carey Wilber. *Guest star*: Nehemiah Persoff (*Michob*).

165 (5 Mar) *Incident at Zebulon*
D: Christian Nyby. *sc*: Dean Reisner. *Guest star*: Robert Cornthwaite (*Dr Laughton Wallace*).

166 (12 Mar) *Incident at Hourglass*
D: Christian Nyby. *sc*: John Hawkins. *Guest star*: John Anderson (*Capt. Rankin*).

167 (26 Mar) *Incident of the Odyssey*
D: Thomas Carr. *sc*: Sam Roeca and Sheldon Stark. *Guest star*: Mickey Rooney (*Pan Macropolous*).

168 (2 April) *Incident of the Banker*
D: Christian Nyby. *sc*: Chris Miller. *Guest star*: Allyn Joslyn (*Albert Ashton-Warner*).

169 (9 April) *Incident of El Toro*
D: Thomas Carr. *sc*: Charles Larson. *Guest star*: James Best (*Art Fuller*).

170 (16 April) *Incident at Deadhorse – Part I*
D: Thomas Carr. *sc*: Paul King. *Guest stars*: Burgess Meredith (*Hannibal Plew*) and Broderick Crawford (*Jud Hammerklein*).

171 (23 April) *Incident at Deadhorse – Part II*

172 (30 April) *Incident of the Gilded Goddess*
D: Christian Nyby. *sc*: Don Brinkley. *Guest star*: Dina Merrill (*Lisa Temple*).

173 (7 May) *Incident at Seven Fingers*
D: Christian Nyby. *sc*: John Hawkins. *Guest star*: William Marshall (*Sgt. Turner*).

174 (14 May) *Incident of the Peyote Cup*
D: Thomas Carr. *sc*: Richard Nelson. *Guest star*: James Gregory (*Brothers*).

Season 1964 – 65

175 (25 Sept) *The Race*
D: Vincent McEveety. *sc*: Robert Lewin. *Guest star*: Warren Oates (*Weed*).

176 (2 Oct) *The Enormous Fist*
D: Bernard Kowalski. *sc*: Sam Ross. *Guest stars*: Lee Van Cleef (*Fred Grant*) and Mark Slade (*Adam Grant*).

177 (9 Oct) *Piney*
D: Philip Leacock. *sc*: Clyde Ware. *Guest star*: Ed Begley (*Piney Kinney*).

178 (16 Oct) *The Lost Herd*
D: Vincent McEveety. *sc*: Archie L. Teglend. *Guest star*: Royal Dano (*Teisner*).

179 (23 Oct) *A Man Called Mushy*
D: Michael O'Herlihy. *sc*: John Mantley. *Guest star*: Sondra Kerr (*Teya*).

180 (30 Oct) *Canliss*
D: Jack Arnold. *sc*: Stirling Silliphant. *Guest star*: Dean Martin (*Gurd Canliss*).

181 (13 Nov) *Damon's Road – Part I*
D: Michael O'Herlihy. *sc*: Robert Lewin and Richard Carr. *Guest star*: Fritz Weaver (*Jonathan Damon*).

182 (20 Nov) *Damon's Road – Part II*

183 (27 Nov) *The Backshooter*
D: Herschel Daugherty. *sc*: Richard Carr. *Guest star*: Louis Hayward (*John Tasker*).

184 (4 Dec) *Corporal Dasovik*
D: Bernard Kowalski. *sc*: Lee Siegal. *Guest star*: Nick Adams (*Corp. Dasovik*).

185 (11 Dec) *The Photographer*
D: Vincent McEveety. *sc*: Clyde Ware. *Guest star*: Eddie Albert (*Taylor Dickson*).

186 (18 Dec) *No Dogs or Drovers*
D: Vincent McEveety. *sc*: Cliff Gould. *Guest star*: Philip Abbott (*Ben Dennis*).

187 (25 Dec) *The Meeting*
D: Michael O'Herlihy. *sc*: Robert Lewin. *Guest star*: Gavin MacLeod (*Rian Powers*).

188 (8 Jan) *The Book*
D: Bernard Kowalski. *sc*: Cliff Gould. *Guest star*: Pat Hingle (*Pop starke*).

189 (15 Jan) *Josh*
D: Herschel Daugherty. *sc*: Robert E. Thompson. *Guest star*: Albert Dekker (*Josh Breedon*).

190 (22 Jan) *A Time for Waiting*
D: Charles Rondeau. *sc*: Sy Salkowitz. *Guest star*: George Grizzard (*Capt. Ballinger*).

191 (29 Jan) *Moment in the Sun*
D: Bernard Girard. *sc*: Bernard Girard. *Guest star*: Gene Evans (*Marshal Shaw*).

192 (5 Feb) *Texas Fever*
D: Harmon Jones. *sc*: John Dunkel. *Guest star*: Royal Dano (*Sam Wentworth*).

193 (12 Feb) *Blood Harvest*
D: Justus Addiss. *sc*: Walter Black. *Guest star*: Steve Forrest (*Adam Cable*).

194 (5 Mar) *The Violent Land*
D: Harmon Jones. *sc*: Buckley Angell. *Guest star*: Davey Davison (*Abby Conroy*).

195 (12 Mar) *The Winter Soldier*
D: Justus Addiss. *sc*: John Dunkel. *Guest star*: Robert Blake (*Pvt Johnson*).

196 (19 Mar) *Prairie Fire*
D: Jesse Hibbs. *sc*: Elliott Arnold and Louis Vittes. *Guest star*: Michael Conrad (Jerry Munson).

197 (26 Mar) *The Retreat*
D: Jim Goldstone. *sc*: John Dunkel. *Guest star*: John Anderson (*Major Cantwell*).

198 (2 April) *The Empty Sleeve*
D: Justus Addiss. *sc*: Louis Vittes. *Guest star*: Burt Douglas (*Tom Cowan*).

199 (9 April) *The Last Order*
D: Robert L. Friend. *sc*: Tom Seller. *Guest star*: Efrem Zimbalist, Jr. (*Jeff McKeever*).

200 (16 April) *Mrs Harmon*
D: Michael O'Herlihy. *sc*: John Mantley. *Guest star*: Barbara Barrie (*Elizabeth Harmon*).

201 (30 April) *The Calf Women*
D: Tony Leader. *sc*: Louis Vittes and Buckley Angell. *Guest star*: Julie Harris (*Emma Teall*).

202 (7 May) *The Spanish Camp*
D: Harmon Jones. *sc*: John Dunkel. *Guest star*: John Ireland (*Dr Joseph Merritt*).

203 (14 May) *El Hombre Bravo*
D: Philip Leacock. *sc*: Herman Groves. *Guest star*: Frank Silvera (*Pajarito*).

204 (21 May) *The Gray Rock Hotel*
D: Stuart Rosenberg. *sc*: Jack Curtis. *Guest star*: Lola Albright (*Lottie*).

Season 1965 – 66

205 (14 Sept) *Encounter at Boot Hill*
D: Sutton Roley. *sc*: Rony Spinner. *Guest star*: Jeff Corey (*Morgan Kane*).

206 (21 Sept) *Ride A Crooked Mile*
D: Justus Addiss. *sc*: N.B. Stone, Jr. *Guest star*: John Drew Barrymore (*Danny Hawks*).

207 (28 Sept) *Six Weeks to Bent Fork*
D: Thomas Carr. *sc*: Mort. R. Lewis. *Guest star*: James Gregory (*Lash Whitcomb*).

208 (5 Oct) *Walk Into Terror*
D: Thomas Carr. *sc*: Joanna Thompson and Jerry Adelman. *Guest star*: Claude Akins (*Jerry Boggs*).

209 (12 Oct) *Escort to Doom*
D: Alan Crosland, Jr. *sc*: Walter Black. *Guest star*: Rip Torn (*Jacob Yellow-Sun*).

210 (19 Oct) *Hostage for Hanging*
D: Herman Hoffman. *sc*: Walter Black. *Guest star*: Mercedes McCambridge (*Ma Gufler*).

211 (26 Oct) *The Vasquez Woman*
D: Bernard McEveety. *sc*: Boris Ingster. *Guest star*: Cesar Romero (*Col. Vasquez*).

212 (2 Nov) *Clash at Broken Gulf*
D: Chuck Haas. *sc*: Louis Vittes. *Guest star*: Nancy Gates (*Cassie Webster*).

213 (9 Nov) *The Pursuit*
D: Justus Addiss. *sc*: John Dunkel. *Guest star*: Ralph Bellamy (*Marshal Hanson Dickson*).

214 (16 Nov) *Duel at Daybreak*
D: Sutton Roley. *sc*: Bob Bloomfield. *Guest star*: Charles Bronson (*Del Lingman*).

215 (23 Nov) *Brush War at Buford*
D: Thomas Carr. *sc*: Mort B. Lewis. *Guest star*: Robert Middleton (*Duke Aberdeen*).

216 (30 Nov) *The Testing Post*
D: Gerd Oswald. *sc*: John and Ward Hawkins. *Guest star*: Dick Foran (*Major Taggart*).

217 (7 Dec) *Crossing at White Feather*
D: Richard Whorf. *sc*: Robert Bloomfield. *Guest star*: Albert Dekker (*Jonas Bolt*).

Clint Eastwood

III. ITALIAN FILMS, 1964 – 7

'To keep the mystique of the character, it was important not to have the guy say too much.'

Per un Pugno Di Dollari
(A Fistful of Dollars)
Italy/West Germany/Spain, 1964

Director: Bob Robertson (Sergio Leone)

Dist: United Artists. *p.c.*: Jolly Film (Rome)/Constantin (Munich)/Ocean (Madrid). *p*. Harry Colombo, George Papi [i.e. Arrigo Colombo, Giorgio Papi]. *p. manager*: Franco Palaggi, Günter Raguse, *sc*: Sergio Leone, Duccio Tessari, *English version*: Mark Lovell, *ph*: Jack Dalmas [Massimo Dallamano]. Techniscope. *col*: Technicolor. *ed*: Bob Quintle [Roberto Cinquini]. *a.d*: Charles Simons [Caro Simi]. *m*: Dan Savio [Ennio Morricone]. *titles*: Luigi Lardani. *sd*: Elio Pacella, Edy Simson. *l.p.*: Clint Eastwood (*The Stranger*), John Welles [Gian Maria Volonté] (*Ramon Rojo*), Marianne Koch (*Marisol*), Pepe Calvo (*Silvanito*), Wolfgang Lukschy (*John Baxter*), Sieghardt Rupp (*Esteban Rojo*), Antonio Prieto (*Benito Rojo*), Margherita Lozano (*Consuela Baxter*), Daniel Martin (*Julian*), Carol Brown [Bruno Carotenuto] (*Antonio Baxter*), Benny Reeves [Benito Stefanelli] (*Rubio*), Richard Stuvvesant (*Chico*), Josef Egger (*Piripero*), Mario Brega. 100 mins. *Dubbed*.

Per Qualche Dollaro in Più
(For a Few Dollars More)
Italy/Spain/West Germany, 1965

Director: Sergio Leone

Dist: United Artists, *p.c.*: P.E.A. (Rome)/Arturo Gonzales (Madrid)/Constantin Film (Munich). *p*: Alberto Grimaldi. *p. manager*: Ottavio Oppo. *assist d*: Tonino Valerii. *sc*: Sergio Leone, Luciano Vincenzoni. *story*: Fulvio Morsella, Sergio Leone. *ph*: Massimo Dallamano. Techniscope. *col*: Technicolor. *ed*: Alabiso Serralonga, Giorgio Serralonga. *a.d*: Carlo Simi. *m*: Ennio Morricone. *m.d.*: Bruno Nicolai. *cost*: Carlo Simi. *sd*: Oscar De Arcangelis. *l.p.*: Clint Eastwood (*The Stranger*), Lee Van Cleef (*Colonel Mortimer*), Gian Maria Volonté (*Indio*), Klaus Kinski (*Hunchback*), Mara Krup (*Hotel Manager's Wife*), Josef Egger (*Old Man over Railway*), Rosemary Dexter (*Colonel's Sister*), Mario Brega, Aldo Sambrell, Luigi Pistilli, Benito Stefanelli, Panos Papadopoulos, Roberto Camardiel, Luis Rodriguez, Diana Rabito, Giovanni Tarallo, Mario Meniconi, Lorenzo Robledo. 130 mins. *Dubbed*.

Il, Bruno, il Brutto, il Cattivo
(The Good, the Bad and the Ugly)
Italy, 1966   Director: Sergio Leone

Dist: United Artists. *p.c.*: Produzioni Europee Associate (Rome). *p*: Alberto Grimaldi. *p.sup*: Carlos Bartolini, Federico Tofi. *p. manager*: Fernando Cinquini. *assistant d*: Giancarlo Santi. *sc*: Age-Scarpelli, Luciano Vincenzoni, Sergio Leone. *English adapt*: Mickey Knox. *ph*: Tonino Delli Colli, Techniscope. *col*: Technicolor. *ed*: Nino Baragli, Eugenio Alabiso. *a.d. cost*: Carlo Simi. *sp. effects*: Eros Bacciucchi. *m*: Ennio Morricone. *m.d*: Bruno Nicolai. *titles*: Ardani. *l.p.*: Clint Eastwood (*Joe*), Eli Wallach (*Tuco*), Lee Van Cleef (*Setenza*), Aldo Giuffrè, Mario Brega, Luigi Pistilli, Rada Rassimov, Enzo Petito, Claudio Scarchelli, Livio Lorenzon, Antonio Castale, Sando Scarchelli, Benito Stefanelli, Chelo Alonso, Silvana Bacci, Al Mulock, Antonio Casas, Aldo Sambrel. 180 mins. *Dubbed.*

Le Streghe
(The Witches)
Segment *Una Sera Come Le Altre (A Night Like Any Other)*
Italy/France, 1966   Directors: Luchino Visconti (Pt 1)
                        Mauro Bolognini (Pt 2), Piero Paolo Pasolini (Pt 3)
                        Franco Rossi (Pt 4) and Vittorio De Sica (Pt 5)

Dist: United Artists. *p.c.*: Dino de Laurentiis (Rome)/Les Productions Artistes Associes (Paris). *p*: Dino de Laurentiis. *sc*: (for Eastwood segment): Cesare Zavattini, Fabio Carpi and Enzio Muzil. *ph*: Giuseppe Rotunno and Giuseppe Maccari. *col*: Technicolor. *m*: Pierro Piccone and Ennio Morricone. Eastwood segment, the fifth *dir*: Vittorio De Sica. *l.p.*: Silvano Mangano (Giovanna), Clint Eastwood (Mario, Mangano's husband), Armando Bottin, Gianno Gori, Paolo Gozina, Angelo Santi, Valentino Macchi. 110 mins; Eastwood segment 19 mins.

IV. BRINGING IT ALL BACK HOME, 1967–71

'I do all the stuff John Wayne would never do ...'

Hang 'em High

USA, 1967   Director: Ted Post

Dist: United Artists. *p.c.*: Leonard Freeman Productions/Malpaso. *p*: Leonard Freeman. *assoc. p*: Robert Stampler. *p. manager*: Frank Mayer, *ass. d*: Richard Bennett, Don Klune, *sc*: Leonard Freeman, Mel Goldberg. *ph*: Leonard South, Richard Kline, *col*: De Luxe. *ed*: Gene Fowler, Jnr. *a.d*: John B. Goodman. *set dec.*: Arthur Krams. *m*: Dominic Frontiere. *sd*: Franklin Milton, Al Strasser, Jnr. *l.p.*: Clint Eastwood (Jed Cooper), Inger Stevens (*Rachel*), Ed Begley (*Captain Wilson*), Pat Hingle (*Judge Adam Fenton*), Arlene Golonka (*Jennifer*), James MacArthur (*Priest*), Charles McGraw, L.Q. Jones, Jack Ging, James Westerfield, Alan Hale, Jnr., Dennis Hopper, Ben Johnson, Ruth White, Bruce Dern, Michael O'Sullivan, Joseph Sirola, Bob Steele, Bert Freed, Russell Thorsen, Ned Romero, Jonathan Lippe, Rick Gates, Bruce Scott, Richard Guison, Todd Andrews, Mark Lenard, Roy Glenn. 114 mins.

Coogan's Bluff

USA, 1968   Director: Don Siegel

P.c.: Universal. *exec.p*: Richard E. Lyons *p*: Don Siegel. *assoc.p*: Irving Leonard. *p. manager*: Robert E. Larson. *ass. d*: Joe Cavalier. *sc*: Herman Miller, Dean Riesner, Howard Rodman. *story*: Herman Miller. *ph*: Bud Thackery. *col*: Technicolor. *ed*: Sam E. Waxman. *a.d*: Alexander Golitzen, Robert C. MacKichan. *set dec.*: John McCarthy, John Austin. *m*: Lalo Schifrin. *m.sup*: Stanley Wilson. *cost*: Helen Colvig. *sd*: Waldon O. Watson, Lyle Cain, Jack Bolger. *l.p.*: Clint Eastwood (*Walt Coogan*), Lee J. Cobb (*McElroy*), Susan Clark (*Julie*), Tisha Sterling (*Linny Raven*), Don Stroud (*Ringerman*), Betty Field (*Mrs Ringerman*), Tom Tully (*Sheriff McCrea*), Melodie Johnson (*Millie*), James Edwards (*Jackson*), Rudy Diaz (*Running Bear*), David F. Doyle (*Pushie*), Louis Zorich (*Taxi Driver*), Meg Myles (*Big Red*), Marjorie Bennett (*Mrs Fowler*), Seymour Cassel (*Young Hood*), John Coe (*Bellboy*), Skip Battyn (*Omega*), Albert Popwell (*Wonderful Digby*), Conrad Bain (*Madison Avenue Man*), James Gavin (*Ferguson*), Albert Henderson (*Desk Sergeant*), James McCallion (*Room Clerk*), Syl Lamont (*Manager*), Jess Osuna (*Prison Hospital Guard*), Jerry Summers (*Good Eyes*), Antonia Rey (*Mrs Amador*), Marya Henriques (*Go-Go Dancer*). 94 mins.

Where Eagles Dare

Great Britain, 1968   **Director: Brian G. Hutton**

Dist: MGM. *p.c.*: Winkast Films. A Jerry Gershwin/Elliot Kastner Picture. *p*: Elliot Kastner. *p. sup*: Ted Lloyd. *2nd Unit p.manager*: Tom Sachs. *2nd Unit d*: Yakima Cannutt. *assistant d*: Colin Brewer. *2nd Unit assistant d*: Anthony Wayne. *sc*: Alistair MacLean, based on his own novel. *ph*: Arthur Ibbetson. Panavision 70. *col*: Metrocolor. *2nd Unit ph*: H.A.R. Thomson. *sp. ph. effects*: Tom Howard. *ed*: John Jympson. *a.d*: Peter Mullins. *set dec*: Arthur Taksen. *sp. effects*: Richard Parker, Fred Hellenburgh. *m/m.d*: Ron Goodwin. *sd*: Jonathan Bates. *sd. rec*: John Bramall. *l.p.*: Richard Burton (*John Smith*), Clint Eastwood (*Lt. Morris Schaffer*), Mary Ure (*Mary Ellison*), Patrick Wymark (*Colonel Turner*), Michael Hordern (*Vice-Admiral Rolland*), Donald Houston (*Christiansen*), Peter Barkworth (*Berkeley*), Robert Beatty (*Cartwright Jones*), William Squire (*Thomas*), Derren Nesbitt (*Major von Hapen*), Anton Diffring (*Colonel Kramer*), Brook Williams (*Sgt. Harrod*), Neil McCarthy (*MacPherson*), Vincent Ball (*Carpenter*), Ferdy Mayne (*Reichsmarschal Rosemeyer*), Ingrid Pitt (*Heidi*), Victor Beaumont (*Colonel Weissner*), Richard Beale (*Telephone Orderly*), Ivor Dean (*German Officer*), Lyn Kennington (*German Woman*), Nigel Lambert (*Young German Soldier*), Michael Rooney (*Radio Operator*), Ernst Walder (*Airport Control Officer*). 155 mins.

Paint Your Wagon

USA, 1969   **Director: Joshua Logan**

Dist: Paramount. *p.c.*: Paramount/Alan Jay Lerner Prods. *p*: Alan Jay Lerner. *assoc.p*: Tom Shaw. *p.manager*: Carl Beringer, Fred Lemoine. *2nd Unit d*: Tom Shaw, Fred Lemoine, *assistant d*: Jack Roe. *sc*: Paddy Chayefsky. Based on the musical play, book and lyrics by Alan Jay Lerner, music by Frederick Loewe. *ph*: William A. Fraker. Panavision 70. *col*: Technicolor. *2nd Unit ph*: Loyal Griggs. *aerial ph*: Nelson Tyler. *ed*: Robert Jones. *production designer*: John Truscott. *a.d*: Carl Braunger. *set dec.*: James I. Berkey. *sp.effects*: Maurice Ayers, Larry Hampton. *m*: Frederick Loewe, *addit.m*: André Previn. *m. arrangements/m.d*: Nelson Riddle. *choral arrangements*: Joseph J. Lilley, *choral m.d*: Roger Wagner. *songs*: "I'm On My Way", "I Still See Elisa", "The First Thing You Know", "Hand Me Down That Can o' Beans", "They Call the Wind Maria", "A Million Miles Away Behind the Door", "There's a Coach Comin' In", "Whoop-Ti-Ay!", "I Talk to the Trees", "The Gospel of No Name City", "Best Things", "Wand'rin' star", "Gold

Fever" by Lerner and Loewe, Lerner and Previn. *cost*: John Truscott. *choreo*: Jack Baker. *titles*: David Stone Martin. *sd*: William Randall, *stereophonic re-rec.*: Fred Hynes. *l.p.*: Lee Marvin (*Ben Rumson*), Clint Eastwood (*Pardner*), Jean Seberg (*Elizabeth*), Harve Presnell (*Rotten Luck Willie*), Ray Walston (*Mad Jack Duncan*), Tom Ligon (*Horton Fenty*), Alan Dexter (*Parson*), William O'Connell (*Horace Tabor*), Ben Baker (*Haywood Holbrook*), Alan Baxter (*Mr Fenty*), Paula Trueman (*Mrs Fenty*), Robert Easton (*Atwell*), Geoffrey Norman (*Foster*), H.B. Haggerty (*Steve Bull*), Terry Jenkins (*Joe Mooney*), Karl Bruck (*Schermerhorn*), John Mitchum (*Jacob Woodling*), Sue Casey (*Sarah Woodling*), Eddie Little Sky (*Indian*), Harvey Parry (*Higgins*), H.W. Gim (*Wong*), William Mims (*Frock-coated Man*), Roy Jenson (*Hennessey*), Pat Hawley (*Clendennon*), and the Nitty Gritty Dirt Band. 164 mins.

Two Mules for Sister Sara

USA, 1969   **Director: Don Siegel**

P.c.: Universal/Malpaso. *p*: Martin Rackin, Carroll Case. *p. manager*: William Davidson, Alfonso Sanchez Tello. *2nd Unit d*: Joe Cavalier, René Cardona. *assistant d*: Joe Cavalier, Manuel Muñoz. *sc*: Albert Maltz. *story*: Budd Boetticher. *ph*: Gabriel Figueroa. *2nd Unit ph*: Gabriel Torres. Panavision. *col*: Technicolor. *ed*: Robert F. Shugrue, Juan José Marino. *a.d*: José Rodriguez Granada. *set dec*: Pablo Galvan. *sp. effects*: Frank Brendel, Leon Ortega. *m*: Ennio Morricone. *m.sup*: Stanley Wilson. *cost*: Helen Colvig, Carlos Chavez. *sd*: Waldon O. Watson, Jesus Gonzalez Gancy, Ronald Pierce. *l.p.*: Shirley MacLaine (*Sara*), Clint Eastwood (*Hogan*), Manolo Fabregas (*Colonel Beltran*), Alberto Morin (*General LeClaire*), Armando Silvestre (*1st American*), John Kelly (*2nd American*), Enrique Lucero (*3rd American*), David Estuardo (*Juan*), Ada Carrasco (*Juan's Mother*), Poncho Cordoba (*Juan's Father*), José Chavez (*Horacio*). 116 mins.

Kelly's Heroes

USA/Yugoslavia, 1970   **Director: Brian G. Hutton**

Dist: MGM-EMI. *p.c.*: The Warriors Company (Hollywood)/Avala Films (Belgrade). A Katzka-Loeb Production. *p*: Gabriel Katzka, Sidney Beckerman *assoc.p*: Irvin Leonard. *p.sup*: Basil Somner. *p.manager*: Terry Lens. *Yugoslav p. manager*: Milenko Stankovic. *2nd Unit d*: Andrew Marton. *assistant d*: John C. Chulay. *Yugoslav assistant d*: Stevo Petrovic. *sc*: Troy Kennedy Martin. *ph*: Gabriel Figueroa. Panavision. *col*: Metrocolor. *2nd*

Unit ph: H.A.R. Thomson. *ed*: John Jympson. *a.d*: Jonathan Barry. *set dec*: Mike Ford. *sp. effects*: Karli Baumgartner. *m/m.d*: Lalo Schifrin. *songs*: "Burning Bridges" by Lalo Schifrin, Mike Curb, sung by The Mike Curb Congregation; "Si tu me dis" by Lalo Schifrin, Gene Lees, sung by Monique Aldebert; "Sunshine", sung by Hank Williams, Jnr. *sd. ed*: Jonathan Bates. *sd. rec*: Cyril Swern, Harry W. Tetrick. *technical adviser*: Major Alexander Gerry. *l.p.*: Clint Eastwood (*Kelly*). Telly Savalas (*Big Joe*), Don Rickles (*Crapgame*), Donald Sutherland (*Oddball*), Carroll O'Connor (*Gen. Colt*), Hal Buckley (*Maitland*), Stuart Margolin (*Little Joe*), Fred Pearlman (*Mitchell*), Tom Troupe (*Job*), Gavin MacLeod (*Moriarty*), Gene Collins (*Babra*), Perry Lopez (*Petchuko*), Dick Balduzzi (*Fisher*), Harry Stanton (*Willard*), Dick Davalos (*Gutkowski*), Len Lesser (*Bellamy*), Jeff Morris (*Cowboy*), Michael Clark (*Grace*), George Fargo (*Penn*), Dee Pollock (*Jonesy*), Shepherd Sanders (*Marvin*), Frank J. Garlotta (*1st Tank Commander*), Sandy Kevin (*2nd Tank Commander*), Phil Adams (*3rd Tank Commander*), Read Morgan (*ADC Driver*), David Hurst (*Col. Dankhopf*), Robert McNamara (*Roach*), James McHale (*Guest*), Ross Elliott (*Booker*), Tom Signorelli (*Bonsor*), George Savalas (*Mulligan*), John G. Heller (*German Lieutenant*), Karl Otto Alberty (*German Tank Commander*), Hugo de Vernier (*French Mayor*), Harry Goines (*Supply Sergeant*), David Gross (*German Captain*), Donald Waugh (*Roamer*), Vincent Maracecchi (*Old Man in Town*). 143 mins.

The Beguiled

USA, 1970   **Director: Don Siegel**

P.c.: Universal/Malpaso. A Jennings Lang Production. *exec.p*: Julian Blaustein. *p*: Don Siegel. *a.p*: Claude Travers. *p. manager/2nd Unit d*: Joe Cavalier. *asst.d*: Burt Astor. *sc*: John B. Sherry, Grimes Grice. Based on the novel by Thomas Cullinan. *ph*: Bruce Surtees. *col*: Technicolor. *ed*: Carl Pingitore. *p.des*: Ted Haworth. *a.d*: Alex Golitzen. *set dec*: John Austin. *m*: Lalo Schifrin. *cos*: Helen Colvig. *sd*: Waldon O. Watson, John Mack. *l.p.*: Clint Eastwood (*John McBurney*), Geraldine Page (*Martha Farnsworth*), Elizabeth Hartman (*Edwina Dabney*), Jo Anne Harris (*Carol*), Darleen Carr (*Doris*), Mae Mercer (*Hallie*), Pamelyn Ferdin (*Amy*), Melody Thomas (*Abigail*), Peggy Drier (*Lizzie*), Pattye Mattick (*Janie*). 105 mins.

Clint Eastwood

V. THE ACTOR – DIRECTOR 1971 –

'In the past, accolades have been bestowed unfairly, primarily on the motion picture directors who have spent the most time and money on their pictures.'

Play Misty for Me

USA, 1971   Director: Clint Eastwood

P.c.: Universal/Malpaso. A Jennings Lang Presentation. *p*. Robert Daley. *assoc.p/p. manager/asst. d*: Bob Larson. *sc*: Jo Heims, Dean Riesner. *story*: Jo Heims. *ph*: Bruce Surtees. *col*: Technicolor. *ed*: Carl Pingitore. *a.d*: Alexander Golitzen. *set dec*: Ralph Hurst. *m*: Dee Barton. *songs*: "Misty" written and performed by Erroll Garner; "The First Time Ever I Saw Your Face" sung by Roberta Flack. *titles*: Universal Title. *sd. rec*: Waldon O. Watson, Robert Martin, Robert L. Hoyt. *l.p.*: Clint Eastwood (*Dave Garland*), Jessica Walter (*Evelyn Draper*), Donna Mills (*Tobie Williams*), John Larch (*Sgt. McCallum*), Jack Ging (*Frank Dewan*), Irene Hervey (*Madge Brenner*), James McEachin (*Al Monte*), Clarice Taylor (*Birdie*), Donald Siegel (*Murphy*), Duke Everts (*Jay Jay*), George Fargo (*Man*), Mervin W. Frates (*Locksmith*), Tim Frawley (*Deputy Sheriff*), Otis Kadani (*Policeman*), Brit Lind (*Angelica*), Paul E. Lippman (*2nd Man*), Jack Kosslyn (*Cab Driver*), Ginna Patterson (*Madelyn*), Malcolm Moran (*Man in Window*), the Johnny Otis Show and the Cannonball Adderly Quintet (*Themselves*). 102 mins.

Dirty Harry

USA, 1971   Director: Don Siegel

Dist: Columbia-Warner. *p.c.*: Warner Bros./Malpaso. *exec.p*: Robert Daley. *p*: Don Siegel. *assoc.p*: Carl Pingitore. *p. manager*: Jim Henderling. *asst.d*: Robert Rubin. *sc*: Harry Julian Fink, Rita M. Fink, Dean Riesner. *story*: Harry Julian Fink, Rita M. Fink, *ph*: Bruce Surtees. Panavision. *col*: Technicolor. *ed*: Carl Pingitore. *a.d*: Dale Hennesy. *set dec*: Robert DeVestel. *m*: Lalo Schifrin. *sd*: William Randall. *l.p.*: Clint Eastwood (*Harry Callahan*), Harry Guardino (*Lt. Bressler*), Reni Santoni (*Chico*), John Vernon (*The Mayor*), Andy Robinson (*Scorpio*), John Larch (*Chief*), John Mitchum (*De Georgio*), Mae Mercer (*Mrs Russell*), Lyn Edgington (*Norma*), Ruth Kobart (*Bus Driver*), Woodrow Parfrey (*Mr Jaffe*), Josef Sommer (*Rothko*), William Paterson (*Bannerman*), James Nolan (*Liquor Proprietor*), Maurice S. Argent (*Sid Kleinman*), Jo de Winter (*Miss Willis*), Craig G. Kelly (*Sgt. Reineke*). 101 mins.

Joe Kidd

USA, 1972   **Director: John Sturges**

P.c.: Universal/Malpaso. *exec.p*: Robert Daley. *p*: Sidney Beckerman. *p.manager*: Ernest Wehmeyer. *asst.d*: Jim Fargo. *sc*: Elmore Leonard. *ph*: Bruce Surtees. Panavision. *col*: Technicolor. *ed*: Ferris Webster. *a.d*: Alexander Golitzen, Henry Bumstead. *set dec*: Charles S. Thompson. *m*: Lalo Schifrin. *titles*: Universal Title. *sd.rec*: Waldon O. Watson, James R. Alexander. *stunt co-ordinator*: Buddy van Horn. *l.p.*: Clint Eastwood (*Joe Kidd*), Robert Duvall (*Frank Harlan*), John Saxon (*Luis Chama*), Don Stroud (*Lamarr*), Stella Garcia (*Helen Sanchez*), James Wainwright (*Mango*), Paul Koslo (*Roy*), Gregory Walcott (*Mitchell*), Dick Van Patten (*Hotel Manager*), Lynne Marta (*Elma*), John Carter (*Judge*), Pepe Hern (*Priest*), Joaquin Martinez (*Manolo*), Ron Soble (*Ramon*), Pepe Callahan (*Naco*), Clint Ritchie (*Calvin*), Gil Barreto (*Emilio*), Ed Deemer (*Bartender*), Maria Val (*Vita*), Chuck Hayward (*Eljay*), Michael R. Horst (*Deputy*). 87 mins.

High Plains Drifter

USA, 1972   **Director: Clint Eastwood**

Dist: CIC. *p.c.*: Malpaso/Universal. *exec.p*: Jennings Lang. *p*: Robert Daley. *p.manager*: Ernest B. Wehmeyer. *asst.d*: Jim Fargo. *sc*: Ernest Tidyman. *ph*: Bruce Surtees. Panavision. *col*: Technicolor. *ed*: Ferris Webster. *a.d*: Henry Bumstead. *set dec*: George Milo. *m*: Dee Barton. *sd*: James R. Alexander. *stunt co-ordinator*: Buddy Van Horn. *l.p.*: Clint Eastwood (*The Stranger*), Verna Bloom (*Sarah Belding*), Mariana Hill (*Callie Travers*), Mitchell Ryan (*Dave Drake*), Jack Ging (*Morgan Allen*), Stefan Gierasch (*Mayor Jason Hobart*), Ted Hartley (*Lewis Belding*), Billy Curtis (*Mordecai*), Geoffrey Lewis (*Stacy Bridges*), Scott Walker (*Bill Borders*), Walter Barnes (*Sheriff Sam Shaw*), Paul Brinegar (*Lutie Naylor*), Richard Bull (*Asa Godwin*), Robert Donner (*Preacher*), John Hillerman (*Bootmaker*), Anthony James (*Cole Carlin*), William O'Connell (*Barber*), John Quade (*Jake Ross*), Jane Aull (*Townswoman*), Dan Vadis (*Dan Carlin*), Reid Cruickshanks (*Gunsmith*), James Gosa (*Tommy Morris*), Jack Kosslyn (*Saddlemaker*), Russ McCubbin (*Fred Short*), Belle Mitchell (*Mrs Lake*), John Mitchum (*Warden*), Carl C. Pitti (*Teamster*), Chuck Waters (*Stableman*), Buddy Van Horn (*Marshal Jim Duncan*). 105 mins.

Clint Eastwood

Breezy

USA, 1973   Director: Clint Eastwood

Dist: CIC. *p.c*: Universal/Malpaso Company. *exec.p*: Jennings Lang. *p*: Robert Daley. *assoc.p*: Jo Heims. *p.manager*: Donald Roberts. *asst.d*: Jim Fargo, Tom Joyner. *sc*: Jo Heims. *ph*: Frank Stanley. *col*: Technicolor. *ed*: Ferris Webster. *a.d*: Alexander Golitzen. *set dec*: James Payne. *m*: Michel Legrand. *song*: 'Breeezy's Song" by Michel Legrand, Marilyn Bergman, Alan Bergman. *sung by*: Shelby Flint. *sd*: James R. Alexander. *l.p.*: William Holden (*Frank Harmon*), Kay Lenz (*Breezy*), Roger C. Carmel (*Bob Henderson*), Marj Dusay (*Betty Tobin*), Joan Hotchkis (*Paula Harmon*), Jamie Smith Jackson (*Marcy*), Norman Bartold (*Man in Car*), Lynn Borden (*Overnight Date*), Shelley Morrison (*Nancy Henderson*), Dennis Olivieri (*Bruno*), Eugene Peterson (*Charlie*), Lew Brown (*Police Officer*), Richard Bull (*Doctor*), Johnnie Collins III (*Norman*), Don Diamond (*Maitre D'*), Scott Holden (*Veterinarian*), Sandy Kenyon (*Real Estate Agent*), Jack Kosslyn (*Driver*), Mary Munday (*Waitress*), Frances Stevenson (*Saleswoman*), Buck Young (*Paula's Escort*), Priscilla Morrill (*Dress Customer*). 107 mins.

Magnum Force

USA, 1973   Director: Ted Post

Dist: Columbia-Warner. *p.c*: Malpaso. *p*: Robert Daley. *p. manager*: John G. Wilson. *2nd Unit d*: Buddy Van Horn. *asst. d*: Wes McAfee. *sc*: John Milius, Michael Cimino. *story*: John Milius. Based on the character created by Harry Julian Fink, Rita M. Fink. *ph*: Frank Stanley. Panavision. *col*: Technicolor. *ed*: Ferris Webster. *a.d*: Jack Collis. *set dec*: John Lamphear. *m*: Lalo Schifrin. *sd*: James Alexander. *l.p.*: Clint Eastwood (*Inspector Harry Callahan*), Hal Holbrook (*Lieutenant Neil Briggs*), Mitchell Ryan (*Charlie McCoy*), David Soul (*Ben Davis*), Felton Perry (*Early Smith*), Robert Urich (*John Grimes*), Kip Niven (*Red Astrachan*), Tim Matheson (*Phil Sweet*), Christine White (*Carol McCoy*), Richard Devon (*Carmine Ricca*), Tony Giorgio (*Frank Palancio*), Albert Popwell (*Pimp*), John Mitchum (*DiGorgio*), Margaret Avery (*Prostitute*), Jack Kosslyn (*Walter*), Clifford A. Pellow (*Lou Guzman*), Adele Yoshioka (*Sunny*), Maurice Argent (*Nat Weinstein*), Bob March (*Estabrook*), Bob McClurg (*Cab Driver*), Russ Moro (*Ricca's Driver*). 122 mins.

Thunderbolt and Lightfoot

USA, 1974 Director: Michael Cimino

Dist: United Artists. *p.c.*: Malpaso Company. *p*: Robert Daley. *p.manager*:
Abner Singer. *asst.d*: Charles Okun, David Hamburger, Arnie Schmitt. *sc*:
Michael Cimino. *ph*: Frank Stanley. Panavision. *col*: DeLuxe. *ed*: Ferris
Webster. *a.d*: Tambi Larsen. *set dec*: James Berkey. *sp.effects*: Sass Bedig.
m: Dee Barton. *song*: "Where Do I Go from Here?" by and sung by Paul
Williams. *titles:* Wayne Fitzgerald. *sd.ed*: Keith Stafford. *sd.rec*: Bert
Hallberg, Norman Webster. *sd.re-rec*: Richard Portman. *stunt co-ordinator*:
Buddy Van Horn. *special action sequences*: Carey Loftin. *l.p.*: Clint
Eastwood (*John "Thunderbolt" Doherty*), Jeff Bridges (*Lightfoot*), George
Kennedy (*Red Leary*), Geoffrey Lewis (*Goody*), Catherine Bach (*Melody*),
Gary Busey (*Curly*), Jack Dodson (*Vault Manager*), Gene Elman and Lila
Teigh (*Tourists*), Burton Gilliam (*Welder*), Roy Jenson (*Dunlop*), Claudia
Lennear (*Secretary*), Bill McKinney (*Crazy Driver*), Vic Tayback (*Mario*),
Dub Taylor (*Gas Station Attendant*), Gregory Walcot (*Used Car Salesman*),
Erica Hagen (*Waitress*), Virginia Baker and Stuart Nisbet (*Couple at Gas
Station*), Alvin Childress (*Janitor*), Irene K. Cooper (*Cashier*), Cliff Emmich
(*Fat Man*), June Fairchild (*Gloria*), Ted Foulkes (*Little Boy*), Karen Lamm
(*Girl on Motorcycle*), Leslie Oliver and Mark Montgomery (*Teenagers*),
Luanne Roberts (*Suburban Housewife*), Tito Vandis (*Counterman*). 115
mins.

The Eiger Sanction

USA, 1975 Director: Clint Eastwood

Dist: CIC. *p.c.*: Universal/Malpaso Company. A Jennings Lang presentation.
exec.p: Richard D. Zanuck, David Brown. *p*: Robert Daley. *p.managers*: Fred
Simpson (US), Wallace Worsley (Switzerland). *asst.d*: Jim Fargo, (US) Craig
Hughes, (Switzerland) Victor Tourjansky. *sc*: Warren B. Murphy, Hal Dresner,
Rod Whitaker. Based on the novel by Trevanian. *ph*: Frank Stanley. Panavision.
col: Technicolor. *mountain sequences ph*: John Cleare, Jeff Schoolfield, Peter
Pilafian, Pete White. *ed*: Ferris Webster. *a.d*: George Webb (US), Aurelio
Crugnola (Switzerland). *set dec*: John Dwyer. *sp.effects*: Ben McMahan. *m*:
John Williams. *sd.rec*: James R. Alexander. *sd.re-rec*: Robert Hoyt. *climbing
adviser*: Mike Hoover. *climbers*: Norman Dyhrenfurth, Dougal Haston, David
Knowles, Bev Clark, Martin Boysen, Guy Neithardt, Charles Scott, Hamish
McInnes. *l.p.*: Clint Eastwood (*Jonathan Hemlock*), George Kennedy (*Ben
Bowman*), Vonetta McGee (*Jemima Brown*), Jack Cassidy (*Miles McHough*),

Heidi Bruhl (*Anna Montaigne*), Thayer David (*Dragon*), Reiner Schoene (*Freytag*), Michael Grimm (*Meyer*), Jean-Pierre Bernard (*Montaigne*), Brenda Venus (*George*), Gregory Walcott (*Pope*), Candice Rialson (*Art Student*), Elaine Shore (*Miss Cerberus*), Dan Howard (*Dewayne*), Jack Rosslyn (*Reporter*), Walter Kraus (*Kruger*), Frank Redmond (*Wormwood*), Siegfried Wallach (*Hotel Manager*), Susan Morgan (*Buns*), Jack Frey (*Cab Driver*). 125 mins.

The Outlaw Josey Wales

USA, 1976   Director: Clint Eastwood

Dist: Columbia-Warner. *p.c.*: Malpaso. For Warner Bros. *p*. Robert Daley. *assoc.p*: Jim Fargo, John G. Wilson. *p. manager*: John G. Wilson. *asst.d*: Jim Fargo, Win Phelps, Alan Brimfield. *sc*: Phil Kaufman, Sonia Chernus. Based on the novel *Gone to Texas* by Forrest Carter. *ph*: Bruce Surtees. Panavision. *col*: DeLuxe. *ed*: Ferris Webster. *p.designer*: Tambi Larsen. *set.dec*: Chuck Pierce. *sp.effects*: Robert MacDonald, Paul Pollard. *m*: Jerry Fielding. *titles/optical effects*: Pacific Title. *sd.ed*: Keith Stafford. *sd.rec*: Bert Hallberg. *sd.re-rec*: Tex Rudloff. *stunt co-ordinator*: Walter Scott. *wrangler*: Rudy Ugland. *l.p.*: Clint Eastwood (*Josey Wales*), Chief Dan George (*Lone Watie*), Sondra Locke (*Laura Lee*), Bill McKinney (*Terrill*), John Vernon (*Fletcher*), Paula Trueman (*Grandma Sarah*), Sam Bottoms (*Jamie*), Geraldine Keams (*Little Moonlight*), Woodrow Parfrey (*Carpetbagger*), Joyce Jameson (*Rose*), Sheb Wooley (*Travis Cobb*), Royal Dano (*Ten Spot*), Matt Clarke (*Kelly*), John Verros (*Chato*), Will Sampson (*Ten Bears*), William O'Connell (*Sim Carstairs*), John Quade (*Comanchero Leader*), Frank Schofield (*Senator Land*), Buck Kartalian (*Shopkeeper*), Len Lesser (*Abe*), Douglas McGrath (*Lige*), John Russell (*Bloody Bill Anderson*), Charles Tyner (*Zukie Limmer*), Bruce M. Fischer (*Yoke*), John Mitchum (*Al*), John Chandler (*1st Bounty Hunter*), Tom Roy Lowe (*2nd Bounty Hunter*), Clay Tanner (*1st Texas Ranger*), Madeline T. Holmes (*Grannie Hawkins*), Erik Holland (*Union Army Sergeant*), Cissy Wellman (*Josey's wife*), Faye Hamblin (*Grandpa*), Danny Green (*Lemuel*). 134 mins.

The Enforcer

USA, 1976   Director: James Fargo

Dist: Columbia-Warner. *p.c.*: Malpaso. For Warner Bros. *p*: Robert Daley, *p.manager*: John G. Wilson *asst.d*: Joe Cavalier, Joe Florence, Billy Ray Smith. *sc*: Stirling Silliphant, Dean Reisner, *story*: Gail Morgan Hickman, S.W. Schurr. Based on characters created by Harry Julian Fink, R.M. Fink.

ph: Charles W. Short. Panavision. *col*: DeLuxe; prints by Technicolor. *ed*: Ferris Webster, Joel Cox *a.d*: Allen E. Smith. *set dec*: Ira Bates. *sp.effects*: Joe Unsinn. *m*: Jerry Fielding. *titles*: Pacific Title. *sd.rec*: Bert Hallberg. *sd.re rec*: Les Fresholtz. *sd.effects ed*: Keith Stafford. *stunt co-ordinator*: Wayne Van Horn *l.p.*: Clint Eastwood (*Inspector Harry Callahan*), Harry Guardino (*Lt. Bressler*), Bradford Dillman (*Capt. McKay*), John Mitchum (*DiGeorgio*), DeVeren Brookwalter (*Bobby Maxwell*), John Crawford (*Mayor*), Tyne Daly (*Kate Moore*), Samantha Doane (*Wanda*), Robert Hoy (*Buchinski*), Jocelyn Jones (*Miki*), M.G. Kelly (*Father John*), Nick Pellegrino (*Martin*), Albert Popwell (*Big Ed Mustapha*), Rudy Ramos (*Mendez*), Bill Ackridge (*Andy*), Bill Jelliffe (*Johnny*), Joe Bellan (*Freddie the Painter*), Tim O'Neill (*Police Sergeant*), Jan Stratton (*Mrs Grey*), Will MacMillan (*Lt. Dobbs*), Jerry Walter (*Krause*), Steve Boff (*Bustanoby*), Tim Burrus (*Henry Lee*), Michael Cavanaugh (*Lalo*), Dick Durock (*Karl*), Ronald Manning (*Tex*), Adele Proom (*Irene DiGeorgio*), Glenn Leigh Marshall (*Army Sergeant*), Robert Behling (*Autopsy Surgeon*), Terry McGovern (*Disc Jockey*), Stan Richie (*Bridge Operator*), John Roselims (*Mayor's Driver*), Brian Fong (*Scoutmaster*), Art Rimdzius (*Porno Director*), Chuck Hicks (*Huey*), Ann Macy (*Madam*), Gloria Prince (*Massage Girl*), Kenneth Boyd (*Abdul*), Bernard Glin (*Koblo*), Fritz Manes (*1st Detective*). 96 mins.

The Gauntlet

USA, 1977   **Director: Clint Eastwood**

Dist: Columbia-Warner. *p.c.*: Malpaso. For Warner Bros. *p*: Robert Daly. *assoc. p*: Fritz Manes. *p.manager*: Joe Cavalier. *asst.d*: Richard Hashimoto, Lynn Morgan, Peter Bergquist, Al Silvani. *sc*: Michael Butler, Dennis Shyrack. *ph*: Rexford Metz. Panavision. *col*: DeLuxe. *ed*: Ferris Webster, Joel Cox. *a.d*: Allen E. Smith. *set dec*: Ira Bates. *sp.effects*: Chuck Gaspar. *m*: Jerry Fielding. *jazz soloists*: Art Pepper, Jon Faddis. *cost*: Glenn Wright. *make-up*: Don Schoenfeld. *titles/opticals*: Pacific Title. *sd.rec*: Bert Hallberg. *sd.re-rec*: Les Fresholtz. *sd.effects ed*: Keith Stafford. *stunt co-ordinator*: Wayne Van Horn. *l.p.*: Clint Eastwood (*Ben Shockley*), Sondra Locke (*Gus Mally*), Pat Hingle (*Josephson*), William Prince (*Blakelock*), Bill McKinney (*Constable*), Michael Cavanaugh (*Feyderspiel*), Carole Cook (*Waitress*), Mara Corday (*Jail Matron*), Douglas McGarth (*Bookie*), Jeff Morris (*Desk Sergeant*), Samantha Doane, Roy Jenson and Dan Vadis (*Bikers*), Carver Barnes (*Bus Driver*), Robert Barrett (*Paramedic*), Teddy Bear (*Lieutenant*), Mildren J. Brion (*Old Lady on Bus*), Ron Chapman (*Veteran Cop*), Don Circle (*Bus Clerk*), James W. Gavin and Tom Friedkin (*Helicopter Pilots*),

Darwin Lamb (*Police Captain*), Roger Lowe (*Paramedic Driver*), Fritz Manes (*Helicopter Gunman*), John Quiroga (*Cab Driver*), Joe Rainer (*Rookie Cop*), Art Rimdzius (*Judge*), Al Silvani (*Police Sergeant*). 109 mins.

Every Which Way But Loose

USA, 1978   Director: James Fargo

P.c.: Malpaso. For Warner Bros. *p*: Robert Daley. *assoc.p*: Fritz Manes, Jeremy Joe Kronsberg. *p.managers*: Billy Ray Smith, Ernest B. Wehmeyer. *location managers*: Sheridan "Dar" Reid, Harry Zubrinsky. *asst.d*: Larry Powell, Wendy Shear, Al Silvani, Alain J. Silver. *sc*: Jeremy Joe Kronsberg. *ph*: Rexford Metz. *col*: DeLuxe. *ed*: Ferris Webster, Joel Cox. *a.d*: Elayne Ceder. *set dec*: Robert de Vestel. *sp.effects*: Chuck Gaspar. *m/songs*: "Every Which Way But Loose" by S. Dorff, M. Brown, T. Garrett, performed by Eddie Rabbitt; "I'll Wake You Up When I Get Home" by S. Dorff, M. Brown; "Behind Closed Doors" by K. O'Dell, performed by Charlie Rich; "Coca Cola Cowboy" by S. Pinkard, I. Dain, S. Dorff, S. Atchley; "Send Me Down To Tucson" by C. Crofford, T. Garrett, performed by Mel Tillis; "Ain't Love Good Tonight" by G. Sklerov, R. Cate, G. Howe, performed by Wayne Parker; "Don't Say You Don't Love Me No More" by P. Everly, J. Paige, performed by Sondra Locke, Phil Everly; "Honky Tonk Fever", "Monkey See, Monkey Do" by C. Crofford, T. Garrett, performed by Cliff Crofford; "I Can't Say No to a Truck Drivin' Man" by C. Crofford, performed by Carol Chase; "I Seek the Night" performed by Sondra Locke; "Red Eye Special" by S. Collins, S. Pinkard, T. Garrett, performed by Larry Collin; "Salty Dog Blues", "Under the Double Eagle" adapted by S. Dorff, T. Garrett; "Six Pack to Go" by Thompson, Lowe, Hart, performed by Hank Thompson. *m.sup*: Snuff Garrett. *m.d*: Steve Dorff, *cost.sup*: Glenn Wright. *make-up*: Don Schoenfeld. *titles/opticals*: Pacific Title. *sd.rec*: Bert Hallberg. *sd.re-rec*: Vern Poore. *sd.effects ed*: Gene Eliot, Marvin I. Kosberg, Joe von Stroheim. *stunt co-ordinator*: Wayne van Horn. *stuntmen*: George Dockstader, Bobby Porter. *l.p.*: Clint Eastwood (*Philo Beddoe*), Sondra Locke (*Lynn Halsey-Taylor*), Ruth Gordon (*Ma*), Geoffrey Lewis (*Orville*), Beverly D'Angelo (*Echo*), Walter Barnes (*Tank Murdock*), George Chandler (*Clerk at DMV*), Roy Jenson (*Woody*), James McEachin (*Herb*), Bill McKinney (*Dallas*), William O'Connell (*Elmo*), John Quade (*Cholla*), Dan Vadis (*Frank*), Gregory Walcott (*Putnam*), Hank Worden (*Trailer Court Manager*), Jerry Brutsche (*Sweeper Driver*), Cary Michael Cheifer (*Kincaid's Manager*), Janet Louise Cole (*Girl at Palomino*), Sam Gilman (*Fat Man's Friend*), Chuck Hicks (*Trucker*), Timothy P. Irvin (*MC at Zanzabar*), Tim Irwin (*Bandleader*),

Billy Jackson (*Bettor*), Joyce Jameson (*Sybil*), Richard Jamison (*Harlan*), Jackson D. Kane (*Man at Bowling Alley*), Jeremy Kronsberg (*Bruno*), Fritz Manes (*Bartender at Zanzabar*), Michael Mann (*Church's Manager*), Lloyd Nelson (*Bartender*), George Orrison (*Fight Spectator*), Thelma Pelish (*Lady Customer*), William J. Quinn (*Kincaid*), Tom Runyon (*Bartender at Palomino*), Bruce Scott (*Schyler*), Al Silvani (*Tank Murdock's Manager*), Hartley Silver (*Bartender*), Al Stellone (*Fat Man*), Jan Stratton (*Waitress*), Mike Wagner (*Trucker*), Guy Way (*Bartender*), George Wilbur (*Church*), Gary Davis, Scott Dockstader, Orwin Harvey, Gene LeBell, Chuck Waters and Jerry Wills (*Bikers*), Manis (*Clyde*). 114 mins.

Escape from Alcatraz

USA, 1979   **Director: Don Siegel**

Dist: CIC. *p.c.*: Malpaso. For Paramount. *exec.p*: Robert Daley. *p*: Donald Siegel. *assoc.p*: Fritz Manes. *unit p.manager*: Jack Terry. *asst.d*: Luigi Alfano, Mark Johnson, Richard Graves. *sc*: Richard Tuggle. Based on the book by J. Campbell Bruce. *ph*: Bruce Surtees. *col*: DeLuxe. *camera op*: Rick Neff, Bob Bergdahl. *ed*: Ferris Webster. *p.designer*: Allen Smith. *set dec*: Edward J. McDonald. *sp.effects*: Chuck Gasper. *m*: Jerry Fielding. *song*: "D Block Blues" by Gilbert Thomas Jnr. *cost*: Glenn Wright. *make-up*: Joe McKinney. *titles/opticals*: Pacific Title. *sd.rec*: Bert Hallberg. *sd.re-rec*: John T. Reitz. *sd.effects ed*: Alan Robert Murray, Bub Asman. *l.p.*: Clint Eastwood (*Frank Morris*), Patrick McGoohan (*Warden*), Roberts Blossom (*Chester Dalton, known as "Doc"*), Jack Thibeau (*Clarence Anglin*), Fred Ward (*John Anglin*), Paul Benjamin (*English*), Larry Hankin (*Charley Butts*), Bruce M. Fischer (*Wolf*), Frank Ronzio (*Litmus*), Fred Stuthman (*Johnson*), David Cryer (*Wagner*), Madison Arnold (*Zimmerman*), Blair Burrows (*Fight Guard*), Bob Balhatchet (*Medical Technical Assistant*), Matthew J. Locrcchio and Stephen Bradley (*Exam Guards*), Don Michaelian (*Beck*), Ray K. Goman (*Cellblock Captain*), Jason Ronard (*Bobs*), Ed Vasgersian (*Cranston*), Ron Vernan (*Stone*), Regie Bagg (*Lucy*), Hank Brandt (*Associate Warden*), Candace Bowen (*English's Daughter*), Joseph Miksak (*Police Sergeant*), Gary Goodrow (*Weston*), Ross Reynolds (*Helicopter Pilot*), Al Dunlap (*Visitors' Guard*), Donald Siegel (*Doctor*), Dan Leegant, John Garabedian, Denis Berkefeldt, Jim Haynie, Tony Dario, Fritz Manes, Dana Derfus, Don Cummins, Gordon Handforth, John Scanlon, Don Watters, Lloyd Nelson, George Orrison, Gary F. Warren, Joe Whipp, Terry Willis, Robert Irvine, Joseph Knowland, James Collier, R.J. Ganzert and Robert Hirschfeld (*Guards*), Dale Alvarez, Sheldon Feldner, Danny Glover, Carl Lumbly, Patrick Valentino, Glenn Wright,

Clint Eastwood

Gilbert Thomas Jnr. and Eugene W. Jackson (*Inmates*). 112 mins.

Bronco Billy

USA, 1980   **Director: Clint Eastwood**

P.c.: Warner Bros. In association with Second Street Films. *exec.p*: Robert Daley. *p*: Dennis Hackin, Neal Dobrofsky. *assoc.p*: Fritz Manes. *p.co-ordinator*: (New York) Manno Productions. *unit p.manager*: Larry Powell. *asst.d*: Tom Joyner, Stanley J. Zabka, Richard Graves, Fritz Manes. *sc*: Dennis Hackin. *ph*: David Worth. *col*: DeLuxe. *camera op*: Jack Green. *ed*: Ferris Webster, Joel Cox. *a.d.*: Gene Lourie. *set dec*: Ernie Bishop. *sp.effects*: Jeff Jarvis. *m/songs*: "Cowboys and Clowns" by Steve Dorff, G. Harju, L. Herbstritt, Snuff Garrett, "Bronco Billy" by M. Brown, Steve Dorff, Snuff Garrett, performed by Ronnie Milsap; "Misery and Gin" by J. Durrill, Snuff Garrett, performed by Merle Haggard; "Barroom Buddies" by M. Brown, C. Crofford, Steve Dorff, Snuff Garrett, performed by Merle Haggard, Clint Eastwood; "Bayou Lullaby" by C. Crofford, Snuff Garrett, performed by Penny De Haven. *m.sup*: Snuff Garrett. *m.d.*: Steve Dorff. *cost*: Glenn Wright. *make-up*: Tom Tuttle. *titles*: Pacific Title. *sd.rec*: Bert Hallberg. *sd.re-rec*: John T. Reitz. *sd.effects ed*: Alan Robert Murray, Bub Asman. *riding sequences*: Alan Cartwright. *roping sequences*: J.W. Stoker. *l.p.*: Clint Eastwood (*"Bronco Billy" McCoy*), Sondra Locke (*Antoinette Lily*), Geoffrey Lewis (*John Arlington*), Scatman Crothers (*"Doc" Lynch*), Bill McKinney (*"Lefty" LeBow*), Sam Bottoms (*Leonard James*), Dan Vadis (*Chief Big Eagle*), Sierra Pecheur (*Lorraine Running Water*), Walter Barnes (*Sheriff Dix*), Woodrow Parfrey (*Dr Canterbury*), Beverlee McKinsey (*Irene Lily*), Douglas McGrath (*Lt. Wiecker*), Hank Worden (*Station Mechanic*), William Prince (*Edgar Lipton*), Pam Abbas (*Mother Superior*), Edye Byrde (*Maid, Eloise*), Douglas Copsey and Roger Dale Simmons (*Reporters at Bank*), John Wesley Elliott Jnr. (*Sanatorium Attendant*), Chuck Hicks and Bobby Hoy (*Cowboys at Bar*), Jefferson Jewell (*Boy at Bank*), Dawneen Lee (*Bank Teller*), Don Mummert (*Chauffeur*), Lloyd Nelson (*Sanatorium Policeman*), George Orrison (*Cowboy in Bar*), Michael Reinbold (*King*), Tessa Richarde (*Mitzi Fritts*), Tanya Russell (*Doris Duke*), Valerie Shanks (*Sister Maria*), Sharon Sherlock (*Licence Clerk*), James Simmerhan (*Bank Manager*), Jenny Sternling (*Reporter at Sanatorium*), Chuck Waters and Jerry Wills (*Bank Robbers*). 116 mins.

Any Which Way You Can

USA, 1980   Director: Buddy Van Horn

P.c.: Malpaso. For Warner Bros. *exec.p*: Robert Daley. *p*: Fritz Manes. *unit p.manager*: Larry Powell. *asst.d*: Tom Joyner, Stan Zabka, David Valdes, Fritz Manes. *sc*: Stanford Sherman. Based on characters created by Jeremy Joe Kronsberg. *ph*: David Worth. *col*: DeLuxe. *camera op*: Jack Green, Douglas Ryan. *ed*: Ferris Webster, Ron Spang. *p.designer*: William J. Creber. *set dec*: Ernie Bishop. *sp.effects*: Chuck Gaspar, Jeff Jarvis. *m.sup*: Snuff Garrett. *m.d*: Steve Dorff. *songs*: "Beers to You" by S. Dorff, J. Durrill, S. Pinkard, S. Garrett, performed by Ray Charles, Clint Eastwood; "Any Which Way You Can" by M. Brown, S. Dorff, S. Garrett, performed by Glen Campbell; "Whiskey Heaven" by C. Crofford, J. Durrill, S. Garrett, performed by Fats Domino; "Cow Patti" by and performed by Jim Stafford; "Acapulco" by L. Collins, M. Leath, performed by Johnny Duncan; "Any Way You Want Me" by L. Offman, performed by Gene Watson; "One Too Many Women in Your Life" by J. Durrill, P. Everly, "Too Loose" by M. Brown, S. Dorff, S. Garrett, performed by Sondra Locke; "Cotton-Eyed Clint" adapted by S. Dorff, S. Garrett; "You're the Reason God Made Oklahoma" by L. Collins, S. Pinkard, performed by David Frizzell, Shelly West; "Orangutan Hall of Fame" by C. Crofford, S. Garrett, performed by Cliff Crofford; "The Good Guys and the Bad Guys" by J. Durrill, S. Garrett, performed by John Durrill. *cost.sup*: Glenn Wright. *make-up*: Joe McKinney. *titles/opticals*: Pacific Title. *sd.rec*: Bert Hallberg. *sd.re-rec*: Vern Poore. *sd.effects ed*: Alan Robert Murray, Bub Asman. *stunt doubles*: Bobby Porter, George Orrison. *animals supplied by*: Gentle Jungle. *animal trainer*: Boone Narr. *animal handlers*: Joe Campassi, Bill Gage, Ken Decroo, Jim Piccolo. *l.p.*: Clint Eastwood (*Philo Beddoe*), Sondra Locke (*Lynn Halsey-Taylor*), Geoffrey Lewis (*Orville Boggs*), William Smith (*Jack Wilson*), Harry Guardino (*James Beekman*), Ruth Gordon (*Ma Boggs*), Michael Cavanaugh (*Patrick Scarfe*), Barry Corbin (*Fat Zack*), Roy Jenson (*Moody*), Billy McKinney (*Dallas*), William O'Connell (*Elmo*), John Quade (*Cholla*), Al Ruscio (*Tony Paoli Snr.*), Dan Vadis (*Frank*), Camila Ashlend (*Hattie*), Dan Barrows (*Baggage Man*), Michael Brockman (*Moustache Officer*), Julie Brown (*Candy*), Glen Campbell (*Himself*), Dick Christie (*Jackson Officer*), Rebecca Clemons (*Buxom Bess*), Reid Cruickshanks (*Bald-headed Trucker*), Michael Currie (*Wyoming Officer*), Gary Lee Davis (*Husky Officer*), Dick Durock (*Joe Casey*), Michael Fairman (*CHP Captain*), James Gammon (*Bartender*), Weston Gavin (*Beekman's Butler*), Lance Gordon (*Biceps*), Lynn Hallowell (*Honey Bun*), Peter Hobbs (*Motel Clerk*), Art La Fleur (*2nd Baggage Man*), Ken Lerner (*Tony Paoli Jnr.*), John McKinney (*Officer*), Robin Menken

(*Tall Woman*), George Murdock (*Sergeant Cooley*), Jack Murdock (*Little Melvin*), Ann Nelson (*Harriet*), Sunshine Parker (*Old Codger*), Kent Perkins (*Trucker*), Anne Ramsey (*Loretta Quince*), Logan Ramsey (*Luther Quince*), Michael Reinbold (*Officer with Glasses*), Tessa Richarde (*Sweet Sue*), Jeremy Smith (*Intern*), Bill Sorrells (*Bakersfield Officer*), Jim Stafford (*Long John*), Michael Talbott (*Officer Morgan*), Mark Taylor (*Desk Clerk*), Jack Thibeau (*Head Muscle*), Charles Walker (*Officer*), Jerry Brutsche, Orwin Harvey, Larry Holt, John Nowak, Walt Robles and Mike Tillman (*Black Widows*). 115 mins.

Honkytonk Man

USA, 1982   Director: Clint Eastwood

P.c.: Malpaso. For Warner Bros. *exec.p*: Fritz Manes. *p*: Clint Eastwood. *unit p. manager*: Steve Perry. *asst.d*: Tony Brown, Tom Seidman. *sc*: Clancy Carlile. Based on his own novel. *ph*: Bruce Surtees. *col*: Technicolor. *camera op*: Jack Green. *ed*: Ferris Webster, Michael Kelly, Joel Cox. *p.designer*: Edward Carfagno. *set dec*: Gary Moreno. *sp. effects*: Wayne Edgar. *m.sup*: Snuff Garrett. *m.d*: Steve Dorff. *m.ed*: Donald Harris. *cost.sup*: Glenn Wright. *women's wardrobe*: Aida Swinson. *make-up*: David Dittmar. *titles/opticals*: Pacific Title. *sd.rec*: Don Johnson. *sd.re-rec*: John Reitz, David Campbell, Joe Citarella. *sd.effects ed*: Alan Robert Murray, Bob Henderson, Bub Asman. *stand-in*: Frank Reinhard. *wrangler*: Jim Medearis. *l.p.*: Clint Eastwood (*Red Stovall*), Kyle Eastwood (*Whit*), John McIntire (*Grandpa*), Alexa Kenin (*Marlene*), Verna Bloom (*Emmy*), Matt Clark (*Virgil*), Barry Corbin (*Derwood Arnspriger*), Jerry Hardin (*Snuffy*), Tim Thomerson (*Highway Patrolman*), Macon McCalman (*Doctor Hines*), Joe Regalbuto (*Henry Axle*), Gary Grubbs (*Jim Bob*), Rebecca Clemons (*Belle*), John Gimble (*Bob Wills*), Linda Hopkins (*Flossie*), Bette Ford (*Lulu*), Jim Boelsen (*Junior*), Tracey Walter (*Pooch*), Susan Peretz (*Miss Maud*), John Russell (*Jack Wade*), Charles Cyphers (*Stubbs*), Marty Robbins (*Smoky*), Ray Price (*Bob Wills Singer*), Shelly West and David Frizzell (*Opry Singers*), Porter Wagoner (*Dusty*), Bob Ferrera (*Oldest Son*), Tracy Shults (*Daughter*), R.J. Ganzert (*Rancher*), Hugh Warden (*Grocer*), Kelsie Blades (*Veteran*), Jim Ahart (*Waiter*), Steve Autry (*Mechanic*), Peter Griggs (*Mr Vogel*), Julie Hoopman (*Whore*), Rozelle Gayle (*Club Manager*), Robert V. Barron (*Undertaker*), DeForest Covan (*Gravedigger*), Lloyd Nelson (*Radio Announcer*), George Orrison and Glenn Wright (*Jailbirds*), Roy Jenson (*Dub*), Sherry Allurd (*Dub's Wife*), Gordon Terry, Tommy Alsup and Merle Travis (*Texas Playboys*), Robert D. Carver (*1st Bus Driver*), Thomas Powels (*2nd Bus Driver*). 123 mins.

Firefox

USA, 1982   Director: Clint Eastwood

P.c.: Malpaso. For Warner Bros. *exec.p*: Fritz Manes. *p*: Clint Eastwood
assoc.p: Paul Hitchcock. *unit p.managers*: Steve Perry, Fritz Manes.
p.manager: (Europe) Dieter Meyer. *Arctic location adviser*: Dr Jack Wheeler.
asst.d: Steve Perry, David Valdes, (Europe) Don French. *sc*: Alex Lasker,
Wendell Wellman. Based on the novel by Craig Thomas. *ph*: Bruce Surtees.
Panavision. *col*: DeLuxe. *camera op*: Jack Green, Doug Smith, Mat Beck,
Bruno George, Mark Gredell, Greg Heschong, David Nowell, Jerry Pooler,
John Sullivan. *anim.ph*: Harry Moreau, Angela Diamos. *process ph*: Bruce
Logan. *sp.visual effects*: (p.) John Dykstra, (sup.) Robert Shepherd. *sp.optical
effects sup*: Roger Dorney. *ed*: Ferris Webster, Ron Spang. *a.d*: John
Graysmark, Elayne Ceder. *asst.a.d.*: (Europe) Thomas Riccabona. *set dec*:
Ernie Bishop. *p.illustrators*: Marty Kline, John Shourt. *scenic artist*: Mike
Speaker. *sp.effects*: Chuck Gaspar, (Europe) Karl Baumgartner. *sp.effects
ed*: Michael Kelly, Denny Kelly, Dennis Michelson, David Bartholomew,
sp.effects co-ordinator: Percy Angress. *electronic sp.effects sup*: Al Miller.
mechanical sp.effects: Bill Shourt, Don Trumbull, Richard Alexander, Mark
Cane, Richard Helmer, Steve Sass, Rick Gilligan. *sp.technical development*:
John Erland. *models*: Grant McCune (sup.); David Beasley, Pete Gerard,
Mike Joyce, Pat McClung, Gary Rhodaback, David Scott, David Sosalla,
Ken Swenson, Dewey Webber. *m/m.d.*: Maurice Jarre. *m.ed*: Donald Harris.
cost.sup: Glen Wright. *make-up*: Christina Smith. *titles/opticals*: Pacific Title.
sd.rec: Don Johnson. Dolby stereo. *sd.re-rec*: Les Fresholtz, Arthur
Piantadosi, Dick Alexander. *sd.effects ed*: Alan Robert Murray, Bub Asman,
Bob Henderson. *scientific advisers*: Durk Pearson, Sandy Shaw. *sp.flight
consultants*: Clay Lacy, Jim Gavin, David Nieman. *l.p.*: Clint Eastwood
(*Mitchell Gant*), Freddie Jones (*Kenneth Aubrey*), David Huffman (*Buckholz*),
Warren Clarke (*Pavel Upenskoy*), Ronald Lacey (*Semelovsky*), Kenneth
Colley (*Colonel Kontarsky*), Klaus Löwitsch (*General Vladimirov*), Nigel
Hawthorne (*Pyotr Baranovich*), Stefan Schnabel (*First Secretary*), Thomas
Hill (*General Brown*), Clive Merrison (*Major Lanyev*), Kai Wulff (*Lt.-
Cononel Voskov*), Dimitra Arliss (*Natalia*), Austin Willis (*Walters*), James
Staley (*Lt.-Commander Fleischer*), Ward Costello (*General Rogers*), Alan
Tilvern (*Air Marshal Kutuzov*), Oliver Cotton (*Dimitri Priabin*), Michael
Currie (*Capt. Seerbacker*), Bernard Behrens (*William Saltonstall*), Richard
Derr (*Admiral Curtin*), Woody Eney (*Major Dietz*), Bernard Erhard (*KGB
Guard*), Hugh Fraser (*Police Inspector Tortyev*), David Gant (*KGB Official*),
John Grillo (*Customs Officer*), Czeslaw Grocholski (*Old Man*), Barrie

Clint Eastwood

Houghton (*Boris Glazunov*), Neil Hunt (*Richard Cunningham*), Vincent J. Isaacs (*Sub Radio Operator*), Alexei Jawdokimov and Phillip Littell (*Code Operators*), Wolf Kahler (*KGB Chairman Andropov*), Eugene Lipinski (*KGB Agent*), Curt Lowens (*Dr Schuller*), Lev Mailer (*Guard at Shower*), Fritz Manes (*Captain*), David Meyers (*Grosch*), Alfredo Michelson (*Interrogator*), Zenno Nahayevsky (*Officer at Plane*), George Orrison (*Leon Sprague*), Tony Papenfuss (*GRU Officer*), Olivier Pierre (*Borkh*), Grisha Plotkin (*GRU Officer*), George Pravda (*General Borov*), John Ratzenberger (*Chief Peck*), Alex Rodine (*Captain of the Riga*), Lance Rosen (*Agent*), Eugene Scherer (*Russian Captain*), Warrick Sims (*Shelley*), Mike Spero (*Russian Guard*), Malcolm Storry (*KGB Agent*), Chris Winfield (*RAF Operator*), John Yates (*Admiral Pearson*), Alexander Zale (*Riga Fire Control Chief*), Igor Zatsepin (*Flight Engineer*), Konstantin Zlatev (*Riga Technician*). 136 mins.

Sudden Impact

USA, 1983   Director: Clint Eastwood

P.c.: Malpaso. For Warner Bros. *exec.p*: Fritz Manes. *p*: Clint Eastwood. *assoc.p/unit p.manager*: Steve Perry. *asst.d*: David Valdes, Paul Moen. *sc*: Joseph C. Stinson. *story*: Earl E. Smith, Charles B. Pierce. Based on characters created by Harry Julian Fink, R.M. Fink. *ph*: Bruce Surtees. *col*: Technicolor. *camera op*: Jack Green. *ed*: Joel Cox. *asst.ed*: John Morrisey. *p.designer*: Edward Carfagno. *set dec*: Ernie Bishop. *sp.effects*: Chuck Gaspar. *m*: Lalo Schifrin. *m.ed*: Donald Harris. *song*: "This Side of Forever" by Lalo Schifrin, DeWayne Blackwell, performed by Roberta Flack. *cost.sup*: Glenn Wright. *cos*: (women) Sue Moore, (men) Darryl Athons. *make-up*: Barbara Guedell. *titles/opticals*: Pacific Title. *asst.sd.ed*: Brooke Henderson. *sd.rec*: Don Johnson. *sd.re-rec*: Les Fresholtz, Dick Alexander, Vern Poore. *sd.effects ed*: Alan Robert Murray, Bob Henderson, Bub Asman. *stunt co-ordinator*: Wayne ("Buddy") Van Horn. *stunts*: Carey Loftin, Fritz Manes, Debby Porter, Christine Baur, Jade David, Scott Dockstader, Jerry Gatlin, Larry Holt, Kristy Horak, Jack Lilley, Paula Moody, George Orrison, Chuck Waters, Al Silvani. *animal handler*: Paul Calabria. *l.p.*: Clint Eastwood (*Harry Callahan*), Sondra Locke (*Jennifer Spencer*), Pat Hingle (*Chief Jannings*), Bradford Dillman (*Captain Briggs*), Paul Drake (*Micky*), Audrie J. Neenan (*Ray Parkins*), Jack Thibeau (*Kruger*), Michael Currie (*Lt. Donnelly*), Albert Popwell (*Horace King*), Mark Keyloun (*Officer Bennett*), Kevyn Major Howard (*Hawkins*), Bette Ford (*Leah*), Nancy Parsons (*Mrs Kruger*), Joe Bellan (*Burly Detective*), Wendell Wellman (*Tyrone*), Mara Corday (*Coffee Shop Waitress*), Russ McCubbin (*Eddie*), Robert Sutton

(*Carl*), Nancy Fish (*Historical Society Woman*), Carmen Argenziano (*D'Ambrosia*), Lisa Britt (*Elizabeth Spencer*), Bill Reddick (*Police Commissioner*), Lois de Banzie (*Judge*), Matthew Child (*Alby*), Michael Johnson and Nick Dimitri (*Assassins*), Michael Maurer (*George Wilburn*), Pat Du Val (*Bailiff*), Christian Phillips and Steven Kravitz (*Hawkins' Cronies*), Dennis Royston, Melvin Thompson, Jophery Brown and Bill Upton (*Young Guys*), Lloyd Nelson (*Desk Sergeant*), Christopher Pray (*Detective Jacobs*), James McEachin (*Detective Barnes*), Maria Lynch (*Hostess*), Ken Lee (*Loomis*), Morgan Upton (*Bartender*), John X. Heart (*Uniform Policeman*), David Gonzales, Albert Martinez, David Rivers and Robert Rivers (*Gang Members*), Harry Demopoulos (*Dr Barton*), Lisa London (*Young Hooker*), Tom Spratley (*Senior Man*), Eileen Wiggins (*Hysterical Female Customer*), John Nowak (*Bank Robber*). 117 mins.

Tightrope

USA, 1984   Director: Richard Tuggle

P.c.: Warner Bros. A Malpaso production. *p*: Clint Eastwood, Fritz Manes. *unit p.manager*: Fritz Manes. *asst.d*: David Valdes, Paul Moen, L. Dean Jones Jnr. *sc*: Richard Tuggle. *ph*: Bruce Surtees. *col*: Technicolor. *2nd Unit ph*: Billy Bragg. *camera op*: Jack Green. *ed*: Joel Cox *p.designer*: Edward Carfagno. *set dec*: Ernie Bishop. *sp.effects*: Joe Unsinn. *m*: Lennie Niehaus. *main and end title themes performed by*: James Rivers Movement. *m.ed*: Donald Harris. *cost.sup*: Glenn Wright. *wardrobe*: (women) Deborah Ann Hopper. *make-up*: Barbara Guedel. *titles/opticals*: Pacific Title. *sd.rec*: William Kaplan. *sd.re-rec*: Les Fresholtz, Dick Alexander, Vern Poore, *sd.effects ed*: Alan Robert Murray, Gordon Davidson, Chet Slomka, Neil Burrow. *stunt co-ordinator*: Wayne Van Horn. *stunts*: Wayne Van Horn, George Orrison. *animal handler*: Paul Calabria. *l.p.*: Clint Eastwood (*Wes Block*), Genevieve Bujold (*Beryl Thibodeaux*), Dan Hedaya (*Detective Molinari*), Alison Eastwood (*Amanda Block*), Jennifer Beck (*Penny Block*), Marco St. John (*Leander Rolfe*), Rebecca Perle (*Becky Jacklin*), Regina Richardson (*Sarita*), Randi Brooks (*Jamie Cory*), Jamie Rose (*Melanie Silber*), Margaret Howell (*Judy Harper*), Rebecca Clemons (*Girl with Whip*), Janet MacLachlan (*Dr Yarlofsky*), Graham Paul (*Luther*), Bill Holliday (*Police Chief*), John Wilmot (*Medical Examiner*), Margie O'Dair (*Mrs Holstein*), Joy N. Houck Jnr. (*Swap Meet Owner*), Stuart Baker-Bergen (*Blond Surfer*), Donald Barber (*Shorty*), Robert Harvey (*Lonesome Alice*), Ron Gural (*Coroner Dudley*), Layton Martens (*Sergeant Surtees*), Richard Charles Boyle (*Dr Fitzpatrick*), Becki Davis (*Nurse*), Jonathan Sacher (*Gay Boy*), Valerie

Thibodeaux (*Black Hooker*), Lionel Ferbos (*Plainclothes Gus*), Eliott Keener (*Sandoval*), Cary Wilmot Alden (*Secretary*), David Valdes (*Manes*), James Borders (*Carfagno*), Fritz Manes (*Valdes*), Jonathan Shaw (*Quono*), Don Lutenbacher (*Dixie President*), George Wood (*Conventioneer*), Kimberly Georgoulis (*Sam*), Glenda Byars (*Lucy Davis*), John Schluter Jnr. (*Piazza Cop*), Nick Krieger (*Rannigan*), Lloyd Nelson (*Patrolman Restic*), David Dahlgren (*Patrolman Julio*), Rod Masterson (*Patrolman Gallo*), Glenn Wright (*Patrolman Redfish*), Angela Hill (*Woman Reporter*), Ted Saari (*TV News Technician*). 114 mins.

City Heat

USA, 1984   Director: Richard Benjamin

P.c.: Malpaso/Deliverance. For Warner Bros. *p/unit p.manager*: Fritz Manes. *location manager*: Paula Shaw. *asst.d*: David Valdes, L. Dean Jones Jnr., Matt Earl Beesley. *sc*: Sam O. Brown [Blake Edwards], Joseph C. Stinson. *story*: Sam O. Brown [Blake Edwards]. *ph*: Nick McLean. *col*: Technicolor. *camera op*: Michael O'Shea. *panaglide op*: Jack Green, Stephen St. John. *ed*: Jacqueline Cambas. *p.designer*: Edward Carfagno. *set dec*: George Gaines. *p.illustrator*: Sherman Labby. *sp.effects*: Joe Unsinn. *m*: Lennie Niehaus. *m.co-ordinator*: Steve Wax. *m.ed*: Donald Harris. *songs*: "City Heat" by Irene Cara, Bruce Roberts, performed by Joe Williams; "Million Dollar Baby" by Billy Rose, Mort Dixon, Harry Warren, performed by Al Jarreau; "Between the Devil and the Deep Blue Sea" by Ted Koehler, Harold Arlen, performed by Eloise Laws; "Embraceable You" by George Gershwin, Ira Gershwin, "Get Happy" by Ted Koehler, Harold Arlen, performed by Irene Cara; "Let's Do It" by Cole Porter, performed by Rudy Vallee; "Montage Blues" by Lennie Niehaus, performed by (piano) Mike Lang, Pete Jolly, Clint Eastwood *cost.design*: Norman Salling. *wardrobe*: (men) Glenn Wright, (women) Arlene Encell. *make-up*: Tom Ellingwood, Dan Striepeke. *titles/opticals*: Pacific Title. *sd.rec*: C. Darin Knight. Dolby stereo. *sd.re-rec*: Les Fresholtz, Dick Alexander, Vern Poore. *sd.effects ed*: Alan Robert Murray, Bob Henderson, Bub Asman, Gordon Davidson. *stunt co-ordinator*: Wayne Van Horn. *stunts*: Michael Cassidy, Vincent Deadrick Jnr., Richard Drown, Bud Ekins, Allan Graf, Chuck Hicks, Julius Le Flore, Fritz Manes, Debby Porter, James Hooks Reynolds, Mic Rodgers, Sharon Schaffer, Wayne Van Horn, Chuck Waters, George Wilbur, Glenn Wilder. *animal handlers*: Paul Calabria, Karin Dew. *l.p.*: Clint Eastwood (*Lieutenant Speer*), Burt Reynolds (*Mike Murphy*), Jane Alexander (*Addy*), Madeline Kahn (*Caroline Howley*), Rip Torn (*Primo Pitt*), Irene Cara (*Ginny Lee*),

Richard Roundtree (*Dehl Swift*), Tony Lo Bianco (*Leon Coll*), William Sanderson (*Lonnie Ash*), Nicholas Worth (*Troy Roker*), Robert Davi (*Nino*), Jude Farese (*Dub Slack*), John Hancock (*Fat Freddie*), Tab Thacker (*Tuck*), Gerald S. O'Loughlin (*Counterman Louie*), Jack Nance (*Aram Strossell*), Dallas Cole (*Redhead Sherry*), Lou Filippo (*Referee*), Michael Maurer (*Vint Diestock*), Preston Sparks (*Keith Stoddard*), Ernie Sabella (*Ballistics Expert*), Christopher Michael Moore (*Roxy Cop*), Carey Loftin (*Roxy Driver*), Harry Caesar (*Locker Room Attendant*), Charles Parks (*Dr Breslin*), Hamilton Camp (*Garage Attendant*), Arthur Malet (*Doc Loomis*), Fred Lerner (*Pitt Roof Sniper*), George Orrison (*Pitt Doorway Thug*), Beau Starr (*Pitt Lookout*), Joan Shawlee (*Peggy Barker*), Minnie Lindsey (*Bordello Maid*), Darwyn Swalve (*Bordello Bouncer*), Wiley Harker and Bob Maxwell ("*Mr Smiths*"), Tom Spratley (*Chauffeur*), Bob Terhune (*Billiard Soldier*), Holgie Forrester (*Little Red*), Harry Demopoulos (*Roman Orgy Patron*), Jim Lewis (*Roxy Patron*), Edwin Prevost (*Butler*), Alfie Wise (*Short Man*), Hank Calia (*Shorter Friend*), Alex Plasschaert (*Shortest Friend*), Daphne Eckler (*Agnes*), Lonna Montrose (*Didi*), Bruce M. Fischer and Art La Fleur (*Bruisers*), Jack Thibeau, Gene LeBell, Nick Dimitri, George Fisher, Bob Herron and Bill Hart (*Garage Soldiers*), Anthony Charnota, Walter Robles and Richard Foronjy (*Poker Players*). 97 mins.

Pale Rider

USA, 1985   **Director: Clint Eastwood**

P.c.: Warner Bros. A Malpaso production. *exec.p*: Fritz Manes. *p*: Clint Eastwood. *assoc.p*: David Valdes. *unit p.manager*: Fritz Manes. *asst.d*: David Valdes, L. Dean Jones Jnr., Matt Earl Beesley. *sc*: Michael Butler, Dennis Shryack. *ph*: Bruce Surtees. Panavision. *col*: Technicolor. *camera op*: Jack Green. *addit.camera op*: Leo Napolitano, Stephen St. John. *ed*: Joel Cox. *p.designer*: Edward Carfagno. *set design*: Bob Sessa. *set dec*: Ernie Bishop. *sp.effects sup*: Chuck Gaspar. *m*: Lennie Niehaus. *m.ed*: Donald Harris. *cost.sup*: Glenn Wright. *wardrobe*: (women) Deborah Ann Hooper, (men) Darryl Athons. *make-up*: Barbara Guedel. *titles/opticals*: Pacific Title. *sd.rec*: C. Darin Knight. Dolby stereo. *sd.re-rec*: Les Fresholtz, Dick Alexander, Vern Poore. *sup.sd.effects ed*: Alan Robert Murray, Bob Henderson. *stunt co-ordinator*: Wayne Van Horn. *stunts*: Kerrie Cullen, Tom Ellison, Leroy Hershkowitz, Bob Herron, Walt La Rue, Jim Winburn. *wrangler*: Jay K. Fishburn. *animal handlers*: Paul Calabria, Karin Dew. *l.p.*: Clint Eastwood (*Preacher*), Michael Moriarty (*Hull Barret*), Carrie Snodgress (*Sarah Wheeler*), Christopher Penn (*Josh LaHood*), Richard Dysart (*Coy LaHood*),

Sydney Penny (*Megan Wheeler*), Richard Kiel (*Club*), Doug McGrath (*Spider Conway*), John Russell (*Marshal Stockburn*), Charles Hallahan (*McGill*), Marvin J. McIntyre (*Jagou*), Fran Ryan (*Ma Blankenship*), Richard Hamilton (*Jed Blankenship*), Graham Paul (*Ev Gossage*), Chuck LaFont (*Eddie Conway*), Jeffrey Weissman (*Teddy Conway*), Allen Keller (*Tyson*), Tom Oglesby (*Elam*), Herman Poppe (*Ulrik Lindquist*), Kathleen Wygle (*Bess Gossage*), Terrence Evans (*Jake Henderson*), Jim Hitson (*Biggs*), Loren Adkins (*Bossy*), Tom Friedkin (*Miner Tom*), S.A. Griffin (*Deputy Folke*), Jack Radosta (*Deputy Grissom*), Robert Winley (*Deputy Kobold*), Billy Drago (*Deputy Mather*), Jeffrey Josephson (*Deputy Sedge*), John Dennis Johnston (*Deputy Tucker*), Mike Adams, Clay Lilley, Gene Hartline, R.L. Tolbert, Cliff Happy, Ross Loney, Larry Randles, Mike McGaughy and Gerry Gatlin (*Horsemen*), Lloyd Nelson (*Bank Teller*), Jay K. Fishburn (*Telegrapher*), George Orrison (*Stationmaster Whitey*), Milton Murrill (*Porter*), Mike Munsey (*Dentist/Barber*), Keith Dillin (*Blacksmith*), Wayne Van Horn (*Stage Driver*), Fritz Manes and Glenn Wright (*Stage Riders*). 116 mins.

Vanessa in the Garden (TV episode for Steven Spielberg's *Amazing Stories)*

USA, 1985   Director: Clint Eastwood

l.p.: Sondra Locke (*Vanessa*), Harvey Keitel and Beau Bridges.

Heartbreak Ridge

USA, 1986   Director: Clint Eastwood

Pc.: Malpaso. For Warner Bros. In association with Jay Weston Productions. *exec.p*: Fritz Manes. *p*: Clint Eastwood. *unit p.manager*: Fritz Manes. *casting exec*: Phyllis Huffman. *asst.d*: Paul Moen, L. Dean Jones Jnr., Michael Looney. *sc*: James Carabatsos. *ph*: Jack N. Green. *col*: Technicolor. *asst.ph*: (2nd Unit) Buzz Feitshans IV, Larry Hezzelwood, Jeff Gershman. *camera op*: Stephen St. John. *ed*: Joel Cox. *p.designer*: Edward Carfagno. *set design*: Robert Sessa. *set dec*: Robert Benton. *sp.effects*: Chuck Gaspar. *m/m.d*: Lennie Niehaus. *m.ed*: Donald Harris. *songs*: "Sea of Heartbreak" by Hal David, Paul Hampton, performed by Don Gibson; "Secret Love", "A Very Precious Love" by Sammy Fain, Paul Francis Webster, "How Much I Care" by Clint Eastwood, Sammy Cahn, performed by Jill Hollier; "I Love You, But I Ain't Stupid" by Mario Van Peebles, Desmond Nakano, performed by Mario Van Peebles; "Bionic Marine", "Recon Rap" by Mario Van Peebles. *cost.sup*: Glenn Wright. *wardrobe*: (men) Darryl Athons, (women) Deborah Ann Hopper. *make-up artist*: Tom Case. *titles/opticals*: Pacific Title.

sup.sd.ed: Alan Murray, Robert Henderson *sd.ed*: Bruce Lacey, D. Michael Horton, Neil Burrow, Teri E. Dorman, Scott Burrow, Richard Oswald. *ADR ed*: Jay Engel. *sd.rec*: William Nelson, (m.) Bobby Fernandez, (ADR) Ron Harris. Dolby stereo. *sd.re-rec*: Les Fresholtz, Dick Alexander, Vern Poore. *stunt co-ordinator*: Wayne Van Horn. *l.p.*: Clint Eastwood (*Sergeant Thomas Highway*), Marsha Mason (*Aggie*), Everett McGill (*Major Powers*), Moses Gunn (*Sergeant Webster*), Eileen Heckart (*Little Mary*), Bo Svenson (*Roy Jennings*), Boyd Gaines (*Lieutenant Ring*), Mario Van Peebles ("*Stitch*" *Jones*), Arlen Dean Snyder (*Master Sergeant Choozoo*), Vincent Irizarry (*Fragetti*), Ramon Franco (*Aponte*), Tom Villard (*Profile*), Mike Gomez (*Quinones*), Rodney Hill (Collins), Peter Koch ("*Swede*" *Johanson*), Richard Venture (*Colonel Meyers*), Peter Jason (*Major Devin*), J.C. Quinn (*Quartermaster Sergeant*), Begoña Plaza (*Mrs Aponte*), John Eames (*Judge Zane*), Thom Sharp and Jack Gallagher (*Emcees*), John Hostetter (Reese), Holly Shelton-Foy (*Sarita Dwayne*), Nicholas Worth (*Jail Binger*), Timothy Fall (*Kid in Jail*), Jon Pennell (*Jail Crier*), Trish Garland (*Woman Marine Officer*), Dutch Mann and Darwyn Swalve (*Bar Tough Guys*), Christopher Lee Michael and Alex M. Bello (*Marines*), Steve Halsey and John Sasse (*Bus Drivers*), Rebecca Perle (*Student in Shower*), Annie O'Donnell (*Telephone Operator*), Elizabeth Ruscio (Waitress), Lloyd Nelson (*Deputy*), Sergeant Major John H. Brewer (*Sergeant Major in Court*), Michael Maurer (*Bouncer in Bar*), Tom Ellison (*Marine Corporal*). 130 mins.

Bird

USA, 1988   **Director: Clint Eastwood**

P.c.: Warner Bros. A Malpaso production. *exec.p*: David Valdes. *p*: Clint Eastwood, *p.assoc*: Tom Rooker. *p.manager*: David Valdes. *location manager*: Antoinette Simmrin. *casting*: Phyllis Huffman. *asst.d*: L. Dean Jones Jnr., Tena Psyche Yatroussis, Marsha Scarborough. *sc*: Joel Oliansky. *ph*: Jack N. Green. *col*: Technicolor. *process ph*: Bruce Logan. *lighting consultant*: Tom Stern. *camera op*: Norman G. Langley. *process projection*: Bill Hansard Snr. *ed*: Joel Cox. *p.designer*: Edward C. Carfagno. *set design*: Judy Cammer. *set dec*: Thomas L. Roysden. *set dresser*: Larry Boyd. *sp.effects*: Joe Day. *m/songs*: "Maryland, My Maryland" arranged and performed by Lennie Niehaus; "Lester Leaps In" by Lester Young; "I Can't Believe that You're in Love with Me" by Clerance Gaskill, Jimmy McHugh; "All of Me" by Seymour Simon, Gerald Marks; "This Time the Dream's on Me" by Harold Arlen, Johnny Mercer, performed by Charlie Parker, Monty Alexander, Ray Brown, John Guerin; "Reno Jam Session" by Lennie Niehaus, performed by Lennie Niehaus, James Rivers, Red Rodney, Pete Jolly, Chuck Berghofer, John Guerin; "Young Bird" by Lennie Niehaus, performed by James Rivers, Pete Jolly. Chuck Berghofer, John Guerin; "Why Do I Love You?" by Jerome Kern, Oscar Hammerstein II, performed by James Rivers, Lennie Niehaus; "Moonlight Becomes You" by Johnny Burke, Jimmy Van Heusen, performed by Ronny Lang, Gary Foster, Bob Cooper, Pete Christlieb, Chuck Findley, Conte Candoli, Rick Baptist, Dick Nash, Bill Watrous, Barry Harris, Chuck Berghofer, John Guerin; "Moose the Mooche" by Charlie Parker, performed by Charles McPherson, Jon Faddis, Walter Davis Jnr., Ron Carter, John Guerin; "Ornithology" by Charlie Parker, Bennie Harris, performed by Charlie Parker, Jon Faddis, Mike Lang, Chuck Domanico, John Guerin, Charlie Shoemaker; "Lover Man" by Jimmy Davis, Roger "Ram" Ramirez, Jimmy Sherman, performed by Charlie Parker, Charles McPherson, Jon Faddis, Walter Davis Jnr., Ron Carter, John Guerin; "April in Paris" by Vernon Duke, E.Y. Harburg; "Laura" by Johnny Mercer, David Raskin; "Parker's Mood" (with strings) by Charlie Parker, performed by Charlie Parker, Barry Harris, Chuck Berghofer, John Guerin, plus strings; "Jewish Wedding" by Lennie Niehaus, performed by Charles McPherson, Red Rodney, Walter Davis Jnr., John Guerin; "One for Red" by Lennie Niehaus, performed by Red Rodney, Mike Lang, Chuck Domanico, John Guerin; "Now's the Time" by Charlie Parker, performed by Charlie Parker, Charles McPherson, Red Rodney, Walter Davis Jnr., Ron Carter, John Guerin; "Albino Red Blues" by Lennie Niehaus, Joel Oliansky, performed by Red Rodney, Walter Davis Jnr., Ron Carter, John Guerin; "Cool Blues", "Ko Ko" by Charlie Parker, performed by Charlie Parker, Walter Davis Jnr., Ron Carter, John Guerin; 'Be My Love" by Nicholas Brodszky, Sammy Cahn, performed by Mario Lanza; "Parker's Mood" by Charlie Parker, performed by King Pleasure, John Lewis, Percy Heath, Kenny Clarke; "Buster's Last Stand" by Lennie Niehaus, performed by (alto sax) Ronny Lang. *m.extract: Firebird Suite* by Igor Stravinsky, performed by the Vienna Symphony Orchestra, (conductor) Wolfgang Sawallisch. *sideline musicians*: John Oliver. *m.sup*: Lennie Niehaus. *m.ed*: Donald Harris. *m.contractor*: Patti Fidelibus. *m.consultant*: Steve Wax. *cost.sup*: (men) Glenn Wright, (women) Deborah Hopper. *wardrobe*: (men) Robert Christenson, Alfred Tiegs, (women) Nancy McArdle. *make-up artist*: Michael Hancock. *titles/opticals*: Pacific Title. *sup.sd.ed*: Alan Robert Murray, Robert G. Henderson. *sd.ed*: Teri E. Dorman, Daivd M. Horton, Joseph A. Ippolito, Virginia Cook-McGowan, Walter Newman, Marshall Winn. *ADR ed*: Jay N. Engel. *sd.rec*: Willie D. Burton, (m.) Bobby Fernandez. Dolby stereo. *sd.re-rec*: Les Fresholtz, Dick Alexander, Vern Poore. *l.p.*: Forest Whitaker (*Charlie "Yardbird" Parker*),

Diane Venora (*Chan Richardson*), Michael Zelniker (*Red Rodney*), Samuel E. Wright (*Dizzy Gillespie*), Keith David (*Buster Franklin*), Michael McGuire (*Brewster*), James Handy (*Esteves*), Damon Whitaker (*Young Bird*), Morgan Nagler (*Kim*), Arlen Dean Snyder (*Dr Heath*), Sam Robards (*Moscowitz*), Penelope Windust (*Bellevue Nurse*), Glenn T. Wright (*Alcoholic Patient*), George Orrison (*Patient with Checkers*), Bill Cobbs (*Dr Caulfield*), Hamilton Camp (*Mayor of 52nd Street*), Chris Bosley (*1st Doorman*), George T. Bruce (*2nd Doorman*), Joey Green (*Gene*), John Witherspoon (*Sid*), Tony Todd (*Frog*), Jo de Winter (*Mildred Berg*), Richard Zavaglia (*Ralph the Narc*), Anna Levine (*Audrey*), Al Pugliese (*Owner, Three Deuces*), Hubert Kelly (*John Wilson*), Billy Mitchell (*Billy Prince*), Karl Vincent (*Stratton*), Lou Cutell (*Bride's Father*), Roger Etienne (*Parisian MC*), Jason Bernard (*Benny Tate*), Gretchen Oehler (*Southern Nurse*), Richard McKenzie (*Southern Doctor*), Tony Cox (*Pee Wee Marquette*), Diane Salinger (*Baroness Nica*), Johnny Adams (*Bartender*), Natalia Silverwood (*Red's Girlfriend*), Duane Matthews (*Engineer*), Slim Jim Phantom (*Grainger*), Matthew Faison (*Judge*), Peter Crook (*Bird's Lawyer*), Alec Paul Rubinstein (*Recording Producer*), Patricia Herd (*Hun*), Steve Zettler (*Owner, Oasis Club*), Ann Weldon (*Violet Welles*), Charley Lang (*DJ at the Paramount*), Tim Russ (*Harris*), Richard Jeni (*Chummy Morello*), Don Starr (*Doctor at Nica's*), Richard Mawe (*Medical Examiner*). 160 mins.

The Dead Pool

USA, 1988   Director: Buddy Van Horn

P.c.: Warner Bros. A Malpaso production. *p*: David Valdes. *p.assoc*: Tom Rooker, Jennifer Van Horn. *p.manager*: David Valdes. *location manager*: John Lehane. *casting*: Phyllis Huffman, (San Francisco) Nancy Hayes, Jan Campi, (Los Angeles) Olivia Harris. *asst.d*: L. Dean Jones Jnr., Tena Psyche Yatroussis, Robert Joseph Mooney, *sc*: Steve Sharon. *story*: Steve Sharon, Durk Pearson, Sandy Shaw. Based on characters created by Harry Julian Fink, R.M. Fink. *ph*: Jack N. Green. *col*: Technicolor. *camera op*: Norman G. Langley, Doug Ryan *sup.ed*: Joel Cox. *ed*: Ron Spang. *p.designer*: Edward C. Carfagno. *set dec*: Thomas L. Roysden. *set dresser*: Barbara Munch. *sp.effects*: Chuck Gaspar, Joe Day, Thomas Mertz, Bruce Robles, Robert Finley. *m*: Lalo Schifrin. *m.ed*: Donald Harris. *song*: "Welcome to the Jungle" by Slash, W. Axl Rose, Steven Adler, Izzy Stradlin, Duff Rose McKagen, performed by Guns 'n' Roses. *cost.sup*: (men) Glenn Wright, (women) Deborah Hopper. *wardrobe*: (men) Darryl Athons, *make-up*: Montague Westmore. *titles/opticals*: Pacific Title. *sup.sd.ed*: Alan Robert Murray,

Robert G. Henderson. *sd.ed*: Joseph A. Ippolito, Walter Newman, Marshall Winn, David M. Horton, Virginia Cook-McGowan, Teri E. Dorman, *ARD ed*: Jay N. Engel. *sd.rec*: Richard S. Church, (m.) Bobby Fernandez. Dolby stereo. *sd.re-rec*: Les Fresholtz, Dick Alexander, Vern Poore, *stunt co-ordinator*: Richard (Diamond) Farnsworth. *helicopter pilots*: Jim Gavin, Craig Hosking. *stunts*: Mike Adams, Hank Baumert, May Boss, Tony Cecere, Vince Deadrick Snr., Scott Dockstader, Steve Geray, Andy Gill, Gene Hartline, Orwin Harvey, Fred Hice, Larry Holt, Jeff Imada, Maria Kelly, Kevin Larson, Walt La Rue, Lane Leavitt, Burt Marshall, Carol L. Neilson, George Orrison, Mark Orrison, Debby Porter, Rex Rossi, Spike Silver, Brian Smrz, Richard Warlock, Chuck Waters, Danny Weselis, Webster Whinery, Danny Wong. *l.p.*: Clint Eastwood (*Inspector Harry Callahan*), Patricia Clarkson (*Samantha Walker*), Liam Neeson (*Peter Swan*), Evan C. Kim (*Al Quan*), David Hunt (*Harlan Rook*), Michael Currie (*Captain Donnelly*), Michael Goodwin (*Lieutenant Ackerman*), Darwin Gillett (*Patrick Snow*), Anthony Charnota (*Lou Janero*), Christopher Beale (*DA Thomas McSherry*), John Allen Vick (*Lieutenant Ruskowski*), Jeff Richmond (*1st Freeway Reporter*), Patrick Van Horn (*2nd Freeway Reporter*), Singrid Wurschmidt (*3rd Freeway Reporter*), James Carrey (*Johnny Squares*), Deborah A. Bryan (*Girl in Rock Video*), Nicholas Love (*Jeff Howser*), Maureen McVerry (*Vicky Owens*), John X. Heart (*Samantha's Cameraman*), Victoria Bastel (*Suzanne Dayton*), Kathleen Turco-Lyon (*Officer at Trailer*), Michael Faqir (*Sergeant at Trailer*), Ronnie Claire Edwards (*Molly Fisher*), Wallace Choy (*Chinese Store Manager*), Melodie Soe (*Chinese Restaurant Hostess*), Kristopher Logan (*1st Gunman*), Scott Vance (*2nd Gunman*), Glenn T. Wright (*Detective Hindmark*), Stu Klitsner (*Minister*), Karen Kahn (*TV Associate Producer*), Shawn Elliott (*Chester Docksteder*), Ren Reynolds (*Perry*), Ed Hodson (*Paramedic at Elevator*), Edward Hocking (*Warden Hocking*), Diego Chairs (*Butcher Hicks*), Patrick Valentino (*Pirate Captain*), Calvin Jones (*1st Pirate Tug Reporter*), Melissa Martin (*2nd Pirate Tug Reporter*), Phil Dacey (*Detective Dacey*), Louis Giambalvo (*Gus Wheeler*), Peter Anthony Jacobs (*Sergeant Holloway*), Bill Wattenburg (*Nolan Kennard*), Hugh McCann (*Young Man on Talk Show*), Suzanne Sterling (*Young Woman on Talk Show*), Lloyd Nelson (*Sergeant Waldman*), Charles Martinet (*1st Police Station Reporter*), Taylor Gilbert (*2nd Police Station Reporter*), George Orrison (*1st Embarcadero Bodyguard*), Marc Alaimo (*2nd Embarcadero Bodyguard*), Justin Whalin (*Jason*), Kris LeFan (*Carl*), Katie Bruce (*Girl on Sidewalk*), Harry Demopoulos (*Doctor in Hospital Room*), John Frederick Jones (*Dr. Friedman*), Martin Ganapoler (*Reporter at Pier*). 91 mins.

Pink Cadillac

USA, 1989   Director: Buddy Van Horn

P.c.: Malpaso. For Warner Bros. *p*: David Valdes. *exec.p*: Michael Gruskoff. *sc*: John Escrow. *ph*: Jack N. Green. *m. co-ord*: Clint Eastwood and David Valdes. *m.perf*: Randy Travis, Hank Williams Jr, Michael Martin Murphy, Southern Pacific, Jill Hollier, J.C. Crowley, Billy Hill, Dion, Robben Ford. *l.p.*: Clint Eastwood (*Tommy Nowak*), Bernadette Peters (*Lou Ann McGuinn*), Timothy Carhart (*Roy*), Michael Des Barres (*Alex*), John Dennis Johnston (*Waycross*).

White Hunter, Black Heart

USA, 1990   Director: Clint Eastwood

P.c.: Malpaso/Rastar. For Warner Bros. *exec.p*: David Valdes. *p*: Clint Eastwood. *co-p*: Stanley Rubin. *p.co-ordinator*: Carol Regan. *p.manager*: Roy Button. *location managers*: (Zimbabwe) Pat Harrison, Murray Russell, (UK) Nick Daubeny. *location co-ordinator*: Marianne Jacobs (Zimbabwe). *2nd Unit d*: (wildlife) Simon Trevor. *casting*: Mary Selway, (US) Phyllis Huffman, (Zimbabwe) Andrew Whalley, *asst.d*: Patrick Clayton, Chris Brock, Tim Lewis, Isaac Mabhikwa. *sc*: Peter Viertel, James Bridges, Burt Kennedy. Based on the novel by Peter Viertel. *ph*: Jack N. Green. *col*: Technicolor. *2nd Unit ph*: (wildlife) Simon Trevor. *visual effects*: Roy Field (sup.), Peter Field. *aerial ph*: Peter Allwork. *camera op*: Jack N. Green, Peter Robinson, (wildlife) Jamie Harcourt. *ed*: Joel Cox. *p.designer*: John Graysmark. *a.d*: Tony Reading. *set dec*: Peter Howitt. *sp.effects sup*: John Evans. *sp.effects technicians*: Kevin Draycott, Barry Whitrod, Gift Nyamandi, Steve Sango. *m*: Lennie Niehaus. *m. performed by*: (percussionists) Emil Richards, Efrain Toro, (flute) Bill Perkins. *song*: "Satin Doll" by Duke Ellington, Johnny Mercer, Billy Strayhorn. *m.ed*: Donald Harris. *choreo*: Arelene Phillips. *cost.design*: John Mollo. *wardrobe*: Ron Beck (sup.), Janet Tebrooke (mistress). *make-up artist*: Paul Engelen (chief), Linda Armstrong. *titles/opticals*: Pacific Title. *sup.sd.ed*: Alan Robert Murray, Robert Henderson. *sd.ed*: Bub Asman, Virginia Cook-McGowan, David M. Horton, Joseph A. Ippolito, Jayme Parker, Marshall Winn. *ADR ed*: James Simcik, Hank Salerno. *sd.rec*: Peter Handford. Dolby stereo. *sd.re-rec*: Les Fresholtz, Vern Poore, Michael Jiron. *consultant*: (whitewater unit) Richard Bell. *stunts*: George Orrison. *doubles*: (Clint Eastwood) Bill Weston, (Boy Mathias Chuma) David Mabukane. *animal handlers*: (monkey) Rob Martens, (elephant) Randall Jay Moore. *horse master*: Roy Street. *pilots*: Tom Danaher, (helicopter) Ian Cochrane. *l.p.*: Clint Eastwood (*John Wilson*), Jeff Fahey (*Pete Verrill*), Charlotte Cornwell (*Miss Wilding*), Norman Lumsden (*Butler George*), George Dzundza (*Paul Landers*), Edward Tudor Pole (*Reissar*), Roddy Maude-Roxby (*Thompson*), Richard Warwick (*Basil Fields*), John Rapley (*Gun-shop Salesman*), Catherine Neilson (*Irene Saunders*), Marisa Berenson (*Kay Gibson*), Richard Vanstone (*Phil Duncan*), Jamie Koss (*Mrs Duncan*), Anne Dunkley (*Scarf Girl*), David Danns (*Bongo Man*), Myles Freeman (*Ape Man*), Geoffrey Hutchings (*Alec Laing*), Christopher Fairbank (*Tom Harrison*), Alun Armstrong (*Ralph Lockhart*), Clive Mantle (*Harry*), Mel Martin (*Margaret MacGregor*), Martin Jacobs (*Dickie Marlowe*), Norman Malunga (*Desk Clerk*), Timothy Spall (*Hodkins*), Alex Norton (*Zibelinsky*), Eleanor David (*Dorshka*), Boy Mathias Chuma (*Kivu*), Andrew Whalley (*Photographer*), Conrad Asquith (*Ogilvy*). 112 mins.

The Rookie

USA, 1990   Director: Clint Eastwood

P.c.: Malpaso. For Warner Bros. *p*: Howard Kazanjian, Steven Siebert, David Valdes. *p.manager*: David Valdes. *location manager*: Antoinette Levine. *2nd Unit d*: Buddy van Horn. *casting*: Phyllis Huffman, (San José atmosphere) Judith Bouley. *asst.d*: Matt Earl Beesley, Frank Capra III, Jeffrey Wetzel, D. Scott Easton, George Fortmuller. *sc*: Boaz Yakin, Scott Spiegel *ph*: Jack N. Green. *col*: Technicolor. *2nd Unit ph*: Don Burgess. *camera op*: Stephen St. John, Vince Baldino, (2nd Unit) Michael Ferris. *ed*: Joel Cox *p.designer*: Judy Cammer *a.d*: Ed Verreaux. *set design*: John Berger, Dawn Snyder. *set dec*: Dan May. *p.illustrator*: Tom Cranham. *sp.effects sup*: John Frazier. *sp.effects*: (foreman) Rocky Gehr, (crew) Hal Selig, Bruce Kuroyama, A.J. Thrasher, Paul Ryan, Steve Riley, Robert Phillips, Patrick Lee. *m*: Lennie Niehaus. *m.ed*: Donald Harris. *songs*: "All the Things You Are" by Jerome Kern, Oscar Hammerstein II; "Red Zone" by Kyle Eastwood, Michael Stevens. *cost.sup*: (men) Glenn Wright, (women) Deborah Hopper. *costumer*: (men) Robert Stewart, (women) Patricia Ann Trbovich. *make-up artists*: Michael Hancock, Ralph Gulko. *titles/opticals*: Pacific Title. *sup.sd.ed*: Alan Robert Murray, Robert G. Henderson. *sd.ed*: Bub Asman, Virginia Cook-McGowan, David M. Horton Snr., Jayme Parker, Marshall Winn. *ADR ed*: James Simcik, Godfrey Marks. *foley ed*: David L. Horton Jnr., Butch Wolf. *sd.rec*: Don Johnson, (m) Bobby Fernandez, (2nd Unit) Michael Evje. Dolby stereo. *sd.re-rec*: Les Fresholtz, Vern Poore, Michael Jiron. *office p.assistant*: Marguerite P. Condon. *stunt co-ordinator*: Terry Leonard. *stunts*: Bobby

Aldridge, John Alden, Robert Apisa, John Ashby, Perry Barndt, Gary Baxley, Sandy Berumen, Simone Boisseree, Brad Bovee, Eddie Braun, Kathy Brock, Troy Brown, Brian Burrows, Phil Chong, Carl Ciarfalio, Roydon Clark, Chuck Courtney, Charlie Croughwell, Phil Culotta, David Darling, Jani Davis, Deborah A. Discoe, Richard Duran, Ken Endoso, Jeannie Epper, Kurt Epper, Stephanie Epper, Donna Evans, Frank Ferrara, Cindy Folkerson, Steve Geray, Andrée Gibbs, Al Goto, William S. Grisco, Orwin Harvey, Eddie Hice, Richard Hill, Larry Holt, Jeff Imada, Steven Ito, Terry Jackson, Dean Jeffries, Gary Jensen, Wayne King, Bill Lane, Walt LaRue, Willie Leong, Clay Lilley, Carey Loftin, Cotton Mather, Michael Maurer, Matt McColm, Mike McGaughy, Cole McKay, John C. Meier, Tom Morga, Cheree L. Nelson, Larry Nicholas, Donna Noguchi, Jimmy Ortega, Debi Parker, David Perna, Denny Pierce, Jeff Ramsey, Mario Roberts, J.P. Romano, Ronnie Rondell, Tom Rosales, Kerry Rossall, Dave Rowden, Bill Ryusaki, George Sack Jnr., Ben Scott, John-Clay Scott, Alex Sharp, Spike Silver, Al Simon, Russell Solberg, Jann Steele, Joe Stone, R.L. Tolbert, Wayne van Horn, Mike Watson, Jim Wilkey, Jerry Wills, Danny Wong, Bill Francis Young, Bill Young's Precision Driving Team. *aerial co-ordinator/pilot*: James Gavin. *pilots*: Thomas Friedkin, Craig Hosking. *l.p.*: Clint Eastwood (*Nick Pulovski*), Charlie Sheen (*David Ackerman*), Raul Julia (*Strom*), Sonia Braga (*Liesl*), Tom Skerritt (*Eugene Ackerman*), Lara Flynn Boyle (*Sarah*), Pepe Serna (*Lieutenant Ray Garcia*), Marco Rodriguez (*Loco*), Pete Randall (*Cruz*), Donna Mitchell (*Laura Ackerman*), Xander Berkeley (*Blackwell*), Tony Plana (*Moralles*), David Sherrill (*Max*), Hal Williams (*Powell*), Lloyd Nelson (*Freeway Motorist*), Pat Duval, Mara Corday and Jerry Schumacher (*Interrogators*), Matt McKenzie (*Wang*), Joel Polis (*Lance*), Roger LaRue (*Maître d'*), Robert Dubac (*Waiter*), Anthony Charnota (*Romano*), Jordan Lund (*Bartender*), Paul Ben-Victor (*Little Felix*), Jeanne Mori (*Connie Ling*), Anthony Alexander (*Alphonse*), Paul Butler (*Captain Hargate*), Seth Allen (*David as a child*), Coleby Lombardo (*David's Brother*), Roberta Vasquez (*Heather Torres*), Joe Farago (*Anchorman*), Robert Harvey (*Whalen*), Nick Ballo (*Vito*), Jay Boryea (*Sal*), Mary Lou Kenworthy (*Receptionist*), George Orrison (*Detective Orrison*). 121 mins.

Bibliography

Primary Sources
Interviews with Clint Eastwood, Sergio Leone, Budd Boetticher, Burt Kennedy and Philip Kaufman, between January 1983 and February 1989.

Secondary Sources
Patrick Agan: *Clint Eastwood, the man behind the myth* (London, 1977)
David Ansen and others: 'Clint, an American Icon' (*Newsweek*, 23 Sept 1985)
Lawrence Alloway: *Violent America, the movies 1946 – 64* (New York, 1971)
De Witt Bodeen: 'Clint Eastwood' (*Focus on Film*, Spring 1972)
Budd Boetticher: *When in Disgrace* (California, 1989)
Joe Bob Briggs: *Joe Bob Goes to the Drive-In* (New York, 1987)
J. Cabrera Infante: *Holy Smoke* (London, 1985)
Tim Cahill: 'Clint Eastwood' (*Rolling Stone*, 4 July 1985)
Jenni Calder: *There Must Be a Lone Ranger* (London, 1976)
Carmel Pine Cone and Carmel Valley Outlook: issues from October 1985 to March 1987.
Forrest Carter: *Gone to Texas* (New York, 1973)
Brian Case: 'Bird Song' (*Time Out*, 2 Nov 1988)
John G. Cawelti: *The Six-Gun Mystique* (Ohio, 1971)
Terry Coleman: 'A die-hard liberal behind the Magnum image' (*Guardian*, 17 Jan 1985)
Tony Crawley: 'Clint Eastwood' (*Ritz*, London, July 1985)
Gerard Devillers: 'Clint Eastwood' (*Films/Portraits*, Paris, Nov-Dec 1978)
Peter Douglas: *Clint Eastwood – Movin' on* (London, 1974)
David Downing and Gary Herman: *Clint Eastwood – All-American Anti-hero* (London, 1977)
Michael Dwyer: 'A fistful of memories' (*Irish Times*, 1 Sept 1990)
Richard Dyer: *Stars* (London, 1981)

Clint Eastwood: 'Play "Misty" for Me' (*Action*, Mar-April 1973)

Umberto Eco: 'The Myth of Superman' (*Diacritics*, New York, Spring 1972)

Leonard Feather: 'Bird – the film' (*Jazz Express*, London, Dec 1987)

Dan Ford: *The Unquiet Man* (London, 1979)

John Fraser: *Violence in the Arts* (Cambridge, 1974)

Christopher Frayling: 'Incident of the Man with No Name' (*Primetime*, March – May 1982)

Christopher Frayling: *Spaghetti Westerns – Cowboys & Europeans from Karl May to Sergio Leone* (London, 1981)

Christopher Frayling: 'Magnum Star' (*Independent Magazine*, London, 19 Nov 1988)

Philip French: *Westerns* (London, 1973 updated 1977)

B.J. Friedman: 'Could Dirty Harry Take Rooster Cogburn?' (*Esquire*, Sept 1976)

Francois Guérif: *Clint Eastwood – the man & his films* (New York, 1986)

Jeff Hayward: 'Easy Rider' (*Films & Filming*, Jan 1990)

Nat Hentoff: 'Bird Lives!' (*American Film*, Sep 1988)

Michael Herr: *Despatches* (New York, 1978)

Iain Johnstone: *The Man with No Name* (London, 1981; revised edition, 1988)

Pauline Kael: reviews of Eastwood's films in *The New Yorker*, 14 Jan 1974 & 23 Jan 1984

Stuart Kaminsky: *Clint Eastwood* (New York, 1974)

Joanne Mathewson (ed.): *The Carmel Campaign Scrapbook* (Carmel, 1986)

Norman Mailer: 'All the Pirates and People' (*Parade*, 23 Oct 1983; reprinted in *Observer Magazine*, 29 Jan 1984)

Derek Malcolm: 'In pursuit of Hollywood's jungle giant (*Guardian*, 28 Aug 1990)

Robert Mazzocco: 'The Supply-Side Star' (*New York Review of Books*, 1 April 1982)

Stephanie McKnight: *The Outlaw Josey Wales* (BFI Education Notes; London, 1986)

Larry McMurtry: *In a Narrow Grave – Essays on Texas* (Austin, 1968)

Joan Mellen: *Big Bad Wolves – masculinity in the American film* (New York, 1977)

Jennifer Meynell: 'Values and Violence – a study of the films of Clint Eastwood' (*Journal of Moral Education*, 7, 2, 1977)

Jack Nachbar (ed.): *Focus on the Western* (New Jersey, 1974)

Tony Rayns: 'Clint Eastwood – Shooting Party' (*Time Out*, 18 April 1990)

Jeffrey Ryder: *Clint Eastwood* (New York, 1987)

Clint Eastwood

Richard Schickel: 'Good Ole Burt: Cool-Eyed Clint' (*Time*, 9 Jan 1978)

Julian Smith: *Looking Away – Hollywood & Vietnam* (New York, 1975)

Deyan Sudjic: *Cult Heroes* (London, 1989)

Richard K. Tharp (ed.) *Reruns – The Magazine of Television History*, (California, April 1981 and October 1981)

David Thomson: 'Cop on a Hot Tightrope' (*Film Comment*, Sept – Oct 1984)

David Thomson: 'Clint Eastwood' (*The Movie*, No. 77, London, 1981)

Peter Viertel: *White Hunter, Black Heart* (with afterword, Middlesex, 1990)

John Vincour: 'Clint Eastwood, Seriously' (*New York Times Magazine*, 24 Feb 1985)

Robert Warshaw: *The Immediate Experience* (New York, 1962)

Richard West: 'Cowboys and Computers' (*The Spectator*, 14 May 1983)

Will Wright: *Sixguns and Society* (California, 1975)

Boris Zmijewsky and Lee Pfeiffer: *The films of Clint Eastwood* (New Jersey, 1982)